NAEYC, CEC, and TESOL Correlation Matrix

Standard Summary*	Chapter Number and Topic
NAEYC Standard 3. Observing, Documenting, and Assessing to Support Young Children and Families Students prepared in early childhood degree programs understand that child observation, documentation, and other forms of assessment are central to the practice of all early childhood professionals. They know about and understand the goals, benefits, and uses of assessment. They know about and use systematic observations, documentation, and other effective assessment strategies in a responsible way, in partnership with families and other professionals, to positively influence the development of every child. 3a: Understanding the goals, benefits, and uses of assessment 3b: Knowing about and using observation, documentation, and other appropriate assessment tools and approaches 3c: Understanding and practicing responsible assessment to promote positive outcomes for each child 3d: Knowing about assessment partnerships with families and with professional colleagues	1 What Makes a High-Quality Early Childhood Education Professional? 1 Professional Standards for Early Childhood Educators 5 Assessing Approaches to Learning 6 Assessing Social and Emotional Development 7 Assessing Cognition 8 Assessing Language 9 Assessing Physical Development
CEC Standard 8: Assessment Specialized knowledge or skills in early childhood special education includes the following: 8a. Assess the development and learning of young children 8b. Select, adapt and use specialized formal and informal assessments for infants, young children, and their families 8c. Participate as a team member to integrate assessment results in the development and implementation of individualized family service plans and individualized education plans 8d. Assist families in identifying their concerns, resources, and priorities 8e. Participate and collaborate as a team member with other professionals in conducting family-centered assessments 8f. Evaluate services with families	
TESOL Domain 4. Assessment Candidates understand issues and concepts of assessment and use standards-based procedures with English-language learners. 4.a. Issues of assessment for English-language learners 4.b. Language proficiency assessment 4.c. Classroom-based assessment Candidates know and can use a variety of performance-based assessment tools and techniques to inform instruction in the classroom.	
NAEYC Standards 4 and 5. Using Developmentally Effective Approaches to Connect with Children and Families; Using Content Knowledge to Build Meaningful Curriculum Students prepared in early childhood degree programs understand that teaching and learning with young children is a complex enterprise, and its details vary depending on children's ages, characteristics, and the settings within which teaching and learning occur. They understand and use positive relationships and supportive interactions as the foundation for their work with young children and families. Students know, understand, and use a wide array of developmentally appropriate approaches, instructional strategies, and tools to connect with children and families and positively influence each child's development and learning. 4a: Understanding positive relationships and supportive interactions as the foundation of their work with children 4b: Knowing and understanding effective strategies and tools for early education 4c: Using a broad repertoire of developmentally appropriate teaching/learning approaches 4d: Reflecting on their own practice to promote positive outcomes for each child Students prepared in early childhood degree programs use their knowledge of academic disciplines to design, implement, and evaluate experiences that promote positive development and learning for each and every young child. Students understand the importance of developmental domains and academic (or content) disciplines in an early childhood curriculum. They know the essential concepts, inquiry tools, and structure of content areas, including academic subjects, and can identify resources to deepen their understanding. Students use their own knowledge and other resources to design, implement, and evaluate meaningful, challenging curricula that promote comprehensive developmental and learning outcomes for every young child.	1 What Makes a High-Quality Early Childhood Education Professional? 1 Professional Standards for Early Childhood Educators 4 Setting Up the Environment 4 Daily Schedule 4 Play 4 Interactions 4 The First Weeks of Preschool 5 Supporting Children's Effective and Diverse Approaches to Learning 5 Creative Arts 5 Social Studies 5 Numeracy 5 Science 5 Literacy 5 Interaction and Play 6 Supporting Children's Effective and Diverse Social and Emotional Development 6 Literacy 6 Numeracy 6 Science 6 Social Studies

(continued)

*From NAEYC. (2009). *Position statement. NAEYC Standards for Early Childhood Professional Preparation Programs*. Washington, DC: Author; reprinted with permission from the National Association for the Education of Young Children (NAEYC). A full-text version of the position statement is available at www.naeyc.org/files/naeyc/file/positions/ProfPrepStandards09.pdf; Council for Exceptional Children, "What Every Special Educator Must Know," www.cec. sped.org, Professional Development, Professional Standards, click on Download the Free PDF under the "Red Book," Sixth Edition, Revised; reprinted by permission; Teachers of English to Speakers of Other Languages. (n.d.). *TESOL/NCATE standards for P–12 teacher education programs*. Retrieved January 29, 2011, from http://www.tesol.org/s_tesol/seccss.asp?CID=219&DID=1689; reprinted by permission.

NAEYC, CEC, and TESOL Correlation Matrix (continued)

Standard Summary*	Chapter Number and Topic
NAEYC Standards 4 and 5 *(continued)* 5a: Understanding content knowledge and resources in academic disciplines 5b: Knowing and using the central concepts, inquiry tools, and structures of content areas or academic disciplines 5c: Using their own knowledge, appropriate early learning standards, and other resources to design, implement, and evaluate meaningful, challenging curricula for each child **CEC Standard 7: Instructional Planning** Specialized knowledge or skills in early childhood special education includes the following: 7a: Implement, monitor and evaluate individualized family service plans and individualized education plans 7b: Plan and implement developmentally and individually appropriate curriculum 7c: Design intervention strategies incorporating information from multiple disciplines 7d: Implement developmentally and functionally appropriate individual and group activities including play, environmental routines, parent-mediated activities, group projects, cooperative learning, inquiry experiences, and systematic instruction **TESOL Domain 3. Planning, Implementing, and Managing Instruction** Candidates know, understand, and use evidence-based practices and strategies related to planning, implementing, and managing standards-based ESL and content instruction. Candidates are skilled in using a variety of classroom organization techniques, program models, and teaching strategies for developing and integrating language skills. They can integrate technology and choose and adapt classroom resources appropriate for their English-language learners.	6 Creative Arts 6 Interaction and Play 7 Supporting Children's Effective and Diverse Cognitive Development 7 Creative Arts 7 Social Studies 7 Numeracy 7 Science 7 Literacy 7 Interaction and Play 8 Supporting Children's Effective and Diverse Language Development 8 Creative Arts 8 Social Studies 8 Numeracy 8 Science 8 Literacy 8 Interaction and Play 9 Supporting Children's Effective and Diverse Motor and Physical Development 9 Creative Arts 9 Social Studies 9 Numeracy 9 Science 9 Literacy 9 Interaction and Play
NAEYC Standard 6. Becoming a Professional Students prepared in early childhood degree programs identify and conduct themselves as members of the early childhood profession. They know and use ethical guidelines and other professional standards related to early childhood practice. They are continuous, collaborative learners who demonstrate knowledgeable, reflective, and critical perspectives on their work, making informed decisions that integrate knowledge from a variety of sources. They are informed advocates for sound educational practices and policies. 6a: Identifying and involving oneself with the early childhood field 6b: Knowing about and upholding ethical standards and other professional guidelines 6c: Engaging in continuous, collaborative learning to inform practice 6d: Integrating knowledgeable, reflective, and critical perspectives on early education 6e: Engaging in informed advocacy for children and the profession **CEC Standard 9: Professional and Ethical Practice** Specialized knowledge or skills in early childhood special education includes the following: 9a: Know organizations and publications relevant to the field of early childhood special education 9b: Recognize signs of child abuse and neglect in young children and follow reporting procedures 9c: Use family theories and principles to guide professional practice; respect family choices and goals 9d: Apply models of team process in early childhood 9e: Advocate for enhanced professional status and working conditions for early childhood service providers 9f: Participate in activities of professional organizations relevant to the field of early childhood special education 9g: Apply research and effective practices critically in early childhood settings 9h: Develop, implement, and evaluate a professional development plan relevant to one's work with young children **TESOL Domain 5. Professionalism** Candidates keep current with new instructional techniques, research results, advances in the field, and public policy issues. Candidates demonstrate knowledge of the history of ESL teaching. Candidates use such information to reflect upon and improve their instruction and assessment practices. Candidates work collaboratively with school staff and the community to improve the learning environment, provide support, and advocate for English-language learners and their families. Candidates take advantage of professional growth opportunities and demonstrate the ability to build partnerships with colleagues and students' families, serve as community resources, and advocate for students and their families.	1 Why Become an Early Childhood Teacher? 1 Who Teaches in Early Childhood Education? 1 Where Do Early Childhood Educators Work? 1 What Makes a High-Quality Early Childhood Education Professional? 1 Professional Standards for Early Childhood Educators 1 Integration of Information: Self-Reflective Guide 2 Integration of Information: Self-Reflective Guide 3 Thoughts About Early Childhood Before the 19th Century 3 Early Childhood Education in the 19th Century 3 Early Childhood Education in the First Half of the 20th Century 3 Early Childhood Education in the Second Half of the 20th Century 3 Integration of Information: Self-Reflective Guide 4 Integration of Information: Self-Reflective Guide 5 Integration of Information: Self-Reflective Guide 6 Integration of Information: Self-Reflective Guide 7 Integration of Information: Self-Reflective Guide 8 Integration of Information: Self-Reflective Guide 9 Integration of Information: Self-Reflective Guide 10 Advocacy 10 Reflection Is Never Ending 10 A Rewarding Challenge

*From NAEYC. (2009). *Position statement. NAEYC Standards for Early Childhood Professional Preparation Programs.* Washington, DC: Author; reprinted with permission from the National Association for the Education of Young Children (NAEYC). A full-text version of the position statement is available at www.naeyc.org/files/naeyc/file/positions/ProfPrepStandards09.pdf; Council for Exceptional Children, "What Every Special Educator Must Know," www.cec.sped.org, Professional Development, Professional Standards, click on Download the Free PDF under the "Red Book," Sixth Edition, Revised; reprinted by permission; Teachers of English to Speakers of Other Languages. (n.d.). *TESOL/NCATE standards for P–12 teacher education programs.* Retrieved January 29, 2011, from http://www.tesol.org/s_tesol/seccss.asp?CID=219&DID=1689; reprinted by permission.

Preschool Education
in Today's World

Preschool Education in Today's World

Teaching Children with Diverse Backgrounds and Abilities

by

M. Susan Burns, Ph.D.
George Mason University
Fairfax, Virginia

Richard T. Johnson, Ed.D.
University of Hawaii at Manoa
Honolulu, Hawaii

and

Mona M Assaf, M.Ed.
George Mason University
Fairfax, Virginia

with invited contributors

·P·A·U·L·H·
BROOKES
PUBLISHING Co.®

Baltimore • London • Sydney

Paul H. Brookes Publishing Co.
Post Office Box 10624
Baltimore, Maryland 21285-0624
USA

www.brookespublishing.com

Typeset by Integrated Publishing Solutions, Grand Rapids, Michigan.
Manufactured in the United States of America by
Sheridan Books, Inc., Chelsea, Michigan.

The individuals described in this book are composites or real people whose situations are masked and are based on the authors' experiences. In all instances, names and identifying details have been changed to protect confidentiality.

Library of Congress Cataloging-in-Publication Data

Burns, M. Susan (Marie Susan).
  Preschool education in today's world : teaching children with diverse backgrounds and
  abilities / by M. Susan Burns, Richard T. Johnson, and Mona M Assaf.
     p.   cm.
  Includes index.
  ISBN-13: 978-1-59857-195-0
  ISBN-10: 1-59857-195-8
  1. Education, Preschool.   2. Multicultural education.   3. Mixed ability grouping in education.
  4. Early childhood special education.   I. Johnson, Richard T., 1956–   II. Assaf, Mona M.   III. Title.
  LB1140.2.B865   2011
  372.21—dc22   2011011267

British Library Cataloguing in Publication data are available from the British Library.

2015   2014   2013   2012   2011

10   9   8   7   6   5   4   3   2   1

Contents

About the Authors xi
Contributors xii
Foreword   *Linda M. Espinosa* xiii
Preface xv
Special Features xvii
Acknowledgments xix
Image Credits xx

1   **Who Provides Early Childhood Education and Care?** 1
     Learning Objectives 1
     Why Become an Early Childhood Teacher? 2
     Who Teaches in Early Childhood Education? 4
         Section Summary 5
     Where Do Early Childhood Educators Work? 5
         Family Child Care 9
         Employment and Salary 9
         Section Summary 11
     What Makes a High-Quality Early Childhood Education
     Professional? 11
         Section Summary 15
     Professional Standards for Early Childhood Educators 15
         Multidimensional Development and Learning 16
         Families and Communities 17
         Observing, Documenting, and Assessing 18
         Instruction 19
         Professionalism 20
         Section Summary 21
     Key Concepts 21
     Integration of Information: Self-Reflective Guide 22
     Helpful Web Sites 22

2   **Who Are the Children and Their Families?** 25
     Learning Objectives 25
     Family, Neighborhood, and Community Characteristics 26
         Family Culture 26
         Home Language 27
         Family Type and Structure 28
             Social Organization of Family 28
             Gay and Lesbian Parents 29
             Siblings 29
             Teenage Parents 29
             Income Level 29
             Child Abuse and Neglect 30
         Section Summary 31

Children with Disabilities. 31
    Sensory Impairments. 34
        Visual Impairment and Blindness 35
        Deafness and Hearing Loss 35
    Physical and Health Disabilities 36
        Cerebral Palsy. 36
        Spina Bifida. 37
        Other Low-Incidence Physical and Health Problems. 37
    Intellectual Disabilities 37
        Down Syndrome 38
        Other Intellectual Disabilities. 38
    Autism Spectrum Disorders. 39
    Attention-Deficit/Hyperactivity Disorder. 39
    Emotional and Behavioral Disorders 40
    Learning Disabilities 40
    Speech and Language Impairments 40
    Multiple Disabilities 41
    Section Summary 41
Key Concepts 41
Integration of Information: Self-Reflective Guide. 42
Helpful Web Sites. 42

3   How Has Early Childhood Education Been Defined over
    the Years? 45
Learning Objectives. 45
Thoughts About Early Childhood Before the 19th Century 46
    Section Summary 48
Early Childhood Education in the 19th Century. 48
    Nursery School and Kindergarten in the United States. 50
    Education of Teachers 50
    Section Summary 51
Early Childhood Education in the First Half of the 20th
Century 51
    Major Theorists. 51
    Significant Events. 54
    Section Summary 55
Early Childhood Education in the Second Half of the 20th
Century 56
    Major Theorists. 56
    Significant Events. 57
    Section Summary 60
Key Concepts 61
Integration of Information: Self-Reflective Guide. 61
Helpful Web Sites. 62

4   Early Childhood Practice Today   with Myra Rogers 65
Learning Objectives. 65
The Big Picture 66
    Setting Up the Environment. 66
        Manipulative and Fine Motor Activities (Math) 66
        Writing Center (Literacy) 67
        Book Center (Literacy). 67
        Science Center. 67

        Water and Sand Center 68
        Art Center 68
        Block Center 69
        Sociodramatic Play Center 69
        Woodworking Center 70
        Centers for Special Projects. 70
        Outdoor Play 70
        Environment for Naps. 70
      Daily Schedule 71
        Example of Full-Day Schedule. 71
        Example of Half-Day Morning Schedule 71
        Example of Half-Day Afternoon Schedule. 72
      Section Summary 72
    The Core of Early Childhood Education Today 73
      Play. 73
      Interactions 74
      Building Relationships with Families 77
      Section Summary 78
    The First Weeks of Preschool 78
      Section Summary 80
    Key Concepts 80
    Integration of Information: Self-Reflective Guide. 81
    Helpful Web Sites. 81

5   Approaches to Learning. 85
    Learning Objectives 85
    Theoretical Accounts: Approaches to Learning. 86
      Social Learning Theory 87
      Information Processing Theory 87
      Social Constructivist Theory 88
      Theory of Mind. 90
      Section Summary 91
    Features of Approaches to Learning 91
      Receptive Processes 92
        Initiative 92
        Curiosity 93
        Attention 93
        Impulse Control 93
      Elaborative Processes 93
        Memory 94
        Organization 94
        Creativity. 95
        Persistence, Frustration, Tolerance, and Private Speech 95
      Expressive Processes 95
        Representation 96
        Familiarity with Clarification Questions 96
      Section Summary 96
    Supporting Children's Effective and Diverse Approaches to
    Learning 96
      Creative Arts 98
      Social Studies 98
      Numeracy 98
      Science 99
      Literacy 99

Interaction and Play. 100
Section Summary. 101
Assessing Approaches to Learning. 101
Adapting Curriculum and Monitoring Progress 102
Section Summary. 104
Key Concepts 105
Integration of Information: Self-Reflective Guide 106
Helpful Web Sites. 108

6   **Social and Emotional Development** 111
Learning Objectives 111
Theoretical Accounts: Social and Emotional Development. 112
Ecological Theory. 112
Psychosocial Theory 115
Critical Theory and Early Education 116
Section Summary. 116
Features of Social and Emotional Development 116
Temperament and Personality 117
Attachment 117
Identity. 118
Resiliency and Protective Factors 119
Section Summary. 120
Supporting Children's Effective and Diverse Social and
Emotional Development 120
Literacy 120
Numeracy 121
Science 121
Social Studies 122
Creative Arts. 122
Interaction and Play. 122
Section Summary. 124
Assessing Social and Emotional Development 124
Adapting Curriculum and Monitoring Progress 126
Section Summary. 128
Key Concepts 128
Integration of Information: Self-Reflective Guide 129
Helpful Web Sites 131

7   **Cognitive Development and Learning**. 133
Learning Objectives. 133
Theoretical Accounts: Cognitive Development and Learning 134
Constructivist Theory 134
Narrative Construction of Reality Theory 135
Dynamic Skills Perspective 136
Brain Development 136
Section Summary. 137
Features of Cognitive Development and Learning 137
Sets. 137
Geometry and Spatial Sense 138
Numbers 138
Vocabulary. 138
Patterns and Measurement 138
Section Summary. 139

Supporting Children's Effective and Diverse Cognitive
Development 139
   Creative Arts 140
   Social Studies 141
   Numeracy 141
   Science 141
   Literacy 142
   Interaction and Play. 142
   Section Summary 143
Assessing Cognition 143
   Adapting Curriculum and Monitoring Progress. 143
   Section Summary 147
Key Concepts 147
Integration of Information: Self-Reflective Guide. 148
Helpful Web Sites. 150

8   **Language Development**   *with Robert A. Stechuk*. 153
Learning Objectives. 153
Theoretical Accounts: Using and Understanding Language. 154
   Ecological Theory. 154
   Social Constructivist Theory 155
   Verbal Behavior Theory. 156
   Section Summary 157
Features of Language Development 157
   Communication 157
   Shared Language Systems 159
   Individual Differences in Language Development. 161
   Language Subsystems. 162
   Metalinguistics 165
   Section Summary 166
Supporting Children's Effective and Diverse Language
Development 166
   Creative Arts. 166
   Social Studies 167
   Numeracy 168
   Science 168
   Literacy 168
   Interaction and Play. 168
   Section Summary 171
Assessing Language 171
   Adapting Curriculum and Monitoring Progress. 175
   Section Summary 177
Key Concepts 178
Integration of Information: Self-Reflective Guide. 179
Helpful Web Sites. 180

9   **Physical Development**   *with Myra Rogers* 183
Learning Objectives. 183
Theoretical Accounts: Physical Development 184
   Ecological Theory. 184
   Brain Development 184
   Section Summary 185

Features of Physical Development 185
    Gross Motor Development 185
    Fine Motor Development 187
    Physical Development, Nutrition, and Physical Fitness 187
    Section Summary 188
Supporting Children's Effective and Diverse Motor and
Physical Development 188
    Creative Arts 189
    Social Studies 190
    Numeracy 190
    Science 190
    Literacy 191
    Interaction and Play 191
    Section Summary 192
Assessing Physical Development 192
    Adapting Curriculum and Monitoring Progress 195
    Section Summary 195
Key Concepts 195
Integration of Information: Self-Reflective Guide 196
Helpful Web Sites 197

10 **Learning in Early Childhood Is Continuous** 201
    International Perspectives 201
    Advocacy 202
    Reflection Is Never Ending 202
    A Rewarding Challenge 203

Glossary 205
Index 211

About the Authors

M. Susan Burns, Ph.D., Associate Professor of Early Childhood Education, George Mason University, Graduate School of Education, MS 4B3, 4400 University Drive, Fairfax, Virginia 22030

Dr. Burns is Associate Professor of Early Childhood Education at George Mason University. Her research centers on the development and learning of young children (birth through Grade 3). Her work includes all children: those with diverse abilities (children with disabilities), those living in poverty, and those from multilingual and multicultural backgrounds. Of particular interest to Dr. Burns are language and early literacy development. She has numerous publications presenting her research in these areas. A former employee at the National Research Council, she is a co-editor of *Eager to Learn: Educating Our Preschoolers, Preventing Reading Difficulties in Young Children,* and *Starting Out Right: A Guide to Promoting Children's Reading Success,* all publications of the National Academy Press of the National Academies of Science. She earned her Ph.D. degree in psychology at Peabody College, Vanderbilt University.

Richard T. Johnson, Ed.D., Professor, Institute for Teacher Education, College of Education, University of Hawaii at Manoa, 1776 University Avenue, Everly Hall 223D, Honolulu, Hawaii 96822

Dr. Johnson is a professor at the University of Hawaii at Manoa, where he is on the faculty of the Institute for Teacher Education. His recent research and field-based work includes no-touch policies in education, risk, childhood subjectivity, and visual culture. He has taught and served extensively in various field-based preservice early childhood/elementary teacher education programs for more than 20 years. He earned his Ed.D. degree at Vanderbilt University.

Mona M Assaf, M.Ed., Head Start Teacher and Doctoral Candidate at George Mason University, Post Office Box 114, Oakton, Virginia 22124

Ms. Assaf has been a Head Start teacher in a large public school district for the last 8 years, and she has conducted research in community Head Start programs. She is passionate about improving educational opportunities for culturally, linguistically, and ability diverse young children and their families.

Contributors

Myra Rogers
Early Childhood Special Education
    Teacher (Retired)
St. Tammany Parish Public School
    System
Bush, Louisiana

Robert A. Stechuk, Ph.D.
Senior Project Officer
Education Development Center, Inc.
55 Chapel Street
Newton, Massachusetts 02458

Foreword

> The greatest discovery made by the United States in the twentieth century was the discovery of its own diversity. If *E pluribus unum* remains, in its widest sense, an abiding aspiration, the country has been brought face to face with the fact that it contains within its borders a multiplicity of ethnicities and ethnic inheritances that the Founding Fathers could never have envisaged. (Elliott, 2011, p. 65)

The author of this opinion, a noted American history professor from Princeton and Oxford universities, was reviewing a recent Revolutionary History text, but his conclusions could just as easily be applied to the history and future of early childhood education in the United States. Our field has been founded on multiple theories of how young children grow and develop; includes a diverse group of professionals with highly variable levels of training and formal education; is practiced in multiple settings that include both private and public auspices; and addresses children and families from more than 400 distinct language groups, all levels of socioeconomic status, and hundreds of cultural and ethnic heritages. We are a diverse field, we serve a diverse population, and we have a diversity of professional points of view. Few child development textbooks systematically address all of this complexity in one volume and, therefore, present a rather simplified and overly processed view of early childhood education.

This new book, *Preschool Education in Today's World: Teaching Children with Diverse Backgrounds and Abilities*, frankly and directly discusses many of the complexities of the field and diversity of those we serve while also raising critical questions that all early childhood education practitioners will need to answer at some point in their career. As we move further into the 21st century, increasingly we will need to shift our thinking from how all children are the same and how we can design practices that "fit" all children to how we are all different and how we should personalize instruction that is more targeted toward individual strengths and needs. I have studied the development of young dual-language learners for several decades, and one finding keeps jumping out: All dual-language learners have unique language histories and patterns of social and cognitive strengths, and they vary on a whole host of learning characteristics, so that to lump them together and recommend one set of "best practices" would seriously undermine effective teaching and learning.

One of the challenges in explicitly addressing issues of complexity within the field and diversity among our targeted populations is to provide enough detail to be clear and to present a comprehensible sequence of topics while not overwhelming the reader with confusing distractions. This new text is refreshing in that it embraces the challenge and yet is quite clear and accessible to all levels of emerging pro-

fessionals. Some topics that have rarely been included in early childhood education texts—such as family child care, employment and salary, dual-language learners, immigrant families, gay and lesbian families, teenage parents, children from
abusive families, and children from low-income families—are discussed frankly
and without underlying bias. This book provides accurate information on difficult
topics that many seasoned early childhood education professionals have never
studied. I also found the sections on how to apply the topic to children with different disabilities to be written at just the right level—accurate and detailed without
being more than a reader can comprehend.

The organization of this book—with guiding questions that introduce each
chapter, brief summaries at the end of each topical section, clear review of the key
concepts at the end of each chapter with a process for integrating the content that
includes self-reflection guides, and many helpful and timely web sites—further
supports good comprehension and recall. The self-reflection guides at the end of
each chapter should be extremely helpful to students as they process the information and apply to their particular situations. Overall, I found this book to be re-
freshingly inclusive, clearly written, and highly readable. It also fills a gap in our
professional literature.

Linda M. Espinosa, Ph.D.
Professor of Early Childhood Education
(Retired; University of Missouri–Columbia),
Author, and Consultant

Reference

Elliott, J.H. (2011). The very violent road to America. *The New York Review of Books, 58*(10), 64–66.

Preface

While preparing this book for publication, my coauthors—Rich Johnson and Mona Assaf—and I had the opportunity to hear President Obama's 2011 State of the Union address. He spoke directly about teachers, the audience for this book.

> Let's also remember that after parents, the biggest impact on a child's success comes from the man or woman at the front of the classroom. In South Korea, teachers are known as "nation builders." Here in America, it's time we treated the people who educate our children with the same level of respect...to every young person listening tonight who's contemplating their career choice: If you want to make a difference in the life of our nation; if you want to make a difference in the life of a child, become a teacher. Your country needs you.

If you are reading this preface, you are in the process of making a serious commitment to our country. Your sense of identity and your willingness to actively choose a future as an early childhood education teacher is important.

The power of early childhood educators and the children and families they serve gives a sense of our commitment to make sure we write a book that future teachers, and possibly current teachers, will find intellectually motivating as well as practical. Writing this book has been a long process and includes the feedback from many who are concerned about the education of young children. I especially have been influenced by Peggy Minnis who, as Director of Early Childhood Education for the District of Columbia Public Schools, kept me "real" in the planning of this book. Peggy and I co-led the instruction of a course for the District of Columbia Public Schools early childhood education, early childhood special education, and Head Start teachers using the content of this book. Peggy's comments, and those of her teachers who attended the course, have guided me throughout the complex process of writing this book, including the last stages of finalizing a higher quality book.

I chose Rich Johnson and Mona Assaf as coauthors of this book because of their rich and varied experiences in early childhood education. As a male teacher, Rich has much to offer with insights regarding the need for young children to have males and females in their everyday lives. Mona, as a current Head Start teacher with licensure in Early Childhood Special Education (0–5 years), K–3 Early Childhood Education, and English as a Second Language (K–12), understands how her expertise is needed every day in her classroom. This expertise was central to the content presented in this book. I also choose Myra Rogers and Robert Stechuk to help us with several chapters in the book. Myra, as a recently retired early childhood special education teacher, added essential practical detail to chapters, especially in the area of setting up the classroom and having appropriate materials available. Robert, an early childhood teacher and administrator in the past, currently provides technical assistance for Head Start programs to work with dual-language learners, among other professional tasks. His expertise was important in our chapter on language development and use. Rich, Mona, Robert, and I have used core pieces of information in this book in our teaching of university courses and providing in-service opportunities for teachers.

We hope you find this book to be helpful. Please know that although the information is very practical, it is informed by thorough research.

Special Features

This textbook includes several helpful features designed to enhance learning. These features will assist readers in understanding the information in this text and applying the knowledge in real-world settings.

Purposeful Integration of Theory, Curriculum, Instruction, and Assessment

Theory, curriculum, instruction, and assessment are integrated throughout the book in such a way to reveal the complexity yet coherence of components in providing high-quality early childhood education.

NAEYC, CEC, and TESOL Correlation Matrix

We provide the reader with a matrix listing the relevant standards from the National Association for the Education of Young Children (NAEYC), the Council for Exceptional Children (CEC), and Teachers of English to Speakers of Other Languages (TESOL) and how the content in this book aligns with those standards. Special emphasis is placed on addressing education for children from 3 to 5 years old. Please remember that early childhood education–related professional standards are addressed fully in a complete professional development program addressing young children birth through Grade 3.

Questions to Consider

Questions one might ask about practice in early childhood education are presented at the beginning of each chapter. These serve to engage the reader in the content from a practical viewpoint.

Learning Objectives

Learning objectives for chapters provide a road map to the content being address in the chapter.

Glossary Terms

Glossary terms and definitions are provided at the end of the book and in bold at first mention in the text to clarify how we are defining particular words.

Case Studies

Brief case examples are included to give life to the concepts presented throughout the book.

Section Summaries

Section summaries provide a review before a switch in topic area so that the reader can review concepts in need of clarification.

Key Concepts

A list of key concepts is included at the end of each chapter to help the reader review concepts in need of clarification.

Web Resources

Readers can find more information on specific topics by visiting the web sites listed in the Helpful Web Sites sections in each chapter.

Self-Reflective Guides

The self-reflective guides at the end of each chapter help the reader review the concepts learned in light of his or her professional and personal needs as an early childhood education professional. Readers are encouraged to write down their answers on a separate sheet of paper so that they have a record of their responses should they wish to review them at a later time.

Acknowledgments

We are thankful to the families and children we have had the pleasure to teach and learn from. They have had a powerful influence on every aspect of this book.

Mona M Assaf

I especially thank the children and families I have worked with for providing me with daily reminders of why early childhood is so important. They have given me emotional support, love, and real-world experiences in which to apply the early childhood theories and practices outlined in this book. On a personal note, I am forever in debt to my mom and Gina, who have been my guiding lights through the process of writing this book. My practice has been forever changed from engaging in the writing of this book; I hope the same applies to you after reading this book.

Richard T. Johnson

I am grateful to my parents, who modeled to me the heartfelt importance and value of care for others, and to all the early childhood educators who care so deeply for those children they will serve throughout their careers.

M. Susan Burns

We all are grateful to our families for putting up with us as we wrote this book. In my case, I thank Ella, Nina, and Sara, especially Ella and Nina, who helped me further understand young children and push my thinking to understand different trajectories of development.

Special thanks to our acquisitions editor Astrid Zuckerman for her patience over the years as progress on this book was slow. Her constant support and enthusiasm for the book was essential. Thanks to Charles Gillmarten for jumping in with help when needed. And thanks to Mackenzie Lawrence, Julie Chávez, and everyone else at Brookes Publishing Co. for their professional and good-humored support.

Image Credits

To all of the early childhood education teachers
who made our "academic knowledge" usable and presentable

Who Provides Early Childhood Education and Care?

Learning Objectives

1. Reflect on yourself, your interests and strengths, and different contexts in which young children are taught
2. Identify the various settings in which ECE takes place
3. Recognize the characteristics of successful early childhood educators
4. Understand the basic standards of different professional groups within ECE

Who teaches and cares for 3- to 5-year-old children? Why do people decide to teach in early childhood education (ECE), early childhood special education (ECSE), and child care? Does it matter whether teachers receive professional development in ECE? How does the professional development of early educators and caregivers affect child development and learning? Are there standards in ECE? How are children all the same? In what ways are they different? What does this mean for how young children are taught?

These are the types of questions being addressed in the introductory chapter of this book on the real world of ECE where we want to ensure that new professionals in this field begin with an understanding of *all* children who may have different cultural backgrounds, multiple home languages, varying socioeconomic statuses, or disabilities, among many other defining characteristics.

bilingual
The ability to speak two languages.

Why Become an Early Childhood Teacher?

Teachers choose ECE for many different reasons, often based on their experiences with young children. For example, someone who is particularly interested in Spanish may decide to work with young children in a **bilingual** school. Someone who is so excited about how her daughter is developing may decide that she wants to teach other young children. And someone else may decide that he should teach young children with disabilities after volunteering at an after-school program for children with autism. Other times, personalized memories of their own teachers affected the decisions of educators to focus on early childhood.

The following comments were adapted from students and teachers from urban, suburban, and rural areas in the northeast and southern United States about why they became ECE teachers and chose to specialize in a particular area. Reflect on the questions in the sidebar as you read their comments. Questions do not correspond to a particular teacher's comments but should be considered across these various, diverse experiences.

❆ ❆ ❆ *I actually never thought I would be a teacher; I never thought I was the teaching type. I didn't see myself in a regular classroom because I thought that I was too shy to be up in front of a bunch of kids all day. But ECE is different. As a preschool teacher, you get to teach by playing with the children rather than teaching at the children. I have always connected with the little ones, so ECE seemed to be perfect for me. I really wanted to get involved with children and families who are living in poverty because I have always seen the potential in each and every child.*

❆ ❆ ❆ *I teach in a Head Start program. Head Start is an amazing program that uses families as an asset. I believe so much in supporting the whole growth of a child and Head Start seems to have answers for it all. They have programs for families, for health, for academics, and for emotional growth. The support I have from my mentor teachers is also amazing! I feel lucky to be in the Head Start program because of the support for my students and their families' growth, as well as my own growth as a teacher.*

❆ ❆ ❆ *I chose ECSE because we often teach kids for more than a year—sometimes up to 3 years. Therefore, I am more likely to experience the reward of seeing the gains these children have made before they leave me. We are able to develop a more empathetic re-*

The sidebar questions:

- Do the teachers' experiences resonate with you?
- Are you interested in addressing the whole child, including concerns of health, family, and education?
- Is it important to you to have the opportunity to work with children and families over multiple years?
- Do you relate to one of these teachers more than others?
- Do you want to teach using multiple languages?
- Do you understand that it is an asset to be bilingual?
- Are you willing to take on the challenge of teaching children from homes with a number of different languages?
- Are you also interested in a related area such as ECE leadership, policy, or research?
- Do you have a positive view of children and families who come from different socioeconomic backgrounds?
- Do you think that children with disabilities can be educated in the same classroom as children without disabilities?
- Are you willing to be active in promoting the early childhood profession?
- Are you a collaborator?
- Are you willing to learn about unfamiliar cultures?
- Do you consider families an asset in the education of young children?
- Do you think that young children are eager to learn and be challenged?
- Do you like to learn from other professionals (e.g., from a physical therapist who professionally serves a child with cerebral palsy)?

lationship with both these children and their families. I really know that I am making a difference.

As an early childhood educator, you will come into contact with children from many cultures.

❋ ❋ ❋ *One of the main reasons that I decided to go into ECE is because I love to witness the emergence of language development in children, from the moment they are born with the eye contact they give and the way they learn to affect those around them with their cries and coos, to the time they start to form words and then phrases and sentences. I also love children's literature and songs, so it is easy for me to try to spread that love to them.*

❋ ❋ ❋ *In a bilingual preschool, planning is very important, as well as openness and communication with the families of your students. I am thrilled to use Spanish and English as a teacher. I get very involved in their home lives, as well as the physical and mental aspects of my students. There are a lot of different aspects to the job. You have to love children and understand how impressionable they are. You have to know that they are young, innocent, and will hear everything you say, even if you cannot tell. You have a great effect on a child during their first few years, so you need to understand how what you do affects them later on.*

❋ ❋ ❋ *The younger child with a disability just seems to tug at my heart the most. Children with disabilities can be friends, teammates, or playmates even though they may do things just a little differently. If* **inclusion** *starts early, the barriers can be broken to ensure that a child with a disability is seen as a person first (using* **person-first language***). In a prekindergarten classroom, students learn to socialize, create, and solve problems. It is fun to help them reach their individual potential.*

inclusion
The placement of children with disabilities in classrooms and programs for children without disabilities.

person-first language
Language used to indicate that a child is a person first, rather than a disability (e.g., a child with autism, not an autistic child).

❋ ❋ ❋ *I applied for* **Teach for America** *because I was compelled by the importance of providing quality education to all students. On the application, I checked a small box that said I would be willing to teach prekindergarten. Because I came into this field by happenstance, I was unsure this would be where I stayed. However, I have grown as an educator, especially through my various classroom experiences, my licensure, and graduate studies. I have become committed to staying in the field. Although I might teach or work on policy issues, I want to continue to work toward young children's success.*

Teach for America
A U.S. organization that trains, supports, and places new teachers in high-need schools.

❋ ❋ ❋ *In my preschool special education program, I was able to see children grow and progress so much. I knew I wanted to teach in a setting where the children received specialized attention and therapy (if needed). The program made a great impact. I could make a difference in the lives of families. I especially like that I work in a program where children with disabilities are included with others in the regular early childhood programs.*

❋ ❋ ❋ *In a child care center, you work with other educators on a day-to-day basis, usually planning all activities together and taking on many roles. This is not babysitting, and I often get angry at people who think that way. You also need to plan activities around the children's interests, which can sometimes be difficult. Some programs are much better than others in this respect; if you work in one that is accredited, then you usually have a good basis. Collaboration is the key.*

Your decision to become an early childhood teacher may be based on many different reasons.

❋ ❋ ❋ From my perspective, early childhood is a key time to make a significant impact on a child's overall progress and to help families. Children in this age range have so much potential to overcome many of the challenges of their disabilities. Also, for families who are just coming to terms with a child's disability, there is a greater need for support and guidance on how to help the child and how to adapt as a family. I really want to be able to help children and families, as well as to make a real impact on their lives.

❋ ❋ ❋ I am thrilled that I made this career change. I'm very happy teaching young children. They are so curious about how the world works and see learning as fun! I have enormous respect for the young brain and the speed at which it can learn.

❋ ❋ ❋ No one ever asked me what I wanted to do with my life career wise, so I never expressed my idea of working with young children with disabilities. I was told that I would be a good nurse. However, during my first semester of nursing school, I passed out on an excursion to the morgue. After that, I decided to head back home and become a full-time teacher's assistant. I worked in a program for children diagnosed with emotional disabilities, and I loved it! So I obtained my degrees in ECE and special education. I absolutely love children—all of them!

instructional assistant
A teacher in the class who assists a lead teacher in providing instruction.

❋ ❋ ❋ Part of the joy and challenge of ECE has been working with people from different cultures—families, their children, **instructional assistants,** and **translators.** It is important to always communicate your passion, teaching practices, and how and why you want all families and children to be active members of your classroom with everyone involved in the process.

translator
A person who is responsible for mediating communication between parties who do not share a common language.

When deciding what area(s) of ECE you are personally and professionally interested in, you may consider your own strengths or your potential to help children and their families. You should reflect on the experiences and the various questions posed previously in this chapter. You may have a yearning to teach in a program with specific groups of children and families, but always be cognizant that you will come into contact with an ever-increasing variety of children and families. Therefore, you need to learn about how children and families are different, as well as how they are the same.

Who Teaches in Early Childhood Education?

In the most recent, comprehensive study investigating who teaches in ECE, Saluja, Early, and Clifford (2002) indicated that there were 284,277 teachers of 3- and 4-year-olds in the United States at that time, 98% of whom were female. The teachers had a median age of approximately 39 years and had worked as ECE teachers for an average of 6.8 years. In this study, the researchers examined five types of ECE programs: public schools, Head Start, other public or independent agencies, churches or synagogues, and for-profit programs. Across program types, some differences in the teachers' ages and length of employment were noted. Teachers in public schools were the oldest (42 years) and were employed longest in their positions (7.8 years), followed by teachers in churches or synagogues. ECE teachers in independent nonprofit agencies and Head Start programs were at their positions for an average of 6.9 and 7.1 years, respectively. The youngest ECE teachers were employed in for-profit centers, with a mean age of 35 years; these teachers also worked in their positions for the least number of years (5.6 years).

In this same report (Saluja et al., 2002), the authors also addressed the racial identities of ECE teachers. Overall, 0.9% of ECE teachers were of American Indian or Native Alaskan background, 1.1% were Asian or Pacific Islander, 5.7% were Hispanic, 10.2% were African American, and 78.4% were Caucasian. When the percentages were disaggregated according to the program types mentioned previously, some differences were noted. In Head Start programs, 35% of teachers were identified as African American, 5.1% as American Indian or Native Alaskan, and 2.7% as Asian or Pacific Islander. Of all the programs, public schools had the greatest percentage of Hispanic ECE teachers (10.5%). Caucasian teachers represented more than 80% of ECE teachers in church and synagogue programs (85.7%), for-profit centers (83.3%), and other public agencies or independent centers (80.5%). Few ECE teachers represented themselves as from mixed backgrounds (3.8%); this percentage was fairly evenly distributed across program types.

❊ ❊ ❊ Section Summary ❊ ❊ ❊

Teachers enter the ECE profession for various personal reasons, yet all include a passion to care and educate young children. The ECE teaching field is female dominated at this time. ECE teachers and other professionals work in varied settings, both public and private. Settings vary in terms of the ethnic variation of their teachers and the length of times teachers stay in their positions.

Where Do Early Childhood Educators Work?

Figure 1.1 shows where 3- and 4-year-old children receive early education and care. The majority of 3-year-old children who are in care outside of their homes attend local public education, private child care, or other center-based programs. In smaller numbers, other children are enrolled in Head Start programs, state-funded public prekindergarten, or ECSE. Similarly, for 4-year-old children, the majority of children are enrolled in public education, private child care, or other center-based programs. A sizable number of 4-year-old children attend state-funded public prekindergarten programs, with others in Head Start or ECSE programs. About 26% of 4-year-old children and 53% of 3-year-old children are not enrolled in **center-based care** (Barnett, Epstein, Friedman, Sansanelli, & Hustedt, 2009).

The number of 3- and 4-year-old children attending preschool has increased dramatically since the 1960s. An analysis of this phenomenon revealed that

> In 1960, just 10% of the nation's 3- and 4-year-old children were enrolled in any type of classroom. Less than a half century later, nearly three-quarters of children enroll in a preschool classroom at age 4 and about half do so at age 3. (Barnett, 2008, p. 1)

center-based care (education) *Care or education that occurs within a child development center with multiple classrooms for preschool, in contrast to home or school settings.*

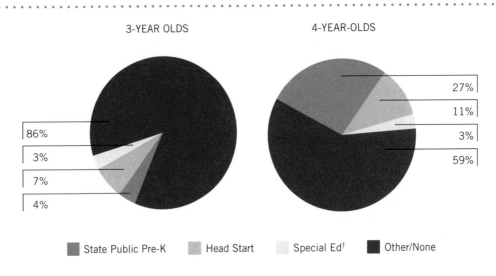

3-YEAR OLDS   4-YEAR-OLDS

86%

3%

7%

4%

27%

11%

3%

59%

■ State Public Pre-K   ■ Head Start   ■ Special Ed†   ■ Other/None

†This is an estimated number of children in special education not enrolled in state-funded pre-K or Head Start. Total enrollment in special education is higher.

Figure 1.1. State prekindergarten and Head Start enrollment as a percentage of the total population. (From Barnett, W.S., Epstein, D.J., Carolan, M.E., Fitzgerald, J., Ackerman, D.J., & Friedman, A.H. [2010]. *The state of preschool 2010: State preschool yearbook* [p. 5]. New Brunswick, NJ: National Institute for Early Education Research; reprinted by permission.)

Research conducted at the National Institute for Early Education Research revealed that approximately 75% of 4-year-old children and 50% of 3-year-old children in the United States attend a preschool center. About half of all 4-year-old children but less than 20% of all 3-year-old children attend public programs, whereas about 35% of both age groups enroll in private preschool options (Barnett, 2008).

Of the total costs of effective ECE, Barnett and Masse (2002) revealed that families pay approximately 55%, the federal government pays about 30%, and state and local governments pay about 15% of the costs of ECE and care. In fiscal year 2001, the government provided about $25 billion for ECE programs, with $16 billion from the federal government and close to $9 billion from state and local governments (estimates in 2002 dollars).

State and federal government funding has played an increasingly larger role in the fiscal support of schooling since the 20th century in the United States. A major shift in education funding resulted in increased government spending on ECE with the implementation of state equalization efforts, as well as federal programs for low-income children and families such as **Title I**, Head Start, and after-school programs. According to the National Center for Education Statistics, expenditures for education rose from $213.4 billion in 1985–1986 to $311.6 billion in 1998–1999, a 46% increase (estimates use constant 1999–2000 dollars).

Federal spending on education from 1965 to 2000 approached $200 billion. The share of ECE revenue that came from the federal government, which was practically nonexistent before the 1970s, hovered near 7% throughout the 1990s. Title I, which helps low-income children and families, is the largest federal program for elementary and secondary education. Established by President Lyndon Johnson in

Title I
The largest federal program for elementary/ secondary education geared to the needs of low-income children and families, which includes funds for prekindergarten education.

Early Childhood Special Education

ECSE provides special classes for young children with disabilities and their families that incorporate early childhood and special education practices. Funded by the **Individuals with Disabilities Education Improvement Act (IDEA) of 2004 (PL 108-446)**, these programs provide early intervention for children with disabilities so that they have access to opportunities needed to reach their potential. The **least restrictive environment** for children receiving education has been required by law for many years. More recently, an emphasis has been placed on inclusive education for children with disabilities, which has taken many different forms, including having typically developing children included in ECSE classes.

1965, the Title I program is intended to help bridge the gap between the educational experiences afforded to low-income communities and affluent communities. Under the law, Title I money enhances allocated state or local education funds. School districts must use Title I funds in schools where at least 75% of the student body qualifies for free or reduced lunches, which is the federal marker for low-income families.

One of the major sources of education revenue historically has been local property taxes. Communities with lower property values thereby have a smaller tax base. Communities with higher property values have a larger tax base and thus can generate more money because of tax revenue. At least 45 states rely heavily on sales taxes to fund education. When sales tax revenues go down, school funding can suffer. Local communities' inequalities can be fixed by state legislation, but this often occurs only after being ordered by state courts. Other sources of revenue for early education vary from state to state. They include parent–teacher associations, booster clubs, state lotteries, school–business partnerships (e.g., vending machines), tobacco settlement money, and local education foundations (e.g., nonprofit groups that raise funds from private sources to benefit local public schools).

The federal government is also involved in child care through the Office of Child Care, which was created in 1995 to provide a central focus for federal child care programs. Welfare reform legislation of the 1990s required most low-income single mothers to work.

A 2010 study by the Government Accountability Office noted that five main programs were accountable for approximately two thirds of federal K–12 and ECE funding. These particular programs and the percentage of federal monies that are allocated toward them include the following:

- *Improving Teacher Quality State Grants:* The U.S. Department of Education provides grants to state educational agencies and local educational agencies to develop and support a high-quality teaching force through activities that strengthen teachers' skills and knowledge, enabling them to improve student achievement in core academic subjects. This program received about $8.7 billion for fiscal years 2006–2008, or 5% of the total.

- *Child Care Mandatory and Matching Funds of the Child Care and Development Fund:* The U.S. Department of Health and Human Services provides grants to states and tribes to help low-income, working families pay for child care so that parents can work, pursue an education, or attend training. A portion of the funds

Individuals with Disabilities Education Improvement Act (IDEA) of 2004 (PL 108-446) *The public law that provides for an appropriate education for children with disabilities. IDEA 2004 reflects changes and clarifications to parent involvement, which is particularly important for ECE.*

least restrictive environment *A basic policy in IDEA to provide an environment in which children with disabilities can function and learn with typically developing children.*

Head Start

Head Start is a comprehensive child development program that started in the 1960s in the United States for children with low socioeconomic status and their families. The goal of the program is to prepare children for kindergarten and provide a successful start to their school experiences. On the initial planning committee in 1962, only two members were early childhood educators; six members were from the medical community, three were psychologists, one was a social worker, and one represented a religious group. The planning committee proposed the following objectives for Head Start (Zigler & Styfco, 2010, p. 37):

- Improving the child's physical health and physical abilities
- Helping the emotional and social development of the child by encouraging self-confidence, spontaneity, curiosity, and self-discipline
- Improving the child's mental processes and skills with particular attention to conceptual and verbal skills
- Establishing patterns and expectations of success for the child that will create a climate of confidence for his future learning efforts
- Increasing the child's capacity to relate positively to family members and others, while at the same time strengthening the family's ability to relate positively to the child and his problems
- Developing in the child and his family a responsible attitude toward society, and fostering constructive opportunities for society to work together in solving their problems
- Increasing the sense of dignity and self-worth within the child and his family

Even before the Education for All Handicapped Children Act of 1975 (PL 94-142) was passed, Head Start included children with disabilities. Head Start was first to include home visits as part of its program structure. At its inception (although not initially implemented), children with middle socioeconomic status were to be included in Head Start based on the understanding that economically integrated experiences are important for children with low socioeconomic status. Considering the racial and ethnic diversity of Head Start programs throughout the United States, it is not surprising that Head Start is at the forefront of program development in education for **dual-language learners**.

Over the years, the drive for a quality program has been paramount, although not realized to the point that Head Start program developers would prefer (Zigler & Styfco, 2010). Frequently, funds allocated to increase teacher quality often end up being used to increase enrollment.

---

dual-language learners
Children who are learning at least two languages.

readiness
The state of being prepared or willing; in early childhood education, often refers to whether children are prepared to be successful in kindergarten.

support activities to improve the quality and availability of care. This program received an estimated $8.8 billion for fiscal years 2006–2008, or 5% of the total.

- *Head Start:* The U.S. Department of Health and Human Services provides grants to promote school **readiness** for low-income preschool children through educational, health, nutrition, social, emotional, and family services. This program received about $19.9 billion for fiscal years 2006–2008, or 12% of the total.

- *Special Education:* The U.S. Department of Education provides grants to assist states in providing special education and related services to children with disabilities. This program received about $32.3 billion for fiscal years 2006–2008, or 19% of the total.

- *Title I Grants to Local Educational Agencies:* The U.S. Department of Education provides grants to help students meet state standards through assistance for individual children deemed most in need, or a schoolwide approach to improve

Universal Prekindergarten

When free, voluntary public preschool is available to all children, this is called **universal pre-kindergarten**. The availability of this program goes beyond a targeted group, such as children with low socioeconomic status or children with disabilities. However, very few states have such programs, despite research that has demonstrated the following results (Barnett, Brown, & Shore, 2004):

- Children of both low and middle socioeconomic statuses benefit from such programs.
- More children attend prekindergarten when it is available to all children regardless of their socioeconomic statuses.
- Children with low socioeconomic status have greater educational achievements when programs are inclusive of children from varied economic backgrounds, as parents are more likely to advocate for high-quality programs.

   Successful programs, such as Sweden's universal preschool, provide additional resources for children who have greater needs while they participate in the inclusive universal program.

the overall instructional program. This program received about $39.5 billion for fiscal years 2006–2008, or 24% of the total.

universal prekindergarten
Voluntary public preschool for all children that is not based on a targeted group, such as income or disability.

Family Child Care

Throughout most of the United States, **family child care** providers who are caring for nonrelatives are required by law to be either registered or licensed by the appropriate county or state government agency. Many states exempt certain providers based on the number of children that will receive services under their charge. Regulations related to issues such as the maximum number of children, maximum number of children in each age group, and training required vary from state to state. Providers who are nonregulated (not licensed or registered) because they are exempt are not illegal. Providers who are required to be licensed or registered and do not comply are illegal. Specific regulations are developed within states (e.g., view Virginia's at http://www.dss.virginia.gov/facility/child_care/licensed/child_day_centers).

family child care
Child care provided in a private home for children who are not related to the home-owner.

   Beyond the governmental licensing and registration, many ECE programs will seek out a rigorous accreditation process that reveals their quality status according to state or federal guidelines. One of the most popular processes for this in the United States is the accreditation process of the **National Association for the Education of Young Children (NAEYC)**. More than 7,000 child care programs, preschools, early learning centers, and other center- or school-based programs have been accredited by NAEYC since it began these services in 1985 (NAEYC, 2010).

National Association for the Education of Young Children (NAEYC)
The main professional organization for early childhood educators.

Employment and Salary

Information from the U.S. Bureau of Labor Statistics (2009) indicated that employment of preschool teachers and preschool education teachers is projected to be higher than average for all occupations through 2018. Employment site and salary are related to teachers' education and training. For example, the lowest level posi-

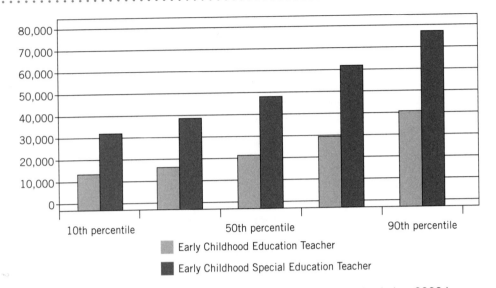

Figure 1.2. Annual wage estimates. (*Source:* U.S. Bureau of Labor Statistics, 2009.)

tions require a high school diploma and a national Child Development Associate (CDA) credential, whereas other positions require a master's degree. Teachers might also have an associate's, bachelor's, or doctoral degree in ECE, child development, applied developmental psychology, or ECSE, depending on their employer and teaching position of interest.

Educational level and employer are related to salary. Head Start is an example that typifies this situation. All Head Start teachers are required to have an associate's degree by 2011, although many community-based programs encourage more advanced degrees. Head Start centers in public schools require a bachelor's degree and certification in ECE through an approved teacher education program or established alternative route. Head Start teachers in public schools receive significantly higher wages than Head Start teachers in community-based programs. ECSE teachers are similarly required to obtain a bachelor's degree and certification in ECSE by an approved special education teacher education program or established alternative. ECSE teachers also make higher salaries than teachers in community-based programs.

Figure 1.2 provides wage estimates for ECE teachers and ECSE teachers. As you can see, ECE teachers have lower wages overall than do ECSE teachers. However, these wages are based on the minimal requirements for each subject area. Therefore, this figure would look quite different if the teachers' levels of education and employers were considered. For example, in many school systems, the salary of an ECE teacher with a master's degree and certification is within the same range as the ECSE teacher who is employed in the same school system with the same requirements and equal level of seniority.

The best-paying employers for ECE teachers include the following:

• Elementary and secondary schools

• Junior colleges

• Local government (Occupational Employment Statistics designation)

• Other residential care facilities

- Colleges, universities, and professional schools (U.S. Bureau of Labor Statistics, 2009)

    For ECSE teachers, the best-paying employers include the following:

- Offices of other health practitioners

- Specialty (except psychiatric and substance abuse) hospitals

- Elementary and secondary schools

- Outpatient care centers

Notice that elementary and secondary schools are top payers across these two areas. They also employ the greatest numbers of ECE teachers receiving top salaries (U.S. Bureau of Labor Statistics, 2009).

❋ ❋ ❋ Section Summary ❋ ❋ ❋

ECE teachers work in many different settings that have different requirements in terms of education and professional development. Services in the different settings are funded at varying levels and from different sources of funds. Teachers across settings have different salary levels, although there is an overall relationship between salary and education level and specialty both among and within settings.

What Makes a High-Quality Early Childhood Education Professional?

When we asked experienced teachers about the characteristics of successful ECE professionals, they mentioned the following qualities:

- Honoring the individual

- Making sure everyone is included

- Teaching kindness

- Building empathy

- Explaining friendship

- Developing a sense of community in the classroom

- Respecting a multicultural environment

- Using words that children can understand

- Using concrete examples

- Providing a medium (e.g., a puppet) that students can use to express themselves

- Getting a good sense of what children know and using that information to teach

- Understanding child development and social emotional development

- Having a vision and a clear sense of purpose

- Respecting the flow of children in transition
- Valuing play
- Being nonjudgmental
- Modeling fairness
- Explaining what the teacher is doing and why
- Encouraging family involvement

High-quality early childhood professionals have the ability to evaluate and intellectually reflect on their practice and the effect they have on young children and their families. They spend time thinking about their practice and reasons behind their actions. They reflect on the outcomes of their teaching and on changes they need to make to improve their teaching (Snow, Griffin, & Burns, 2005). In addition, they understand how to support children's acquisition of the broad array of skills and knowledge they need to become successful learners (Bowman, Donovan, & Burns, 2000). Their teaching is intentional in that they have specified the goals for children's learning and development that will be the result of their teaching (Epstein, 2007).

Teachers who are sensitive and who create positive environments in their classroom are more in touch with children's social and academic needs, as well as their abilities. At a practical level, these teachers make sure that multiple, diverse interactions occur with all children on various levels. Effective teachers build a classroom community in which children and families are respected. Kindness is taught and practiced. Effective teachers promote positive teacher–parent relationships; have learned to work with children and families from different cultures; received professional development in cultural diversity, teaching children with special needs, and teaching students acquiring English as a second language; and hold high expectations for their students.

The education and training of ECE teachers makes a difference. More training has been linked to increased effectiveness (Bowman et al., 2000). However, training is only one of the necessary components for teachers to be able to provide high-quality prekindergarten experiences for all children and their families (Early et al., 2007). Teacher salary is also related to teacher quality. Competitive salaries make it possible for employers to attract and retain high-quality teachers (Whitebook, Phillips, & Howes, 1993). Early childhood teachers in preschools and center-based programs tend to have higher education levels and higher salaries than those in family child care homes (Fuller & Strath, 2001). According to the National Institute for Early Education Research (2004),

- Better-educated preschool teachers with specialized training are more effective.
- Preschool programs employing teachers with 4-year college degrees have been shown to be highly effective and good economic investments for the taxpayer.
- Low educational qualifications and a lack of specific preparation in preschool limit the educational effectiveness of many preschool teachers.
- In 19 out of 38 states that finance prekindergarten programs, educational requirements for prekindergarten teachers are lower than for kindergarten teachers.

Table 1.1.   Teacher qualifications in Maryland, Louisiana, and Washington

State	Teacher		Teacher's assistant degree required
	Degree required	Area of study	
Maryland	Bachelor's degree	Prekindergarten	High school diploma
Louisiana	Bachelor's degree	Prekindergarten or kindergarten	High school diploma
Washington	Associate's or bachelor's degree	Prekindergarten	Associate's degree in child development or equivalent

Source: Barnett et al. (2009).

- Leading educators and researchers have called for improved educational standards for preschool teachers.

- Better compensation is required to hire and retain more effective teachers.

Pianta, Barnett, Burchinal, and Thornburg (2009) follow up on these results, adding that without quality, evidence-based professional development, differences between teachers who complete a 4-year degree versus a 2-year degree do not exhibit different teaching practices and associated improved child outcomes.

Table 1.1 shows teacher qualifications from three states chosen as examples of actual implementation of quality criteria. For example, in 2009, Maryland required ECE teachers to have a bachelor's degree with specialization in ECE, which ranks as high quality. However, Maryland also only requires a high school diploma for teachers' assistants, which is less than the specified high-level indicator of CDA or equivalent. Louisiana required that ECE teachers have a bachelor's degree (high quality) but specialization in kindergarten was allowed (lower quality), as was a high school diploma for teachers' assistants (lower quality). Washington allowed an associate's or bachelor's degree for teachers (mixed quality) with specialization in prekindergarten (high quality) as well as a CDA or equivalent for teachers' assistants (high quality). Nationwide in 2009, 26 of the 51 states required a bachelor's degree (high quality) for teachers, 44 of the 51 states required a specialization for prekindergarten teachers (high quality), and 14 of the 51 states required teachers' assistants to have a CDA or equivalent (high quality; Barnett et al., 2009). Again, improvements in this area need to be accompanied by a full venue of professional development and support, including an effective teacher preservice education program, to ensure **high-quality ECE** (Early et al., 2007).

Preschool teachers working in both public and private programs are required by the majority of states to hold a bachelor's degree in ECE; most programs also require certification in this field. These requirements vary from public to private entities with progression from initial to advanced certification but share commonalities that focus on enhancing the quality of care and assessing this quality through standardized criteria (e.g., NAEYC, Council for Exceptional Children [CEC], Teachers of English to Speakers of Other Languages [TESOL]).

NAEYC and other accreditation groups move to increase the quality of ECE. For example, the *Caring for Our Children* (CFOC) report (American Academy of Pediatrics, American Public Health Association, & National Resource Center for Health and Safety in Child Care, 2002) recommended quality program services for young children and addressed issues of staff qualifications and the relationship to

high-quality ECE
Programs deemed high quality given a particular valid and reliable measure or understanding of quality in early childhood education.

program quality. Specific qualifications for caregivers serving children ages 3–5 build upon general qualifications.

> Caregivers shall demonstrate the ability to apply their knowledge and understanding of the following, to children within the program setting:
>
> a. Typical and atypical development of 3- to 5-year-old children;
>
> b. Social and emotional development of children, including children's development of independence and their ability to adapt to their environment and cope with stress;
>
> c. Cognitive, language, early literacy, and mathematics development of children through activities in the classroom;
>
> d. Cultural backgrounds of the children in the facility's care by demonstrating cultural competence through interactions with children and families and through program activities. (p. 10)

In this book, we provide teachers with the resources to assess whether they are providing opportunities to encourage the learning and development needed by all young children and families. A number of early childhood rating scales are mentioned, which can be used to determine the quality of programs (Snow & Van Hemel, 2008). The following measures are discussed in greater detail in subsequent chapters:

- Assessment Profile for Early Childhood Programs (Abbott-Shim & Sibley, 1992): This is an observational checklist to assess preschool program global quality, including quality of and access to appropriate materials and space, balance and variety of activities, curriculum and role of teacher and learner, and providing for individual children's needs.

- Classroom Assessment Scoring System™ (CLASS™; Pianta, La Paro, & Hamre, 2008): This is a classroom observation system that addresses a teacher's emotional support, classroom organization and management, and quality of instruction across curriculum areas, including concept development, quality of feedback, and language modeling.

- Classroom Practices Inventory (Hyson, Hirsh-Pasek, & Rescorla, 1990): This measure is used to identify didactic preschool practices (e.g., memorization and drill) over reliance on large group instruction and developmentally appropriate practices (e.g., child choice, open-ended and manipulative activities), according to the 1987 guidelines of the NAEYC (Bredekamp, 1987).

- Early Childhood Environment Rating Scale, Revised Edition (Harms, Clifford, & Cryer, 2005): This is a frequently used and well-known rating scale of global program quality (e.g., space furnishings, child care routines, daily schedule), as well as quality of classroom activities (e.g., use of manipulatives, books) and teacher–child interactions (conversation and reasoning).

- Early Childhood Classroom Observation Measure (Stipek & Byler, 2004): This is an observational and rating measure that addresses classroom management, social climate, and learning climate and instruction (literacy and math), including whether instruction is didactic, is totally based on child-initiated learning, or is interactive with the child and based on child understanding.

- Early Language and Literacy Classroom Observation (ELLCO; Smith, Brady, & Anastasopoulos, 2008): This observation instrument provides detailed information on language and literacy instruction, including book reading and discussion, writing, and oral language, as well as assessment in these areas.

- Emerging Academic Snapshot (Ritchie, Howes, Kraft-Sayre, & Weiser, 2001): This time-sampling observational instrument focuses on the social and academic opportunities of children in the preschool classroom, such as children's exposure to instruction and engagement in academic activities across curriculum areas. It can be used with individual children or groups of children and can provide important information for teachers to examine their teaching methods.

- Preschool Classroom Mathematics Inventory (Frede, Weber, Hornbeck, Stevenson-Boyd, & Colon, 2005): This observational instrument assesses instructional opportunities that are related to numbers, such as counting; exploring numbers by comparing, grouping, and recounting; and other mathematical concepts such as classification, seriation, measurement, and time.

Effective early childhood teachers make sure that every child is included in multiple, diverse interactions.

In addition to these more formalized measures, teachers are also encouraged to record their teaching and family interactions to reflect upon the opportunities they are providing. You will want to look at whether you have positive, meaningful conversations with children and parents and whether you are responsive to their needs and interests, including **prior knowledge** about their culture, language(s), and abilities. You might ask a trusted peer to watch the recording an additional time with you so that you can both reflect on strengths, weaknesses, and possibilities for improvement.

prior knowledge
Information that was previously obtained.

❊ ❊ ❊ Section Summary ❊ ❊ ❊

ECE teachers and other professionals strive to be high-quality professionals through active participation in ongoing education experiences and professional development. Being a high-quality professional includes a mixture of **knowledge, skills, and dispositions** found to have an impact on young children's learning and developmental outcomes. In high-quality environments, teachers and other professionals address children's prior knowledge, interests, and needs, and they use effective teaching strategies that reflect best practices and respect and that involve families.

knowledge, skills, and dispositions
Characteristics that are considered by professional groups and researchers to determine the quality of teachers.

Professional Standards for Early Childhood Educators

Across all teaching professions, there are standards for the knowledge, skills, and dispositions that are considered to be important for teachers. This section addresses three of the prominent sets of national standards directly relevant to ECE: the NAEYC (n.d.), the CEC (n.d.) Early Childhood Specialty, and TESOL (n.d.). One might ask why all three of these areas are important for all ECE professionals. High-quality practices in ECE include children with disabilities in classes with typically developing peers, and children who speak languages in addition to English in their homes are also included in ECE throughout the United States.

In addition to these standards that apply across developmental and academic domains, standards for teacher education proposed by the International Reading Association on early literacy and the **National Council of Teachers of Mathematics** on early mathematics have relevance to ECE professionals.

National Council of Teachers of Mathematics (NCTM)
A professional organization for mathematics teachers.

This section introduces the central themes of these professional standards and clarifies the knowledge and skills deemed to be important for early childhood educators. As an ECE professional, you will be influenced by the host of different integrated national, state, and local standards that help to define professional fields and affect the ongoing development of field-based and theoretical practices in ECE. In the following themes, we demonstrate the commonalities of these professional standards. All professional standards are presented here in the briefest form possible; see references for further details.

Multidimensional Development and Learning

Evident in NAEYC, TESOL, and CEC standards is the understanding that *all* children have important developmental trajectories and learning needs (see Figure 1.3). ECE teachers and other professionals need to adhere to multidimensional perspectives of development and learning if they are to provide learning environments and opportunities that are effective for *all* young children.

NAEYC Standard 1:

Promoting child development and learning: Students prepared in early childhood degree programs are grounded in a child development knowledge base. They use their understanding of young children's characteristics and needs and of the multiple interacting influences on children's development and learning to create environments that are healthy, respectful, supportive, and challenging for each child.

TESOL Domain 1:

Candidates know, understand, and use the major theories and research related to the structure and acquisition of language to support English-language learners' language and literacy development and content area achievement. Issues of language structure and language acquisition development are interrelated. The divisions of the standards into the following do not prescribe an order:
1A. Language as a system
1B. Language acquisition and development

CEC Standard 2:

Development and characteristics of learners: Specialized knowledge or skills in early childhood special education includes the following:
2A. Theories of typical and atypical early childhood development
2B. Effect of biological and environmental factors on prenatal, perinatal, and postnatal development
2C. Influence of stress and trauma, protective factors and resilience, and supportive relationships on the social and emotional development of young children
2D. Significance of sociocultural and political contexts for the development and learning of young children who are culturally and linguistically diverse
2E. Impact of medical conditions on family concerns, resources, and priorities
2F. Childhood illnesses and communicable diseases

In their professional development, teachers and caregivers need to be given the opportunity to learn about young children's needs and characteristics and the multiple ways these affect their learning and development. Finally, they need to know how to use this information to develop effective learning environments for young learners.

Figure 1.3. Theme 1: Multidimensional development and learning. ESOL, English for speakers of other languages. (From NAEYC. [2009]. *Position statement. NAEYC Standards for Early Childhood Professional Preparation Programs.* Washington, DC: Author; reprinted with permission from the National Association for the Education of Young Children [NAEYC]. A full-text version of the position statement is available at www.naeyc.org/files/naeyc/file/positions/ProfPrepStandards09.pdf; Council for Exceptional Children, "What Every Special Educator Must Know," www.cec.sped.org, Professional Development, Professional Standards, click on Download the Free PDF under the "Red Book," Sixth Edition, Revised; reprinted by permission; Teachers of English to Speakers of Other Languages. (n.d.). *TESOL/NCATE standards for P–12 teacher education programs.* Retrieved January 29, 2011, from http://www.tesol.org/s_tesol/seccss.asp?CID=219&DID=1689; reprinted by permission.

Families and Communities

Families, communities, and culture are an important source of knowledge about the children in the care of ECE teachers and other professionals. Building relationships with young children's families and their broader communities is central to provide learning environments and opportunities that are effective for *all* young children. NAEYC, TESOL, and CEC standards are very much aligned in support of these ideas (see Figure 1.4), providing integrated foundational principles for practice.

NAEYC Standard 2:

Building family and community relationships: Students prepared in early childhood degree programs understand that successful early childhood education depends upon partnerships with children's families and communities. They know about, understand, and value the importance and complex characteristics of children's families and communities. They use this understanding to create respectful, reciprocal relationships that support and empower families and to involve all families in their children's development and learning.

TESOL Domain 2:

Culture as it affects student learning: Candidates know, understand, and use in their instruction, major theories and research related to the nature and role of culture, and how cultural groups and individual cultural identities affect language learning and school achievement.

CEC Standard 3:

Individual learning differences: Specialized knowledge or skills in early childhood special education includes the following:

3A. Use intervention strategies with young children and their families that affirm and respect family, cultural, and linguistic diversity

Young children are greatly influenced by their families and communities, and our understanding and respect are necessary to provide effective ECE. We might not even realize initially the diversity that we will encounter as early childhood educators and that as informed professionals will make teaching more effective.

Figure 1.4. Theme 2: Families and communities. (From NAEYC. [2009]. *Position statement. NAEYC Standards for Early Childhood Professional Preparation Programs.* Washington, DC: Author; reprinted with permission from the National Association for the Education of Young Children [NAEYC]. A full-text version of the position statement is available at www.naeyc.org/files/naeyc/file/positions/ProfPrepStandards09.pdf; Council for Exceptional Children, "What Every Special Educator Must Know," www.cec.sped.org, Professional Development, Professional Standards, click on Download the Free PDF under the "Red Book," Sixth Edition, Revised; reprinted by permission; Teachers of English to Speakers of Other Languages. (n.d.). *TESOL/NCATE standards for P–12 teacher education programs.* Retrieved January 29, 2011, from http://www.tesol.org/s_tesol/seccss.asp?CID=219&DID=1689; reprinted by permission.

Observing, Documenting, and Assessing

In this theme, we again witness strong commonalities across these professional standards (see Figure 1.5). TESOL's fourth domain emphasizes that educators should understand issues and concepts of assessment and use standards-based procedures with students. NAEYC's third standard highlights observing, documenting, and assessing to support young children and families. In addition, CEC's 8th standard highlights how candidates should assess the development and learning of young children by selecting, adapting, and using specialized formal and informal assessments for infants, young children, and their families. At a time when systematic assessment issues are of key importance to all educators, knowledge and experience in using assessment is central for ECE teachers and other professionals and is an integral part of high-quality ECE practice.

NAEYC Standard 3:

Observing, documenting, and assessing to support young children and families: Students prepared in early childhood degree programs understand that child observation, documentation, and other forms of assessment are central to the practice of all early childhood professionals. They know about and understand the goals, benefits, and uses of assessment. They know about and use systematic observations, documentation, and other effective assessment strategies in a responsible way, in partnership with families and other professionals, to positively influence the development of every child.

TESOL Domain 4:

Candidates understand issues and concepts of assessment and use standards-based procedures with English-language learners.

Standard 4A. Issues of assessment for English-language learners

Standard 4B. Language proficiency assessment

Standard 4C. Classroom-based assessment

Candidates know, use and can design a variety of performance-based assessment tools and techniques to inform instruction in the classroom.

CEC Standard 8:

Specialized knowledge or skills in early childhood special education includes the following:

8A. Assess the development and learning of young children

8B. Select, adapt and use specialized formal and informal assessments for infants, young children, and their families

8C. Participate as a team member to integrate assessment results in the development and implementation of individualized family service plans and individualized education plans

8D. Assist families in identifying their concerns, resources, and priorities

8E. Participate and collaborate as a team member with other professionals in conducting family-centered assessments

8F. Evaluate services with families

Each young child is unique in what and how he or she expresses what has been learned and how he or she develops. Teachers and caregivers of young children need to understand the benefits and misuses of assessment for this age group. The need to understand how observing/assessing learning across contexts with multiple methods will give representative information about young children. This knowledge is used ethically in partnership with families and other professionals.

Figure 1.5. Theme 3: Observing, documenting, and assessing. ESL, English as a second language; ESOL, English for speakers of other languages. (From NAEYC. [2009]. *Position statement. NAEYC Standards for Early Childhood Professional Preparation Programs.* Washington, DC: Author; reprinted with permission from the National Association for the Education of Young Children [NAEYC]. A full-text version of the position statement is available at www.naeyc.org/files/naeyc/file/positions/ProfPrepStandards09.pdf; Council for Exceptional Children, "What Every Special Educator Must Know," www.cec.sped.org, Professional Development, Professional Standards, click on Download the Free PDF under the "Red Book," Sixth Edition, Revised; reprinted by permission; Teachers of English to Speakers of Other Languages. (n.d.). *TESOL/NCATE standards for P–12 teacher education programs.* Retrieved January 29, 2011, from http://www.tesol.org/s_tesol/seccss.asp?CID=219&DID=1689; reprinted by permission.

Instruction

Planning and implementing instruction is a critical part of daily, weekly, and annual activity planning for teachers in ECE (see Figure 1.6). The standards across NAEYC, TESOL, and CEC address effective instruction. Planning with the various sources of knowledge—for example, evidence-based practice, curriculum materials, families, theory, and assessment data—is crucial. Carefulness and flexibility with implementing plans is important. ECE teachers and other professionals should assess the effectiveness of their instruction and reflect on improvement of it on a day-to-day basis.

NAEYC Standards 4 & 5:

Using developmentally effective approaches to connect with children and families: Students prepared in early childhood degree programs understand that teaching and learning with young children is a complex enterprise, and its details vary depending on children's ages, characteristics, and the settings within which teaching and learning occur. They understand and use positive relationships and supportive interactions as the foundation for their work with young children and families. Students know, understand, and use a wide array of developmentally appropriate approaches, instructional strategies, and tools to connect with children and families and positively influence each child's development and learning.

Using content knowledge to build meaningful curriculum: Students prepared in early childhood degree programs use their knowledge of academic disciplines to design, implement, and evaluate experiences that promote positive development and learning for each and every young child. Students understand the importance of developmental domains and academic (or content) disciplines in an early childhood curriculum. They know the essential concepts, inquiry tools, and structure of content areas, including academic subjects, and can identify resources to deepen their understanding. Students use their own knowledge and other resources to design, implement, and evaluate meaningful, challenging curricula that promote comprehensive developmental and learning outcomes for every young child.

TESOL Domain 3:

Planning, implementing, and managing instruction: Candidates know, understand, and use evidence-based practices and strategies related to planning, implementing, and managing standards-based ESL and content instruction. Candidates are skilled in using a variety of classroom organization techniques, program models, and teaching strategies for developing and integrating language skills. They can integrate technology and choose and adapt classroom resources.

CEC Standard 7:

Instructional planning: Specialized knowledge or skills in early childhood special education includes the following:

7A. Implement, monitor and evaluate individualized family service plans and individualized education plans

7B. Plan and implement developmentally and individually appropriate curriculum

7C. Design intervention strategies incorporating information from multiple disciplines

7D. Implement developmentally and functionally appropriate individual and group activities including play, environmental routines, parent-mediated activities, group projects, cooperative learning, inquiry experiences, and systematic instruction

Early childhood education teachers and caregivers build meaningful curriculum through use of children's prior knowledge, interests, and developmental and learning needs as provided by children and their families in conjunction with the content, concepts, and skills found necessary through research in early childhood education.

Figure 1.6. Theme 4: Planning instruction. ESL, English as a second language. (From NAEYC. [2009]. *Position statement. NAEYC Standards for Early Childhood Professional Preparation Programs.* Washington, DC: Author; reprinted with permission from the National Association for the Education of Young Children [NAEYC]. A full-text version of the position statement is available at www.naeyc.org/files/naeyc/file/positions/ProfPrepStandards09.pdf; Council for Exceptional Children, "What Every Special Educator Must Know," www.cec.sped.org, Professional Development, Professional Standards, click on Download the Free PDF under the "Red Book," Sixth Edition, Revised; reprinted by permission; Teachers of English to Speakers of Other Languages. (n.d.). *TESOL/NCATE standards for P–12 teacher education programs.* Retrieved January 29, 2011, from http://www.tesol.org/s_tesol/seccss.asp?CID=219&DID= 1689; reprinted by permission.

Professionalism

Professionalism demands that ECE teachers and other professionals build upon their reflections on all standards by networking with others in the ECE field (see Figure 1.7). Numerous resources are available through professional organizations, such as research-to-practice articles, which examine ethics of the profession and provide opportunities to advocate for young children and their families.

NAEYC Standard 6:

Becoming a professional: Students prepared in early childhood degree programs identify and conduct themselves as members of the early childhood profession. They know and use ethical guidelines and other professional standards related to early childhood practice. They are continuous, collaborative learners who demonstrate knowledgeable, reflective, and critical perspectives on their work, making informed decisions that integrate knowledge from a variety of sources. They are informed advocates for sound educational practices and policies.

TESOL Domain 5:

Professional development, partnerships, and advocacy:

Candidates keep current with new instructional techniques, research results, advances in the field, and public policy issues. Candidates demonstrate knowledge of the history of ESL teaching. Candidates use such information to reflect upon and improve their instruction and assessment practices. Candidates work collaboratively with school staff and the community to improve the learning environment, provide support, and advocate for English-language learners and their families. Candidates take advantage of professional growth opportunities and demonstrate the ability to build partnerships with colleagues and students' families, serve as community resources, and advocate for students.

CEC Standard 9:

Professional and ethical practice: Specialized knowledge or skills in early childhood special education includes the following:

9A. Know organizations and publications relevant to the field of early childhood special education

9B. Recognize signs of child abuse and neglect in young children and follow reporting procedures

9C. Use family theories and principles to guide professional practice; respect family choices and goals

9D. Apply models of team process in early childhood

9E. Advocate for enhanced professional status and working conditions for early childhood service providers

9F. Participate in activities of professional organizations relevant to the field of early childhood special education

9G. Apply research and effective practices critically in early childhood settings

9H. Develop, implement and evaluate a professional development plan relevant to one's work with young children

Your professional organizations invite and demand that you become involved in the early childhood education field, learning new information that is available, and integrating it into prior learning in a reflective and critical manner. Early childhood professionals uphold ethical and professional standards and engage advocacy for children and the profession.

Figure 1.7. Theme 5: Professionalism. ESL, English as a second language; ESOL, English for speakers of other languages. (From NAEYC. [2009]. *Position statement. NAEYC Standards for Early Childhood Professional Preparation Programs*. Washington, DC: Author; reprinted with permission from the National Association for the Education of Young Children [NAEYC]. A full-text version of the position statement is available at www.naeyc.org/files/naeyc/file/positions/ProfPrepStandards09.pdf; Council for Exceptional Children, "What Every Special Educator Must Know," www.cec.sped.org, Professional Development, Professional Standards, click on Download the Free PDF under the "Red Book," Sixth Edition, Revised; reprinted by permission; Teachers of English to Speakers of Other Languages. (n.d.). *TESOL/NCATE standards for P–12 teacher education programs*. Retrieved January 29, 2011, from http://www.tesol.org/s_tesol/seccss.asp?CID=219&DID=1689; reprinted by permission.

✱ ✱ ✱ Section Summary ✱ ✱ ✱

From this brief review of just a few standards that are a vital part of ECE, we witness the relevance of these standards as they stand alone and their immense power as they are integrated. Together, the integration of these standards can assist ECE practitioners to advance their practices throughout their careers. As teachers, you will be working in an established professional field. Research has validated these educational and professional standards, which support the historic and current status of ECE. Understanding these professional criteria and embedding them into your practical experiences will provide a higher quality experience for your students and their families.

KEY CONCEPTS

- Teachers enter the ECE profession for reasons that are personal, yet all include a passion to care and educate young children.
- ECE teachers and other professionals work in varied settings, both public and private. Settings vary in terms of the ethnic variation of their teachers and the length of time teachers stay in their positions.
- Different ECE settings have unique requirements in terms of education and professional development.
- Teachers and other professionals have different salary levels based on setting and education levels, with additional variation based on specialty.
- ECE teachers and other professionals strive to be high-quality professionals through education and professional development.
- Being a high-quality professional includes a mixture of knowledge, skills, and dispositions found to have impact on young children's learning and developmental outcomes. In high-quality environments, ECE teachers and other professionals address children's prior knowledge, their interests, and needs, and they use effective teaching strategies that reflect best practices and respect and that involve families.
- Standards are a vital part of ECE. ECE professionals continuously work to address and improve on those standards that reflect the diversity of children who are in their care.

Integration of Information

You just worked through what might be your first introduction to ECE. What do you think? If you are revisiting this field, is the information the same as you previously learned? Does this professional field seem like the one for you?

Self-Reflective Guide

This self-reflective guide will help you assess whether you learned the information in this chapter. It also provides an opportunity to identify areas in which you want or need more information. Are there some new ideas learned that will affect your immediate practice with children?

1. Reflect on your identity and sense of self, your interests and strengths, and different contexts in which young children are taught, thinking about your interests. Make a few notes.

2. Recognize the various settings in which ECE takes place. List one setting where you think you would like to teach and why. List another where you think you would not like to teach and why.

3. Identify the characteristics of high-quality ECE professionals. List the most important characteristics of high-quality early childhood teachers and caregivers.

4. You now know that different professional groups set professional standards for early childhood professionals. List several NAEYC, TESOL, and CEC standards that seem particularly important to you at this point in your professional development.

5. Identify other information you learned that can have an immediate effect on your current practice if you are a practicing teacher or caregiver at this time.

6. List some areas you want to explore further. Who can help you learn about your concerns?

Helpful Web Sites

Council for Exceptional Children

www.cec.sped.org

The CEC is the major professional association focused on children with disabilities and their families. The site provides many resources for teachers, including discussion forums to share information and discuss their experiences.

The Division for Early Childhood

www.dec-sped.org

This professional organization, which is a division of the Council for Exceptional Children, focuses on young children with disabilities and special needs and their families. The site provides many sources, including information on research, policy, and advocacy, for appropriate educational practices for young children with disabilities.

Frank Porter Graham Child Development Institute

www.fpg.unc.edu

This site includes policy and practice information about early childhood education for young children and their families.

National Association for the Education of Young Children

www.naeyc.org

The NAEYC is the major professional association focused on young children. This site provides information on most topics related to ECE, including research, policy, and practice.

National Institute for Early Education Research

http://nieer.org

This site includes research, policy, and practice information about early childhood education for young children and their families.

Teachers of English to Speakers of Other Languages

www.tesol.org

This site includes resources for providing appropriate educational experiences for dual-language learners.

References

Abbott-Shim, M., & Sibley, A. (1992). *Assessment Profile for Early Childhood Programs.* Atlanta, GA: Quality Assist.

American Academy of Pediatrics, American Public Health Association, & National Resource Center for Health and Safety in Child Care. (2002). *Caring for our children. National health and safety performance standards: Guidelines for out-of-home child care* (2nd ed.). Elk Grove Village, IL: American Academy of Pediatrics.

Barnett, W.S. (2008). *Preschool education and its lasting effects: Research and policy implications.* Boulder, CO: Education and the Public Interest Center & Education Policy Research Unit.

Barnett, W.S., Brown, K., & Shore, R. (2004, April). The universal vs. targeted debate: Should the United States have preschool for all? *Preschool Policy Matters, 6.*

Barnett, W.S., Epstein, D.J., Carolan, M.E., Fitzgerald, J., Ackerman, D.J., & Friedman, A.H. (2010). *The state of preschool 2010: State preschool yearbook.* New Brunswick, NJ: National Institute for Early Education Research.

Barnett, W.S., Epstein, D.J., Friedman, A.H., Sansanelli, R.A., & Hustedt, J.T. (2009). *The state of preschool 2009: State preschool yearbook.* New Brunswick, NJ: National Institute for Early Education Research.

Barnett, W.S., & Masse, L.N. (2002). Funding issues for early childhood care and education programs. In D. Cryer & R.M. Clifford (Eds.), *Early childhood education & care in the USA* (pp. 137–166). Baltimore: Paul H. Brookes Publishing Co.

Bowman, B.T., Donovan, M.S., & Burns, M.S. (2000). *Eager to learn: Educating our preschoolers.* Washington, DC: National Academies Press.

Bredekamp, S. (1987). *Developmentally appropriate practice in early childhood programs serving children from birth through age 8* (Exp. ed.). Washington, DC: National Association for the Education of Young Children.

Council for Exceptional Children. (n.d.) *Professional standards.* Retrieved January 29, 2011, from http://www.cec.sped.org/Content/NavigationMenu/Professional Development/ProfessionalStandards/

Early, D.M., Maxwell, K.L., Burchinal, M., Alva, S., Bender, R.H., Bryant, D., et al. (2007). Teachers' education, classroom quality, and young children's academic skills: Results from seven studies of preschool programs. *Child Development, 78*(2), 558–580.

Education for All Handicapped Children Act of 1975, PL 94-142, 20 U.S.C. §§ 1400 *et seq.*

Epstein, A. (2007). *The intentional teacher: Choosing the best strategies for young children's learning.* Washington, DC: National Association for the Education of Young Children.

Frede, E., Weber, M., Hornbeck, A., Stevenson-Boyd, J., & Colon, A. (2005). *Preschool Classroom Mathematics Inventory.* Unpublished instrument. (Available from the first author at efrede@nieer.org)

Fuller, B., & Strath, A. (2001). The child-care and preschool workforce: Demographics, earnings, and unequal distribution. *Educational Evaluation and Policy Analysis, 23*(1), 37–55.

Harms, T., Clifford, R., & Cryer, D. (2005). *Early Childhood Environment Rating Scale* (Rev. Ed.). New York: Teachers College Press.

Hyson, M.C., Hirsh-Pasek, K., & Rescorla, L. (1990). Academic environments in preschool: Challenge or pressure? *Early Education and Development, 1,* 401–423.

Individuals with Disabilities Education Improvement Act (IDEA) of 2004, PL 108-446, 20 U.S.C. §§ 1400 *et seq.*

National Association for the Education of Young Children. (2010). *Let's celebrate! 25 years of NAEYC accreditation of programs for young children.* Retrieved January

26, 2011, from http://www.naeyc.org/files/academy/file/YCNov2010.pdf

National Association for the Education of Young Children. (n.d.). *Early childhood teacher certification.* Retrieved January 29, 2011, from, http://www.naeyc.org/positionstatements/psAssocOfTeacherEducators

National Institute for Early Education Research. (2004). Should the U.S. have preschool for all? Potential win-win for kids, taxpayers. Retrieved December 4, 2010, from http://nieer.org/psm/index.php?article=64

Pianta, R.C., Barnett, W.S., Burchinal, M., & Thornburg, K.R. (2009). The effects of preschool education: What we know, how public policy is or is not aligned with the evidence base, and what we need to know. *Psychological Science in the Public Interest, 10*(2) 49–88.

Pianta, R.C., La Paro, K.M., & Hamre, B.K. (2008). *Classroom Assessment Scoring System™ (CLASS™).* Baltimore: Paul H. Brookes Publishing Co.

Ritchie, S., Howes, C., Kraft-Sayre, M., & Weiser, B. (2001). *Emerging Academic Snapshot.* Unpublished instrument, University of California, Los Angeles.

Saluja, G., Early, D.M., & Clifford, R.M. (2002). Demographic characteristics of early childhood teachers and structural elements of early care and education in the United States. *Early Childhood Research and Practice, 4*(1), 2–20.

Smith, M.W., Brady, J.P., & Anastasopoulos, J. (2008). *Early Language and Literacy Classroom Observation (ELLCO) pre-K user's guide.* Baltimore: Paul H. Brookes Publishing Co.

Snow, C.E., Griffin, P., & Burns, M.S. (2005). *Knowledge to support the teaching of reading: Preparing teachers for a changing world.* Indianapolis: Jossey-Bass.

Snow, C.E., & Van Hemel, S.B. (2008). *Early childhood assessment: Why, what, and how.* Washington, DC: National Academies Press.

Stipek, D.J., & Byler, P. (2004). The early childhood classroom observation measure. *Early Childhood Research Quarterly, 19*(3), 375–397.

Teachers of English to Speakers of Other Languages. (n.d.) *TESOL/NCATE standards for P-12 teacher education programs.* Retrieved January 29, 2011, from http://www.tesol.org/s_tesol/seccss.asp?CID=219&DID=1689

U.S. Bureau of Labor Statistics. (2009). *Occupational outlook handbook, 2010-11 edition: Teachers—preschool, except special education.* Retrieved June 24, 2010, from http://www.bls.gov/oco/ocos317.htm

Whitebook, M., Phillips, D., & Howes, C. (1993). *National child care staffing study revisited: Four years in the life of center-based child care.* Washington, DC: Center for the Child Care Workforce.

Zigler, E., & Styfco, S.J. (2010). *The hidden history of Head Start.* New York: Oxford University Press.

Who Are the Children and Their Families?

2

Learning Objectives

1. Reflect on the multilingual and multicultural characteristics of the families and children that you might teach

2. Recognize that children come from families with different structures, which may affect how children and their families relate to you

3. Identify some aspects of neighborhoods, communities, and families that might present particular challenges for you as a teacher

4. Consider that children in your classroom might have disabilities and what that means in terms of how you thought of your role as an ECE professional

5. Identify and learn about the different types of disabilities that young children may have

6. Recognize the main points of the laws related to young children with disabilities

7. Understand the special education eligibility process for children with disabilities

8. Understand the basic concept of inclusion and why it is important for ECE professionals

W ho are the children served by early childhood education (ECE) professionals? What about children and families from different cultures? Is there basic information that I need to keep in mind? Are some kinds of families better than others? What about all the different languages that children and families speak at home? What do I need to know about teaching multilingual children? What are some of the disabilities that children might have? What is inclusion and do I need to do it?

These are the types of questions being addressed in this chapter on children and families in ECE. In this chapter, we present characteristics of neighborhoods, communities, and families that affect the children served in

ECE settings, emphasizing aspects of such contexts that are important to consider so that ECE teachers respect all children and their families. We also introduce information regarding young dual-language learners and multilingual children and their families. Many of these characteristics are strengths of families. However, we also discuss some factors that may negatively affect a child's development, such as child abuse, neglect, and living in communities with high levels of poverty (low **socioeconomic status**).

In the second part of this chapter, we discuss children with disabilities, including sensory disabilities such as visual impairment and deafness; physical disabilities such as cerebral palsy; and intellectual disabilities such as Down syndrome, autism spectrum disorders, attention-deficit/hyperactivity disorder, emotional disorders, learning disabilities, and speech and language impairments. Finally, we provide an overview of the process by which young children get referred for special educational services.

socioeconomic status (SES)
An individual's income and educational levels, as well as level of professional status in employment.

Family, Neighborhood, and Community Characteristics

ECE professionals serve not only their students but also students' families and the communities in which they live and teach. Therefore, ECE professionals need to be able to interact effectively with diverse children, families, and colleagues. The following sections describe the importance of characteristics within the students' families, neighborhoods, and communities.

Family Culture

Students' cultures add richness and complexity to ECE. For example, suppose that you are working in a Head Start classroom with 22 three-year-old children, of which 14 children are in a formal school setting for the first time. Most of the 22 children are Hispanic, Asian American, or African American; a few are recently immigrated Asian and Pacific Islander children. In the ongoing consideration of culture in this particular classroom and in the larger context of your school and surrounding community, your thoughts focus on diversity. As a practitioner serving young children and the larger communities you live and work in, your awareness of and sensitivity to the populations you serve is affected by your ability to interact effectively with diverse children, families, and colleagues (Gay, 2010).

cultural values
A cultural preference that guides thoughts and actions.

Your awareness of cultural differences and **cultural values** is referred to as your *cultural competence*.

cultural competence
Having the awareness, insight, knowledge and skills to interact with others from a different cultural group than one's own.

By considering the demographics of the United States, you can better understand how society might view culture and cultural competence. It is important to note that estimates of immigrant populations from the 2010 U.S. Census are ongoing at the time of this writing; however, surprises in the data have been found from data that have been released. For example, consider the recent finding from the Pew Hispanic Center: "The number of Hispanics counted in the 2010 Census has been larger than expected in most states for which the Census Bureau has released detailed population totals so far" (Passel & Cohn, 2011, p. 1). Because the 2010 Census data have not been fully released at the time of publication of this book, in some situations we rely on findings from previous census data in the information presented in this chapter. Below are such findings for Hispanic students.

- The high school graduation rate for Hispanic students is 52% (Bauman & Graf, 2003).

- Approximately 25% of Hispanic students have less than a ninth-grade education (U.S. Census Bureau, 2009).

- Hispanic students attend segregated schools. For example, in four metropolitan areas in Texas—Laredo, McAllen-Edinburg-Pharr, Brownsville-Harlingen, and El Paso—more than 90% of Hispanic students attend segregated schools (Diversitydata.org & Harvard School of Public Health, 2008–2009).

- The poverty level for Hispanic families in 2000 was 21% (National Center for Education Statistics [NCES], 2003).

- Hispanic students score significantly below national norms on academic achievement tests of reading, math, science, social studies, and writing at Grades 3, 7, and 11 (NCES, 2003).

What do numbers like these mean, and how will they influence your interactions with children and families? Many of the statistics speak to culture and **cultural awareness.** Teachers can affect the specific trajectory of their students based on their actions and inactions. For example, historically many teachers referred kindergarten children for special education simply because they did not speak English, had no preschool experience, or scored low on a placement examination. Many of these grade-level decisions were premised on a lack of cultural awareness and an unwillingness to address diversity in the classroom, but they can affect a child's educational outcomes for life (Harry & Klinger, 2006).

Cultural awareness is especially important when you work with immigrant families. About 20% of children in the United States have immigrant parents (Suarez-Orozco, 2001). A recent analysis of census data (Passel & Taylor, 2010) sets the number of children (17 years and younger) of immigrant parents at 23%. Of these, 16% have parents with legal immigrant status, and 7% have parents with unauthorized status. These children function within several different cultural contexts. Immigrant families may experience considerable stress when their hopes of increased financial, social, and **educational opportunities** in their new country of residence are not realized. Moreover, immigrant children may encounter racism and other biases, especially in educational contexts, which may lead to less investment in education (Suarez-Orozco, Suarez-Orozco, & Todorova, 2008).

cultural awareness
The awareness of cultural richness in a particular setting such that it is a source of new learning as well as a marker for respecting cultural differences.

educational opportunities
Learning and development opportunities that children have been given.

multilingualism
The ability to speak more than one language.

Home Language

In the United States, about one in five children speak a language other than English at home (Espinosa, 2009). In Head Start and Early Head Start, about one in three children come from families with a home language other than English (Ballentyne, Sanderman, D'Emilio, & McLaughlin, 2008). **Multilingualism** is very common worldwide and is an asset in children's language and literacy mastery. Young children often can switch between languages depending on who they are speaking with and switch between two or more languages during a bilingual conversation, which is a sign of advanced language proficiency. However, multilingual children's language use is not all the same. Comprehension and production of English varies depending on when the child started learning additional languages. Figure 2.1 depicts this process of additional language use in the context of learning English as a second language.

When determining learning objectives for the children in your classroom, reflect on the multilingual and multicultural characteristics of their families.

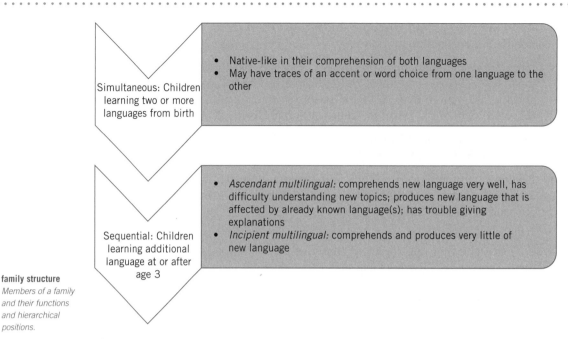

- Native-like in their comprehension of both languages
- May have traces of an accent or word choice from one language to the other

Simultaneous: Children learning two or more languages from birth

- *Ascendant multilingual:* comprehends new language very well, has difficulty understanding new topics; produces new language that is affected by already known language(s); has trouble giving explanations
- *Incipient multilingual:* comprehends and produces very little of new language

Sequential: Children learning additional language at or after age 3

Figure 2.1. Language learning process for multilingual children.

family structure
Members of a family and their functions and hierarchical positions.

extended families
Families that include parents and children, as well as grandparents, cousins, aunts and uncles, nieces and nephews, and more distant relatives living together and taking part in care of children.

nuclear families
Families that include parents and their children, including single parents and same-sex parents.

Recognize that children may come from different family structures.

Family Type and Structure

The multiplicity of different **family structures** in today's world will affect your teaching experiences and interactions with the host of different children and families that you will serve throughout your career. Depending on where you choose to work, you will interact with many different kinds of families, including nuclear and **extended families**, families who have just recently immigrated to the United States, families who speak little or no English in the home, gay and lesbian families with same-sex parents, and families with a history of child abuse or neglect.

Social Organization of Family

Nuclear families consist of parents and their children, including single-parent households and gay and lesbian partners with children. Extended families include parents, children, grandparents, cousins, nieces and nephews, and more distant relatives. Although nuclear families are the predominant family type in the United States, the number of extended-family households has been increasing for a variety of reasons, which may be financial or cultural. For example, when both parents work outside the home, the grandmother may become the primary caregiver.

Parenting styles within nuclear families have also shifted dramatically in recent years as the number of single-parent households have increased. Between 1970 and 2000, there was a 510% increase in single fathers raising children and a 330% increase in single mothers raising children (Fields, 2003).

Gay and Lesbian Parents

Most gay and lesbian families are classified as nuclear families. Research studies have revealed no differences in developmental outcomes for children of gay and lesbian parents when compared with children raised by heterosexual parents. However, children of gay and lesbian parents tend to be targets of peer teasing in school and the community, and they may be shunned by the parents of their peers. Classroom contextual findings revealed that children of gay and lesbian parents tend to be more inclusive of same-sex adults; for example, the child would be more likely to envision two mothers in a dramatic playtime scenario (Patterson, 2006).

Siblings

Sibling interactions and relationships allow for types of development that would be less likely to happen outside of this context in the home. For example, when siblings argue within the family context and are overseen by parents and/or older siblings, these children may learn important social skills that will assist them on the playground, in the community, or in the classroom. Therefore, the sibling role to socialize can be an important aspect of healthy development for all siblings (McHale & Crouter, 1996). Even arguments and disagreements within the family structure provide children with firsthand examples of how they can intellectually and creatively defend themselves beyond those familial bounds, using those learning experiences as assistive processes.

siblings
Individuals who share one or both parents (biological or otherwise)

Similar contextual learning experiences occur when siblings interact with each other in more education-related contexts, such as homework time. Research has highlighted the potential positive cognitive issues that can be addressed within sibling relationships, such as sibling contexts whereby tutoring and modeling of learning experiences affects the younger child's learning experiences (Howe, Brody, & Recchia, 2006).

Teenage Parents

Teenage parents may not be prepared, equipped, or interested in raising children. Significant delays in cognitive, language, and social-emotional development have been found for the children of teenage parents (Furstenberg, Hughes, & Brookes-Gunn, 1992).

teenage parents
Individuals between the ages of 13 and 19 who have children.

Income Level

A family's income level often is influenced by the parents' education levels and occupations. It also is associated with the opportunities young children receive in ECE. Therefore, families with higher incomes may be afforded higher quality opportunities in early childhood. However, family income level is not the sole indicator of the quality of ECE opportunities that children receive. Targeted programs for low-income children are often of high quality, similar to those for children in middle-income families (Bowman, Donovan, & Burns, 2000). Also, although children with high socioeconomic status tend to receive better ECE opportunities, this

resilient
The ability to learn and develop even in difficult, negative, or frustrating circumstances.

does not mean that they are **resilient** to future social and behavior problems. In fact, some of the problems these children experience stem from an overemphasis on achievement in school as children get older and problems are expressed in depression and substance abuse in adolescence (Luther & Becker, 2002).

The effect of income level is not the same for all children; it varies according to family, neighborhood, and community experiences. However, children with low socioeconomic status during the preschool years may be more greatly affected in later years (Stipek, 2001). Consider the following example (Goodman, 2010):

> Able-bodied, outgoing and accustomed to working, Alexandria Wallace wants to earn a paycheck. But that requires someone to look after her 3-year-old daughter, and Ms. Wallace, a 22-year-old single mother, cannot afford childcare. Last month, she lost her job as a hair stylist after her improvised network of baby sitters frequently failed her, forcing her to miss shifts. She qualifies for a state-run subsidized childcare program, but like many other states, Arizona has slashed that program over the last year. Ms. Wallace's daughter, Alaya, is on a waiting list of nearly 11,000 eligible children.

As this case illustrates, a parent's ability to provide access to early schooling opportunities can be affected profoundly by changing income status. Income has the potential to affect children's access to high-quality ECE, especially if the family is living in a neighborhood where high-quality educational programs are not available (Snow, Burns, & Griffin, 1998; White, 1982).

Child Abuse and Neglect

Child abuse and neglect is a global problem. Around the world, children are neglected, mistreated, forced into prostitution, forced into being a child soldier fighting in a war, forced to work, or killed because of their gender or ethnic origin.

Although the view of child abuse and what constitutes its presence vary, the following conditions are often included in its definition: sexual abuse (e.g., incest, sexual touching); physical abuse; failure to provide adequate food, clothing, or shelter; abandonment by a parent or caregiver; emotional abuse (e.g., repeated belittling or insulting); psychological neglect; parental substance abuse; child prostitution; children living on the street; physical beating of a child by any adult; forcing a child to beg; children serving as soldiers; and female circumcision. Depending on the country or culture, there are marked differences in the percentages of people who define each of the above categories as abusive. However, globally there is relatively high agreement (80%–100%) on the following definition of child abuse and neglect: sexual abuse, physical abuse, abandonment by caregiver, child prostitution, and children living on the street (Lightfoot, Cole, & Cole, 2009).

Most child abuse occurs when parents set out to physically punish children. In places such as Japan, where physical punishment is less prevalent than other countries, lower incidences of child abuse occur (Wagatsuma, 1981). A key indicator of potential child abuse is stress, such as chronic poverty, marital discord, recent job loss, and social isolation (English, Marshall, & Stewart, 2003; Zagorsky, 2010).

Many abused children can recover from these negative actions with assistance from adults and peers. McGloin and Widom (2001) have addressed the incidence of successful developmental outcomes for maltreated children. They found that 22% of maltreated children had positive outcomes in young adulthood, though maltreated females were more likely than maltreated males to have positive outcomes. To help assist children recover from the trauma of child abuse, it is important that children have at least one sustained positive relationship with an adult who can attempt to help them move through their trauma. Children also should be housed in stable family residences and actively participate in positive experiences in school. These recovery tools help children work through the pain and trauma of these events and assist them in moving forward developmentally as they recover from abuse and neglect (Howes & Ritchie, 2002).

❊ ❊ ❊ Section Summary ❊ ❊ ❊

In this section, we presented characteristics of neighborhoods, communities, and families that may affect the children served in early childhood settings. We emphasized aspects of such contexts that are important for ECE professionals to consider so that they respect all children and their families. We also introduced information regarding dual-language young learners and multilingual children and their families. Many of these community, neighborhood, and family characteristics are strengths of families. However, some factors such as low community income levels may limit educational opportunities, and child abuse or neglect may negatively affect development.

Children with Disabilities

Young children's typical development varies considerably across many factors. Chess and Thomas (1996) conceptualized this by identifying **temperament** and its subcategories:

temperament
An individual's manner of behaving or thinking.

- Activity level (amount of activity)

- Rhythmicity (regularity of behaviors; e.g., eating, sleeping)

- Approach/withdrawal (patterns of outgoing versus shy behavior)

- Adaptability (ability to adjust to changes)

- Sensory thresholds (amount of stimulation needed to evoke a reaction)

- Quality of mood (general mood)

- Intensity of mood expression (level of response to stimulation)

- Distractibility (degree to which something diverts attention)

- Persistence/attention span (ability to focus on and stick with a task)

A child might be on the extreme of typical in one or two of these subcategories, yet still fall within the typical range of development (Chess & Thomas, 1996). However, this variability in development makes it difficult to diagnose a disability. Also, diagnosis of mild disabilities becomes more difficult when there are societal biases against various groups of children. This may result in particular groups (e.g., African American boys) being over-identified with disabilities (Harry & Klinger, 2006).

Disabilities Occurring on a Continuum

Disabilities occur on a continuum. In many cases, a young child may have a language or behavior problem. However, similar to the diagnosis of high blood pressure, there is a cutoff point in terms of level of severity for which a disability is indicated.

This section focuses on children with disabilities that are most often eligible for services under the Individuals with Disabilities Education Improvement Act (IDEA) of 2004 (PL 108-446). IDEA serves children with disabilities from birth through age 21. Preschool children were included in the law starting in 1990, when public school systems were required to provide services for 3- to 5-year-old children with disabilities. In 2001, 620,195 children ages 3–5 were served under IDEA, representing 5.2% of the total population of 3- through 5-year-olds in the United States (Office of Special Education and Rehabilitative Services, 2003). Approximately 708,000 preschool-age children were served under IDEA in 2007 (U.S. Department of Education, 2007).

Children who are eligible to be served by IDEA receive an **individualized education program (IEP)**, which is developed to meet the educational needs of the child with a disability. The IEP includes specific goals, objectives, **accommodations**, **adaptations**, services, and procedures for identifying progress. The law requires the education of children with disabilities to take place in the least restrictive environment, which is interpreted as being as close in proximity to children with typical development of the same age to the extent possible—that is, inclusion. The IEP team consists of a number of team members and includes parents (see Figure 2.2). ECE programs might also serve children who have **individualized family service plans (IFSPs)** from their early intervention program. An IFSP is simi-

individualized education program (IEP)
A written plan for a child with a disability including assessments, services, and placements for provision of an education.

accommodations
Changes made in the early childhood environment (both indoor and outdoor) so that children with disabilities can participate (e.g., wheelchair ramp).

adaptations
Any means used to help a child with a disability (e.g., wheelchairs, communication devices, special eating utensils).

individualized family service plan (IFSP)
A written plan for an infant or toddler with a disability that focuses on early intervention that is family centered; can also be substituted for an IEP for 3- to 5-year-old children.

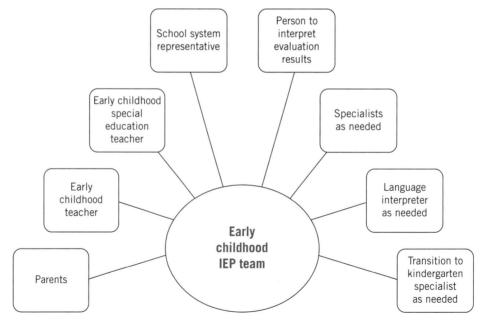

Figure 2.2. Members of the IEP team.

lar to an IEP but is designed to meet the needs of infants and toddlers, many of whom will receive services (e.g., special education, speech and language, occupational and physical therapies, psychological and mental health, parent and family training and counseling) in their homes or as outpatients in clinics. The IFSP helps families to reach their goals so that they can support their children with disabilities.

Certain conditions that are not defined as a disability by IDEA (e.g., wearing glasses to correct vision) might be addressed in a 504 plan, depending on the circumstances. A 504 plan refers to a specific section (Section 504) from the **Americans with Disabilities Act (ADA) of 1990 (PL 101-336),** which guarantees the rights of individuals with a mental or physical disability and prohibits discrimination against Americans with disabilities. Application of this law to ECE programs means that disability must be taken into account in program entry criteria that screen out children with disabilities either explicitly or implicitly (Wood & Youcha, 2009). Indicating that a program does not accept children with disabilities is an explicit way to screen. Having a program that does not have the necessary accommodations for children with disabilities is an implicit way to screen out children with disabilities. Consider the guidelines for play areas and accessibility as modified to represent early childhood programs, which are presented in Figure 2.3. Without such accommodations, certain children may not have access to this and other areas in their ECE program. Throughout this text we assume that children with disabilities will be included in most ECE classrooms and include information about how to be successful including children with disabilities. Odom (2002) provided details on how this happens effectively by giving teachers and specialists ongoing support to coordinate efforts to meet the needs of young children with disabilities.

Americans with Disabilities Act (ADA) of 1990 (PL 101-336) *Federal legislation that requires accommodations so that individuals with disabilities have access to goods and services available to the general public.*

Item	Yes	No	Comments
Equipment access			
Access path: minimum of 60 inches wide			
Hard, resilient surface			
Slope: no greater than 1:16 maximum (or 1 foot in height for every 16 feet in length) and 1:20 minimum (or 1 foot in height for every 20 feet in length)			
Transfer points			
Grab bars			
Transfer platform: 11–14 feet for children younger than 5 years			
Surface			
Shock-absorbing surface under equipment that is more than 20 inches off the ground			
Rest areas			
Close proximity to play equipment			
Description and comments			

Figure 2.3. Checklist for accessibility of play areas. (From Wood, K.I., & Youcha, V. [2009]. *The ABCs of the ADA: Your early childhood program's guide to the Americans with Disabilities Act.* Baltimore: Paul H. Brookes Publishing Co.; adapted by permission.)

Definition of Early Childhood Inclusion

In their joint position statement, *Early Childhood Inclusion* (2009), the Division for Early Childhood and the National Association for the Education of Young Children use the following definition of *early childhood inclusion:*

> Early childhood inclusion embodies the values, policies, and practices that support the right of every infant and young child and his or her family, regardless of ability, to participate in a broad range of activities and contexts as full members of families, communities, and society. The desired results of inclusive experiences for children with and without disabilities and their families include a sense of belonging and membership, positive social relationships and friendships, and development and learning to reach their full potential. The defining features of inclusion that can be used to identify high quality early childhood programs and services are access, participation, and supports. (p. 9)

They also provide the following recommendations to improve early childhood services:

- Create high expectations for every child to reach his or her full potential.
- Develop a program philosophy on inclusion.
- Establish a system of services and supports.
- Revise program and professional standards.
- Achieve an integrated professional development system.
- Influence federal and state accountability systems.

To read more about these recommendations or to read the position statement in its entirety, please visit http://www.naeyc.org/files/naeyc/file/positions/DEC_NAEYC_EC_updatedKS.pdf.

In the following sections, we first discuss young children with disabilities that are of low incidence—that is, very few children have these disabilities. Low-incidence disabilities include sensory, physical, and health impairments and intellectual disabilities. Next, we discuss disabilities that were previously low incidence but are currently increasing, including autism spectrum disorders (ASDs), attention-deficit/hyperactivity disorder (ADHD), and emotional and behavioral disorders. Finally, we discuss high-incidence disabilities, such as learning disabilities and speech and language impairments.

We present information on each disability in enough detail so that you have basic information about the children who will enter ECE programs, given that young children with disabilities are most often served in inclusive preschool programs. More detailed information can be found on the web site of the National Dissemination Center for Children with Disabilities (http://www.nichcy.org/disabilities/specific/Pages/default.aspx).

Sensory Impairments

Sensory impairments include visual and hearing impairments, such as blindness and deafness.

Visual Impairment and Blindness

Children are considered to have a visual impairment if their typical development is affected by visual problems, even after correction. Visual impairments include low vision, legal blindness, and total blindness. Low vision is when a child is unable to see things (or for an older child, read) at a typical distance even with the aid of corrective lenses. Legal blindness is when a child has very limited vision but, for example, might be able to distinguish dark and light. Total blindness is when a child has a complete inability to see.

Visual impairments can be congenital (i.e., a problem present at birth) or adventitious (i.e., a problem that develops after birth). Problems can be genetically based or caused by environmental effects (e.g., injury, which usually happens with one eye). The U.S. Preventive Services Task Force recommends screening for visual impairment in children younger than age 5. Traditional vision testing can be completed with cooperative, verbal children who are as young as 3 to 4 years (U.S. Preventive Services Task Force, 2011). Further testing is completed by an ophthalmologist, who is a medical doctor specializing in eye disorders.

Children with visual impairments often receive services from occupational therapists who help them learn fine motor manipulation, **coordination**, and gross motor mobility skills; touch and hearing needs to be developed in preschool activities. Children might also get education-related services from **assistive technology** specialists, who can provide such things as computer accommodations (possibly including braille) and audiobooks (Pogrund & Fazzi, 2002).

coordination
Effective interaction of movements (e.g., eye–hand coordination to build with blocks, eye–foot coordination to kick a soccer ball).

assistive technology
A type of adaptation that is specific to an individual with a disability so that he or she can function in activities that would be impossible or very difficult to participate in without such a device.

Deafness and Hearing Loss

Children who are deaf do not process linguistic information through hearing, although they can respond to auditory stimuli. Children with hearing loss might use alternative communication systems as well as oral communication systems. Development is impaired if an alternative means of communication, such as American Sign Language, is not used beginning in infancy. Therefore, it is extremely important that deafness is identified early; screening should take place shortly after birth as well as during annual physical examinations. Hearing problems can be genetically based or acquired, especially if ear infections in early childhood are untreated and chronic.

Deaf Culture

Within the deaf community, deafness is not considered a disability that needs to be fixed. It is an identity—a unique group in society that speaks through sign language.

Cochlear Implants

Cochlear implants are electronic devices that stimulate the auditory nerve in the cochlea of the inner ear. A microphone is worn, and it transmits to the surgically implanted device. Cochlear implants maximize spoken language.

Further testing is performed by audiologists, who can locate the particular type of hearing loss, determine the degree of hearing loss, and recommend amplification devices. Children who are deaf or have hearing loss receive services from pediatricians, language pathologists, and assistive technology specialists who will provide such things as accommodations for telephone use and video relay service. Additional supports in literacy development—particularly decoding, concept development, and vocabulary—are provided through early intervention.

Physical and Health Disabilities

Cerebral Palsy

Cerebral palsy is an injury to the nervous system that affects children's ability to use their muscles; it happens during the prenatal and perinatal periods. The nervous system injury has an effect on some muscles but not others. Some children are more severely affected on their lower body, whereas others have more severe effects on their upper body. Impact can be mild, in which case a child may be clumsy or have stiff heel cords. Moderate forms affecting the lower body might require a child to wear braces, or the child might walk with a limp. In severe cases, a child might need to use a wheelchair for mobility. There are several types of cerebral palsy, including spastic, in which there is too much muscle tone or tightness, and athetoid, which makes body movements slow and often uncontrolled.

Cerebral palsy is diagnosed during the early childhood years, typically by a physical therapist who examines muscle tone, body movements, and the presence of primitive reflexes that the young child retains past the time period when they most often disappear. Most children with cerebral palsy who enter ECE settings have had prior years of physical and occupational therapy, as well as speech therapy. Physical therapists address large muscles (e.g., those used in sitting, walking, and balance), occupational therapists address fine motor skills (e.g., eating, playing with building blocks), and speech-language pathologists address communication and language skills. In addition, children have often received developmental and educational intervention, along with an evaluation for any required assistive technology. Assistive technology may range from wheelchairs to custom-made spoons.

What are Augmentative and Alternative Communication and Assistive Technology?

Augmentative and alternative communication (AAC) devices help individuals who are not able to speak or write by using devices such as picture symbol systems (see Chapter 8) or electronic communication systems. Stephen Hawking, the famous physicist, is someone you may have seen using an AAC electronic communication device.

Assistive technology includes any item that is used to increase, maintain, or improve the functional capabilities of an individual with a disability. Small items include picture books with tabs for turning pages. Major devices include a special chair for sitting in the classroom that helps a child regulate movement.

New treatments for cerebral palsy are currently being developed. These may be combined with more traditional treatments to produce better outcomes. For example, botulinum toxin (Botox) injections have been used in spastic muscles to reduce the spasticity, which allows other related muscles to develop the strength needed to function properly.

Spina Bifida

Spina bifida is caused by an incomplete closure of the spinal column. In milder forms, the spinal cord does not seem damaged or can be repaired with little or no damage to the spinal cord. In the severe form, myelomeningocele, there is damage to the spinal cord. It is this group of children who have physical disabilities, such as weakness, paralysis, and loss of sensation below the point of the incomplete closure, which may be associated with loss of bowel and bladder control. In addition to myelomeningocele, many children also have hydrocephalus, which is the accumulation of fluid on the brain. This condition can be controlled by the surgical implant of a shunt to drain the fluid.

Assistive technology includes any item that is used to increase, maintain, or improve the functional capabilities of an individual with a disability.

Myelomeningocele is most often diagnosed at birth. Early intervention requires children to learn mobility skills, which is often accomplished with the help of braces, crutches, and wheelchairs. The bowel and bladder require special supports when a child with myelomeningocele is in a classroom setting. Many of these children also have attention, language, and cognitive impairments and learning difficulties, which require additional interventions. As with cerebral palsy, children with spina bifida are provided services by physical therapists, occupational therapists, and speech-language pathologists, and usually require the use of assistive technology such as braces.

Other Low-Incidence Physical and Health Problems

Teachers should be aware of some additional disabilities, although incidence is low in the preschool years, especially for children in inclusive programs. One is traumatic brain injury, which is caused by the head being hit (e.g., car accident) or being shaken. The results of such experiences can affect all areas of development. Another condition is epilepsy, which is caused when the brain has a sudden, brief internal insult to it. The brain does not work properly during this time, which affects all developmental areas such as movement. In severe cases, the child is unconscious, which is called an epileptic seizure.

Intellectual Disabilities

Children are believed to have intellectual disabilities when they have significant limitations in mental functioning and cannot take care of themselves in ways that other children of the same age are able, such as dressing. Most children with intellectual disabilities have accompanying communication, social, and motor delays. Levels of cognitive delay vary, with some children functioning close to the typical range but others having more severe delays. Children's intellectual disabilities may be congenital, such as Down syndrome and fetal alcohol syndrome. Other problems occur during or after birth, such as meningitis and mercury poisoning. In addition to the syndromes mentioned in the previous section, other conditions associated with intellectual impairment include fragile X syndrome, Prader-Willi syndrome, phenylketonuria, toxoplasmosis, encephalitis, lead poisoning, and brain injury.

Some forms of intellectual disabilities are identified at birth (e.g., Down syndrome), whereas others are noticed in routine screenings during pediatric visits. A screening such as the Ages & Stages Questionnaires® (Squires & Bricker, 2009) can be used by pediatricians as part of well-baby visits. If the screening indicates a delay, children then can be more formally diagnosed by a psychologist, with intellectual ability and adaptive functioning assessed for significant delays.

Children with intellectual disabilities get services from speech-language pathologists, occupational therapists, and physical therapists as required given their particular needs. Special education and developmental intervention are suggested; assistive technology needs (e.g., AAC) also are assessed and provided by an assistive technology specialist. Services can be provided in a special education setting, at home, or at a child care facility. Preschool programs have positive effects on the development of children with cognitive impairments (Pianta, Barnett, Burchinal, & Thornburg, 2009).

Down Syndrome

Down syndrome is a genetic problem in which the child has 47 instead of the typical 46 chromosomes, with the extra chromosome present in the 21st chromosome. Individuals with Down syndrome have unique physical features such as poor muscle tone, eyes that slant upward, tongues that are large relative to the size of their mouths, as well as wide hands, digits, and feet. Many individuals with Down syndrome have health problems, including respiratory and heart problems. There is a large range of delays for children with Down syndrome, ranging from mild to severe. Educational interventions and related services are the same as those mentioned for other intellectual disabilities (Berglund, Eriksson, & Johansson, 2001).

Other Intellectual Disabilities

There are additional intellectual disabilities that teachers need to be aware of as they serve children in inclusive programs. Fetal alcohol syndrome is one such disability; it is caused by the mother's alcohol intake during pregnancy. Children with fetal alcohol syndrome have brain damage with cognitive impairment and delays in development. Fetal alcohol effects is a related disorder associated with some but not all signs of fetal alcohol syndrome.

Positive Behavioral Supports and Functional Behavioral Assessment

Positive behavioral support in the early education environment is provided so that problem behaviors are minimized and appropriate behaviors are promoted. In a functional behavioral assessment, the team working with the child identifies and agrees on the behavior that needs to be changed and determines when, where, and under what circumstances the behavior occurs. Data are then collected to confirm that the team's proposal was actually correct; next, a proposal is developed regarding why the behavior occurs (i.e., what is the function of the behavior). The team then identifies appropriate behavior(s) that will fulfill the same function for the child. Finally, this plan is implemented and the success of the intervention is evaluated and refined as needed.

Autism Spectrum Disorders

Although historically of low incidence, children with ASDs are being identified at much higher rates than in the past (National Institute of Child Health and Human Development, 2005). Young children with ASDs have difficulty communicating, understanding language, and relating to others. These difficulties are neurological in nature with a wide range of severity—from young children having unusual play behavior and communicating at reduced levels to children who spend most of their time engaged in repetitive and stereotypic behavior and do not speak. Diagnosis of ASDs most often takes place between the ages of 3 and 5, but they can be diagnosed at younger ages.

Behavioral interventions are implemented for many young children with ASDs, so a behavioral specialist is often part of an intervention team. In addition, speech-language pathologists and occupational therapists are typically involved in the treatment. Assistive technology also may be implemented, such as augmentative and assistive technology or the Picture Exchange Communication System (Pyramid Educational Consultants; see Chapter 8).

How Are Young Children Identified with Disabilities?

Some children with disabilities are identified at birth, whereas others are identified during the preschool period. Still other children are identified during kindergarten through the high school years. Another means of identification of young children with disabilities is through Child Find, although this service is directed toward identifying infants and toddlers. Child Find fulfills the requirement by IDEA Part C that children (infants and toddlers) are systematically found in communities and evaluated in order to provide proper interventions (Child Find, n.d.). Teachers may identify children who they think need special education; school systems often have teams to help with this process. For example, a response to intervention plan (most often referred to as an RTI) may be created to determine if the identified needs are met through structured instruction, especially for children with suspected learning disabilities. (For more information on RTIs, visit http://iris.peabody.vanderbilt.edu/resources.html and click on the RTI tab on the left.) Children suspected of having a disability might also receive a screening during which they are assessed briefly to see if they should be referred for a full evaluation. If a full evaluation is warranted, children are tested, most often by a school psychologist. Data then are collected on development and interpreted to determine whether the child meets the criteria to be eligible for special education services.

Attention-Deficit/Hyperactivity Disorder

Preschool children with ADHD are hard to diagnose because many of the behaviors that are specified as indicators of ADHD (e.g., problems paying attention, very active and impulsive, problems sitting still, spending little time on difficult tasks, constantly talking) are also exhibited by typically developing children. Recall the conceptualization of temperament by Chess and Thomas (1996) presented earlier and consider just three of the categories of temperament: activity level (amount of activity), rhythmicity (regularity of behaviors; e.g., eating, sleeping), and persistence/attention span (ability to focus on and stick with a task). Many children may show what seems to be extreme behavior in these categories, and one might wonder if they have ADHD because of their behavior, but really their behavior is within the normal range. Chapter 5 presents detailed information on these types of behavior, as well as how preschool children need instructional opportunities to develop in these areas.

A child with ADHD can be inattentive, hyperactive/impulsive, or both inattentive and hyperactive/impulsive. A complete evaluation is needed to diagnose ADHD because other difficulties could be mistaken for ADHD, such as living in a stressful situation, not receiving proper nutrition and sleep, or immaturity. If you have a child with ADHD in your classroom, you will need the support of a behavioral therapist to design any necessary behavioral plans. Children might also be working with a psychiatrist or counselor.

Emotional and Behavioral Disorders

internalized problems
A child who has internalized problems tends to be withdrawn or fearful, and might have associated health problems.

Children with emotional and behavioral disorders have a core identifier: The problems have continued to be present over long periods of time (i.e., at least 6 months). Children may exhibit externalized problems (e.g., aggression, including fighting and destroying property), **internalized problems**, or self-injurious behavior. Internalized behavior might include withdrawal, in which the child does not interact with others or has excessive fear or anxiety. As with ADHD, it is important to be sure that the behavior/feeling is not within the typical range of temperament. Even the level of problems diagnosed as an emotional disorder exists within a range of severity. Children can have severe emotional problems in which they have excessive anxiety, thought disorders such as schizophrenia, or abnormal mood swings. As with ADHD, diagnosis requires a full evaluation, including a psychiatrist, psychologist, and other mental health professionals. ECE professionals and parents also work with this team.

Learning Disabilities

phonology
The study of speech sounds and how they are sequenced and structured in words.

morphology
Meaning units in words.

syntax
The order and combination of words that creates sentences.

semantics
Study of the meaning of language.

Children with learning disabilities have been traditionally thought of as those children having specific learning problems in particular skill areas, such as reading, writing, listening, speaking, reasoning, or math. Because these are often defined in terms of academic outcomes most relevant to school-age children, preschool children have not traditionally fit into this group. Most children with learning disabilities have been identified as having speech and language problems in the preschool years (presented next). However, this is a developing area, and more children with learning disabilities are now being identified in the preschool years.

Speech and Language Impairments

pragmatics
Language use and function of language across contexts.

receptive language
Listening and understanding oral language or visually receiving and understanding sign language or print.

Speech and language impairments in young children are often identified by novices as articulation or pronunciation problems. However, speech and language problems can stem from all areas of language, including **phonology**, **morphology**, **syntax**, **semantics**, and **pragmatics** (see Chapter 8). Problems can occur in both the areas of **receptive language** (understanding) and expressive language (speaking; McCauley & Fey, 2006). As with other disabilities, children can have mild speech and language problems or ones that are more severe.

Multiple Disabilities

Children often have multiple disabilities, such as cerebral palsy and visual impairment. As with all disabilities, they may vary in severity; services and IEP plans will reflect the child's relevant needs. Also, it is important to note that children can have a disability and also have exceptional cognitive functioning or talents across a number of different areas such as music, art, mathematics, body kinesthetics, and personal/social areas (Gardner, 1983).

❋ ❋ ❋ Section Summary ❋ ❋ ❋

Young children with disabilities have different developmental characteristics and needs. Understanding children with disabilities is central in ECE practice today. In this section, we discussed children with disabilities, giving specific information about different areas of disability including sensory impairments, such as visual impairment and deafness; physical impairments, such as cerebral palsy; cognitive impairments, such as Down syndrome; as well as ASDs, ADHD, emotional disorders, learning disabilities, and speech and language impairments. Finally, we provided an overview of the process by which young children get referred for special educational services.

Young children with disabilities have unique developmental characteristics and needs.

KEY CONCEPTS

- The characteristics of the neighborhoods, communities, and families that ECE children come from are rich and provide knowledge that is important for ECE professionals to consider so that they respect all children and their families.

- Some children and their families speak more than one language and have multicultural backgrounds.

- Children live in all types of family structures, including nuclear and extended families, and recognizing all family types is important.

- Factors such as low community income levels may limit educational opportunities for young children.

- Child abuse or neglect may negatively affect development.

- Young children with disabilities have different developmental characteristics and needs. Understanding children with disabilities is central in ECE practice today. Young children with disabilities are included in many if not most ECE programs.

- Disabilities vary. Young children can have sensory impairments, such as visual impairments and deafness; physical impairments, such as cerebral palsy; and cognitive impairments, such as Down syndrome. In addition, children can have autism spectrum disorders, attention deficits/hyperactivity disorder, emotional disorders, learning disabilities, and speech and language impairments. Some young children enter ECE with identified disabilities whereas others may be identified while in your ECE program.

Integration of Information

You have just read the chapter about the children and families that we serve in ECE programs. Does this description match what you had expected? Do you think you will enjoy working with the diverse children and families served in ECE programs?

Self-Reflective Guide

This self-reflective guide will help you assess whether you learned the information in this chapter. It also provides an opportunity to identify areas in which you want or need more information. Are there some new ideas learned that will affect your immediate practice with children?

1. Reflect on the multilingual and multicultural characteristics of the families and children that you might teach. Are you interested in learning about the richness of the new cultures and languages? Why? Make a few notes.

2. Recognize that children come from families with different structures, which might have an effect on how children and their families relate to you. What are the family structures of the young children you are familiar with? List some.

3. Identify some aspects of neighborhoods, communities, and families that might pose particular challenges for you as a teacher. List one of these. Make a few notes on why this situation might be a challenge for you.

4. Consider that children in your classroom might have disabilities and what that means in terms of how you thought of your role as an ECE professional. Does this change your thoughts? How? Make a few notes.

5. Identify and learn about the different types of disabilities. List one disability that is particularly intriguing to you. Make a few notes about that disability.

6. Recognize the main points of the laws related to young children with disabilities. What is IDEA? What is section 504 of the ADA?

7. Understand the process that children with disabilities went through to be eligible for special education. What questions do you have about your role in this process? Make a few notes.

8. Understand the basic concept of inclusion and why it is an important one for early childhood professionals to be familiar with. How do you feel about the inclusion of children with disabilities in your classroom or potential classroom? Make a few notes.

Helpful Web Sites

Early Childhood Learning & Knowledge Center

> http://eclkc.ohs.acf.hhs.gov/hslc
> The Early Childhood Learning & Knowledge Center was developed by the Office of Head Start and provides informative on early childhood practices, especially in relation to children's diversity of culture, language, and ability.

The Family Center on Technology and Disability

www.fctd.info
This site offers information on assistive and instructional technologies for children with disabilities.

IDEA 2004

http://idea.ed.gov
This site, which is sponsored by the U.S. Department of Education, includes information on Part B (ages 3–21) and Part C (birth to age 3) of IDEA 2004.

The IRIS Center

iris.peabody.vanderbilt.edu
Through Peabody College at Vanderbilt University, this site provides information on a wide range of topics regarding the education of children with disabilities.

National Association for Bilingual Education

www.nabe.org
This site provides resources for bilingual children and those who are English language learners in the areas of policy, pedagogy, research, and professional development.

National Association for Multicultural Education

www.nameorg.org
This site provides teaching resources, research, and information on education and advocating for multicultural education for all children and families.

National Dissemination Center for Children with Disabilities

www.nichcy.org
This site includes information on different types of disabilities, as well as IDEA and effective intervention strategies.

References

Americans with Disabilities Act (ADA) of 1990, PL 101-336, 42 U.S.C. §§ 12101 et seq.

Ballentyne, K.G., Sanderman, A.R., D'Emilio, T., & McLaughlin, N. (2008). Dual language learners in the early years: Getting ready to succeed in school. Washington, DC: National Clearinghouse for English Language Acquisition.

Bauman, K.J., & Graf, N.L. (2003). Educational attainment: 2000. Census 2000 brief. Washington, DC: U.S. Census Bureau.

Berglund, E., Eriksson, M., & Johansson, I. (2001). Parental reports of spoken language skills in children with Down syndrome. Journal of Speech, Language, and Hearing Research, 44(1), 179–191.

Bowman, B.T., Donovan, M.S., & Burns, M.S. (2000). Eager to learn: Educating our preschoolers. Washington, DC: National Academies Press.

Chess, S., & Thomas, A. (1996). Temperament: Theory and practice. New York: Brunner-Mazel.

Child Find. (n.d.). About Child Find. Retrieved January 31, 2011, from http://www.childfindidea.org/overview.htm

Diversitydata.org & Harvard School of Public Health. (2008–2009). Segregation of public primary school students, Hispanic students' exposure by race/ethnicity. Retrieved January 18, 2011, from http://diversitydata.sph.harvard.edu/Data/Rankings/Show.aspx?ind=42

Division for Early Childhood & the National Association for the Education of Young Children. (2009). Early childhood inclusion: A joint position statement of the Division for Early Childhood (DEC) and the National Association for the Education of Young Children (NAEYC). Chapel Hill: The University of North Carolina, FPG Child Development Institute. Retrieved March 29, 2011, from http://www.naeyc.org/files/naeyc/file/positions/DEC_NAEYC_EC_updatedKS.pdf

English, D.J., Marshall, D.B., & Stewart, A.J. (2003). Effects of family violence on child behavior and health during early childhood. Journal of Family Violence, 18, 43–57.

Espinosa, L. (2009). Getting it RIGHT for young children from diverse backgrounds: Applying research to improve practice. New York: Prentice Hall.

Fields, J. (2003). *Children's living arrangements and characteristics: March 2002*. Washington, DC: U.S. Census Bureau.

Furstenberg, F.F., Hughes, M.E., & Brookes-Gunn, J. (1992). The next generation: The children of teenage mothers grow up. In M. Rosenheim & M. Testa (Eds.), *Early parenthood and coming of age in the 1990s* (pp. 113–135). New Brunswick, NJ: Rutgers University Press.

Gardner, H. (1983). *Frames of mind: The theory of multiple intelligence*. New York: Basic Books.

Gay, G. (2010). *Culturally responsive teaching: Theory, research, and practice* (2nd ed.). New York: Teachers College Press.

Goodman, P. (2010). *Cuts to child care subsidy thwart more job seekers*. Retrieved May 24, 2010, from http://www.nytimes.com/2010/05/24/business/economy/24childcare.html?hp

Harry, B., & Klinger, J.K. (2006). *Why are so many minority students in special education?* New York: Teachers College Press.

Howe, N., Brody, M.-H., & Recchia, H. (2006). Effects of task difficulty on sibling teaching in middle childhood. *Infant and Child Development, 15*(5), 455–470.

Howes, C., & Ritchie, S. (2002). *A matter of trust: Connecting teachers and learners in the early childhood classroom*. New York: Teachers College Press.

Individuals with Disabilities Education Improvement Act (IDEA) of 2004, PL 108-446, 20 U.S.C. §§ 1400 *et seq.*

Lightfoot, C., Cole, M., & Cole, S. (2009). *The development of children*. New York: Worth.

Luther, S., & Becker, B. (2003). Privileged but pressured? A study of affluent youth. *Child Development, 73*, 1593–1610.

McCauley, R.J., & Fey, M.E. (2006). Treatment of language disorders in children. Baltimore: Paul H. Brookes Publishing Co.

McGloin, J.M., & Widom, C.S. (2001). Resilience among abused and neglected children grown up. *Development and Psychopathology, 13*(4), 1021–1038.

McHale, S., & Crouter, A. (1996). The family contexts of children's sibling relationships. In G.H. Brody (Ed.), *Sibling relationships: Their causes and consequences* (pp. 173–196). Norwood, NJ: Ablex.

National Center for Education Statistics. (2003). *Status and trends in the education of Hispanics*. Washington, DC: U.S. Department of Education Institute of Education Sciences.

National Institute of Child Health and Human Development. (2005, May). *Autism overview: What we know*. (NIH Pub. No. 05-5592.) Washington, DC: U.S. Department of Health and Human Services.

Odom, S. (2002). *Widening the circle: Including children with disabilities in preschool programs*. New York: Teachers College Press.

Office of Special Education and Rehabilitative Services. (2003). *Twenty-fifth annual report to Congress on the implementation of the Individuals with Disabilities Education Act*. Washington DC: Author. Retrieved January 31, 2001, from http://www2.ed.gov/about/offices/list/osers/osep/research.html

Passel, J.S., & Cohn, D. (2011). *How many Hispanics? Comparing new census counts with the latest census estimates*. Washington, DC: Pew Hispanic Center.

Passel, J.S., & Taylor, P. (2010). *Unauthorized immigrants and their U.S.-born children*. Washington, DC: Pew Hispanic Center.

Patterson, C.J. (2006). Children of lesbian and gay parents. *Current Directions in Psychological Science, 15*, 241–144.

Pianta, R.C., Barnett, W.S., Burchinal, M., & Thornburg, K.R. (2009). The effects of preschool education: What we know, how public policy is or is not aligned with the evidence base, and what we need to know. *Psychological Science in the Public Interest, 10*(2) 49–88.

Pogrund, R.L., & Fazzi, D.L. (2002). *Early focus: Working with young children who are blind or visually impaired*. New York: AFB Press.

Snow, C.E., Burns, M.S., & Griffin, P. (1998). *Preventing reading difficulties in young children*. Washington, DC: National Academies Press.

Squires, J., & Bricker, D. (2009). *Ages & Stages Questionnaires®, Third Edition (ASQ-3™): A parent-completed child-monitoring system*. Baltimore: Paul H. Brookes Publishing Co.

Stipek, D. (2001). Pathways to constructive lives: The importance of early school success. In A.C. Bower and D.J. Stipek (Eds.), *Constructive & destructive behavior: Implications for family, school, & society* (pp. 291–315). Washington, DC: American Psychological Association.

Suarez-Orozco, M. (2001). Globalization, immigration, and education: The research agenda. *Harvard Educational Review, 71*, 345–365.

Suarez-Orozco, M., Suarez-Orozco, M.M., & Todorova, I. (2008). *Learning a new land: Immigrant students in American society*. Cambridge, MA: The Belknap Press of Harvard University Press.

U.S. Census Bureau. (2009). *American community survey*. Retrieved March 25, 2011, from http://www.census.gov/acs/www

U.S. Department of Education. (2007). *Twenty-ninth annual report to Congress on the implementation of the Individuals with Disabilities Education Act, Parts B and C. 2007*. Retrieved April 13, 2011, from http://www2.ed.gov/about/reports/annual/osep/2007/parts-b-c/index.html#preface

U.S. Preventive Services Task Force. (2011). *Screening for visual impairment in children ages 1 to 5 years: Recommendation statement*. Retrieved March 25, 2011, from http://www.uspreventiveservicestaskforce.org/uspstf11/vischildren/vischildrs.htm

Wagatsuma, H. (1981). Child abandonment and infanticide: A Japanese case. In J.E. Korgin (Ed.), *Child abuse and neglect: Cross-cultural perspectives* (pp. 120–138). Berkeley, CA: University of California Press.

White, K.R. (1982). The relation between socioeconomic status and academic achievement. *Psychological Bulletin, 91*(3), 461–481.

Wood, K.I., & Youcha, V. (2009). *The ABCs of the ADA: Your early childhood program's guide to the Americans with Disabilities Act*. Baltimore: Paul H. Brookes Publishing Co.

Zagorsky, J. (2010, October). *What happens to child maltreatment when unemployment goes up?* Paper presented at the 2010 American Academy of Pediatrics National Conference and Exhibition, San Francisco.

How Has Early Childhood Education Been Defined over the Years?

3

Learning Objectives

1. Identify major philosophers, theorists, educators, and researchers who influenced ECE prior to and during the 19th and 20th centuries
2. Reflect on how these individuals changed the field during their time
3. Know the major U.S. laws and policies that have influenced ECE and when they were introduced over the years
4. Know private sector actions that affected ECE
5. Identify major themes in the history of ECE

What were the common thoughts about early childhood before the 19th century? Do these ideas still affect us today? What were the popular themes in early childhood education (ECE) during the 19th century? Did they have curriculum back then? How did teachers instruct young children in the 19th century? Who were the main people influencing thoughts about ECE in the 20th century? Are there key people whose ideas still affect programs today? What were the main changes in ECE during the 20th century? How much have the themes in ECE changed in the past few centuries?

These are the types of questions being addressed in this chapter on the history of ECE and care. We begin by mentioning major figures known to influence ECE over the 19th and 20th centuries, then highlight major events during these time periods, including government and private sector influence. Our goal in this chapter is to provide a background for the practices, concerns, and laws regarding ECE today—issues that will have an impact on your personal and professional practices with young children.

Thoughts About Early Childhood Before the 19th Century

Around the world, ECE programs have been dramatically influenced by a long history of philosophers, theorists, and specialists, dating back many centuries. These historical figures theorized, discussed, and wrote about various aspects of the importance of the early years in a child's life. This section provides a timeline and brief overview of some of the important people whose ideas and writings were heavily influential in current ECE practices.

Plato

Dating back many centuries, Plato (428–348 B.C.) was one of the earliest historical figures with an important link with modern ECE. Before the first century, in *The Republic* (2003), Plato discussed the ideal society—a society that placed a heavy emphasis on making sure children's potential was developed. Plato's works also related to the importance of play in a child's life and discussed the balance between physical and mental well-being on overall development. These values and understandings are basic to quality ECE practices today.

Comenius

John Amos Comenius (1592–1670) was a theorist who had a focus on early childhood as part of his pedagogical interests. His belief was that children were inherently good and that education should take place early in life, before children's minds could be corrupted by society. Sensory training was proposed as a necessary component, followed by preparation for learning, with formal learning not being forced too early. His ideas preceded more recent theorists who proposed that there are stages in which children develop and learn. Of particular importance to Comenius was supporting children's natural interests in learning rather than using harsh methods that might diminish it. Young children were believed to develop from within and learn at their own pace. Comenius wrote the first picture book (see Figure 3.1), which was a type of encyclopedia that included illustrations of the natural world as well as an illustrated alphabet (Pettersson, 1993). Comenius advocated universal education—education for all rather than education based on gender, socioeconomic status, or ability level. This idea was depicted in his book *School of Infancy* (1956/1984), which included an emphasis on education for young children, especially in the home. The importance of parents as a child's first teacher is also a value that is very strongly held by most educators today.

Locke

script
The cultural processes involved in functioning in the world learned through experience and interactions with knowledgeable peers and adults (e.g., going to the grocery store, going to the library).

Shortly after this time, John Locke's (1632–1714) theories assisted in further understanding children. Locke looked at societal problems and felt that children were being treated badly. In contrast with Comenius's idea of children learning from within, Locke attributed children's complete learning to the environment in which they are placed. He believed that children are born as blank slates, and parents, teachers, and society in general **script** their respective experiences. While Comenius viewed all children as inherently good, Locke viewed them as neither good nor bad—but rather what experiences have made of them. The idea that life's early experiences influence later development was known as *tabula rasa* (Locke, 1979).

Given this perspective, the role of the social environment was considered paramount in ECE; however, the exact social experiences provided young children did not vary significantly from those described by Comenius. Locke said that people become what their experiences permit them to become. Experience, in this regard, dictates what all people become later in life. This idea is especially important when you consider how badly children were treated in the past. For many centuries, children simply were seen as miniature adults, without being respected or appreciated as children.

⚜:❀:(4):❀:⚜

Cornix cornicatur. die Krähe krechzet.	*á á*	Aa
Agnus balat. das Schaf blöcket.	*bé é é*	Bb
Cicáda ſtridet. der Heuſchreck zitſchert.	*ci ci*	Cc
Upupa, dicit der Widhopf/ ruft	*dù du*	Dd
Infans éjulat. das Kind weinert.	*é é é*	Ee
Ventus flat. der Wind wehet.	*fi fi*	Ff
Anſer gingrit. die Gans gackert.	*ga ga*	Gg
Os halat. der Mund hauchet.	*háh háh*	Hh
Mus mintrit. die Maus pfipfert.	*i i i*	Ii
Anas tetrinnit. die Ente ſchnackert.	*kha khá*	Kk
Lupus úlulat. der Wolff heulet.	*lu ulu*	Ll
Urſus múrmurat. der Beer brummet.	*mum mum*	Mm

Figure 3.1. First picture book written by Comenius.

Rousseau

Another major influence on ECE was Jean Rousseau (1712–1778), who is often referred to as the father of ECE. In his book, *Emile* (1762/2007), Rousseau philosophized that man is by nature good, but that society corrupts him. Rousseau believed that no child should have a formal education until 12 years of age; children should be left to develop naturally. Rousseau believed that adults should not interfere or teach children earlier or the children would be destroyed. He felt that education should be child centered and should flow from a child's natural surroundings. Growth should be allowed to happen without undue interference or restriction from the social environment. Rousseau was the first person to actually describe stages of childhood, which by their very nature pay respect to children's growth and development as children, not as miniature adults. Of particular importance was Rousseau's idea that young children actually think differently from older peers and adults, which should be taken into account when providing educational experiences. Rousseau believed that young children needed concrete rather than abstract information to interact with and that they needed time for free play—both concepts that continue to be important aspects of ECE.

✳ ✳ ✳ Section Summary ✳ ✳ ✳

In this historical review of ECE prior to the 19th century, we described dramatic influences from a long history of philosophers, theorists, and specialists, dating back many centuries. These historical figures—Plato, Comenius, Locke, and Rousseau—discussed and wrote about various aspects of the importance of the early years in a child's life.

Early Childhood Education in the 19th Century

ECE in the 19th century was clearly built upon the foundation of thought developed before this time. It also shares a number of similarities with many of today's current practices (see Figure 3.2).

Pestalozzi

Johann Pestalozzi (1746–1827) was inspired by Rousseau, and he also devoted much practical experience toward working with and for children. He was a Swiss educational reformer who influenced the beginning point of kindergarten programs. However, when it came to educating the preschool-age child, he was more pragmatic. Pestalozzi proposed that it was fine to teach skills while at the same addressing the whole child. Learning was proposed as moving from concrete to abstract, with children learning by doing. Home and school environments were closely linked. School often was constructed to be similar to the home, where groups of children participated, roles of teachers and parents were closely aligned, and all aspects of development were viewed as important (Cleverly & Phillips, 1986).

Owen

The role of education in social reform was evident in the early 1800s. Robert Owen (1771–1858) started programs for 1-year-old children as part of community development involving cooperative employment. The programs were based on the ideas of Pestalozzi. One goal was to provide experiences for the children of uneducated parents so that the children would develop the beliefs and behaviors necessary to be successful in society, therefore leading to societal improvement. The educational experience provided for preschool-age children was based on the exploration of the concrete world accompanied by conversation between the children and teachers, thereby building curiosity. The mode of instruction was free: Children were not required to participate but did so because they were self-motivated by nature (Spodek, Sarachi, & Peters, 1998).

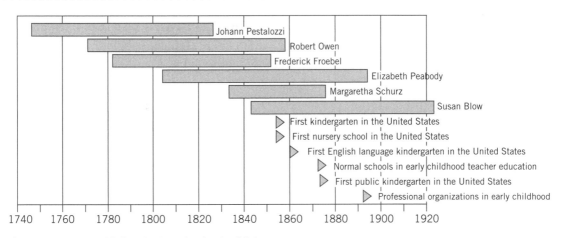

Figure 3.2. Early childhood education in the 19th century.

The "garden of children"—that is, kindergarten—best describes the philosophy of Frederick Froebel (1782–1852), who is known by many as the father of kindergarten education. Froebel actually studied under Pestalozzi and was heavily influenced by him. Froebel's view of children's learning and development was like that of a flower unfolding from a seed. In his work, he stressed the importance of pleasant surroundings, self-activity, and physical training. Childhood was not merely a preparation for adulthood; it was valued in and of itself. Froebel paid careful attention to documenting his practical work with children and writing extensively about his own theoretical understandings of early education. Froebel's first kindergarten began in Germany in 1837. America's first private English-language Froebelian kindergarten opened in Boston in 1860 (Froebel, 1826/1887).

Froebel

Unlike Pestalozzi, however, Froebel believed that free play was not the best basis for meeting all young children's learning needs. He developed particular materials consistent with his philosophy; these "gifts" or curricular materials were devised to assist him in effectively educating children. Included among these materials were six balls of yarn, a cube, a cylinder, and a sphere to use for learning comparing and contrasting materials. He was the first to use blocks as part of the educational program. Froebel stressed learning through play in his kindergarten curriculum. Between 1820 and 1840, Froebel developed a series of 20 educational toys and activities; the second through the sixth of these toys included an intricate block system. With the growth of the kindergarten movement, his block system came into widespread use.

Together, these three voices—Pestalozzi, Owen, and Froebel—had a significant impact on ECE, the threads of which are seen in current professional practices. Of particular importance is the view of the inherent goodness of young children in all cases, and that we need to support this goodness through the experiences we provide young children in the environment and through daily interactions. Clearly, from this rich history of ECE, a continuing demand is being made for society to consider the needs of young children because they are different from the needs of older children. Even in the 19th century, the roles of teachers and caregivers were viewed as being active rather than passive in providing rich experiences for young children. The creation of materials such as Froebel's blocks was the beginning of specific models for necessary activities and curriculum to support these influential theoretical notions.

Nursery School and Kindergarten in the United States

Schurz

Margarethe Schurz (1833–1876) learned Froebel's methods in Europe and used them to provide rich experiences for her daughter and four additional neighborhood children. In addition to some of Froebel's direct activities, she also involved the children in learning games with simple rules, group activities, and singing. All experiences were geared toward the children being prepared for primary school. Other parents requested that Schurz make these experiences available for their children, so in 1854 she opened up the first kindergarten in the United States in Watertown, Wisconsin. The program included 4- to 6-year-old immigrant children and was conducted in the students' home language of German.

At this same time, nursery schools were introduced to provide care for young children of mothers who were working, as factory systems grew in the United States (Cleverly & Phillips, 1986). Mothers often worked long hours each day, and the younger children were neglected. Day nurseries were established so that mothers could leave their children in a safe place while they worked. One of the first day nurseries in the United States was established in New York City in 1854. Other cities followed, and in 1898 the National Federation of Day Nurseries was founded, which later became the National Association for the Education of Young Children (NAEYC).

Peabody

In 1860, Elizabeth Peabody (1804–1894) opened up the first English-language kindergarten in Boston, Massachusetts. Like Schurz's kindergarten, this was a private school based on Froebel's ideas. Peabody was influenced by Schurz when they met at a meeting on Froebel's philosophy. Although many of Peabody's activities were similar to Schurz's, concepts such as developing eye–hand coordination, habits of politeness, self-control, and understanding of numeracy were also introduced in Peabody's program for 4- to 6-year-old children. Peabody was known in the United States for promoting information about kindergarten to the larger society (Hewes, 1995).

Blow and Harrison

In 1873, the first public kindergarten opened in St. Louis, Missouri. It was founded by Susan Blow (1843–1916), who was an active leader in education in Missouri. Blow also incorporated Froebelian methods. In addition, she used furniture that was sized for young children (e.g., low tables, short benches) in classrooms that were brightly painted and included aspects of the natural world (e.g., plants), as well as books and toys. Learning occurred using all of these materials, the Froebelian blocks and similar materials, and the songs and games used by Schurz and Peabody (Nourot, 2005). In addition, the students learned about hygiene, nutritious eating habits, and the importance of exercise.

intentional teaching
Teaching that takes into account children's individual needs and interests, which includes differentiated instruction and culturally responsive practice.

Many of the ECE practices used in these first U.S. kindergarten programs remain popular today, especially in programs that integrate child-centered practices geared toward **intentional teaching** to prepare young children for primary school. However, particularly during the late 19th century, some programs provided only basic supports so that learning and development would unfold naturally, whereas others provided teacher-directed group instruction in a factory-like approach.

Education of Teachers

Toward the end of the 19th century, formal teacher training programs began to open in the United States. These programs started in the 1870s and had roots in the European programs, with Froebel's methods having a significant impact. The programs varied somewhat, but the basics included 1 year of coursework and an additional 1 year of practice teaching. Examples of these programs included the Oshkosh Normal School, the New York Seminary for Kindergarteners, and Hull House kindergarten training (which later became the University of Chicago Normal School). Toward the end of the 19th century, similar schools opened in numerous sites across the country.

Another indicator of the rise of the ECE profession was the establishment of professional organizations for early childhood educators in the late 19th century. One of the first associations was the International Kindergarten Union, which later became the Association for Childhood Education International (ACEI). As with the kindergarten programs established in the United States and the increasing number of teacher education programs, the first professional organizations were greatly affected by Froebel's methods and ideas (Nourot, 2005).

✳ ✳ ✳ Section Summary ✳ ✳ ✳

During the 19th century, thoughts about ECE were deeply influenced by the work of Pestalozzi and Froebel. Early childhood programs based on their ideas were opened in the United States, with some being taught in German. Simultaneously, nursery schools were started to meet the needs of factory workers, with some taking ideas from Owen, who proposed that day nurseries would improve the children's standing in society. At the end of the 19th century, efforts toward professionalizing the field of ECE were developed.

Early Childhood Education in the First Half of the 20th Century

ECE theory in the first part of the 20th century was clearly influenced by earlier ideas but also shared a number of similarities with today's practices and intellectual thoughts (see Figure 3.3).

Major Theorists

The major theorists influencing ECE during the first part of the 20th century included Sigmund Freud, John Dewey, Maria Montessori, and Arnold Gesell. These theorists are discussed briefly here though their work provides a foundation for work presented in the following sections of this chapter and chapters to follow.

Sigmund Freud (1856–1939) was a Jewish Austrian psychoanalyst who founded the psychoanalytic school of psychiatry. In his work, Freud proposed that the human psyche could be divided into three parts: the id, ego, and superego, which he discussed in his 1920 essay *Beyond the Pleasure Principle* (1920/1961), and fully elaborated upon in *The Ego and the Id* (1923/1949). His theorizing focused on the fact that,

Freud

> There is more to childhood than innocent play . . . young children continually find themselves embroiled in internal conflicts between impulses toward sexuality and aggression, on the one hand, and socially sanctioned pressures to gain parental approval and be productive, on the other hand. (As quoted in McDevitt & Ormrod, 2004, p. 13)

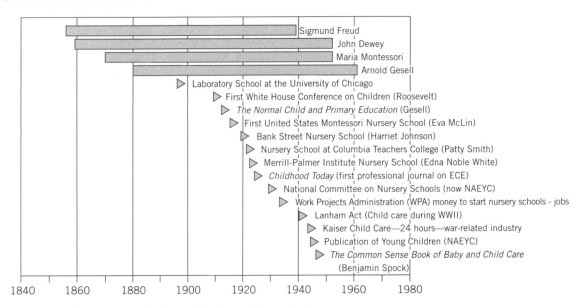

Figure 3.3.   Early childhood education in the first half of the 20th century.

Freud's work theorized psychodynamic perspectives related to childhood and later life. Like many of the other theorists discussed in this chapter, Freud focused on the importance of early experiences and how they affect the development of later characteristics and behaviors. Emotional development is a central part of the psychodynamic theory. With Freud's seminal work, teachers and researchers in laboratory schools began addressing how emotional development was of central importance to children's overall healthy development.

Dewey

John Dewey (1859–1952) was a great American philosopher who wrote about progressive education. His philosophy and his works had a tremendous effect on all education, and his ideas continue to thrive today. Dewey was greatly influenced by Rousseau and Froebel. Dewey felt that education was the fundamental method of social progression and reform, in the spirit of social cooperation (Dewey, 1938). He felt that education should be strongly connected and integrated with life and that education should come from children's powers and interests. Dewey believed that learning is natural and should come through experiencing the world. To Dewey, social life is the unconscious unity in all a child does, so it should be the center of importance at school.

Like Froebel, Dewey had great respect for the child as a person. School was explained by Dewey as primarily a social function: School life should grow out of home life, and it should continue the activities with which the child is already familiar with in the home. Dewey felt that the purpose of school is to prepare young children for their future responsibilities and for success in life. These views were counter to the typical education of children as being passive, receptive, and absorbing of knowledge—all of which Dewey saw as a major reason for children's lack of interest in school.

Montessori

Maria Montessori (1870–1952) was an Italian physician who worked with children with special needs who lived in low-income neighborhoods. In her work, Montessori had such great success with Italian children that she thought her theory of child development and her instructional methods could be applied to all children. Therefore, she developed her original methods of working with children into a structured system that is still used in various forms throughout the world. Montessori's method of early education focused on her stage-based notions of child development. She felt that appropriate stimuli in a controlled, disciplined environment would enhance a child's early development (Montessori, 1965).

Montessori followed through on this so effectively that she actually personalized the early childhood environment by scaling the space and materials down to a child's size. Montessori organized and coordinated a set of materials aimed at helping children to establish order and meaning in their worlds. There is very little freedom of movement in a Montessori classroom. Children work individually, gathering materials from low shelves available to all. Order and attractiveness are important characteristics of all good Montessori classrooms. Montessori's classroom materials are visually and tactilely attractive, self-directive, and self-corrective. These materials were created to develop coordination; stimulate activity and curiosity; increase attention span; develop the abilities to think, judge, reason, and compare; develop a growth of confidence; and foster independence. Children in Montessori classrooms emphasize highly active involvement with a variety of materials and as much independence as possible within a routine-based environment. The child's autonomous functioning in the environment is the goal of Montessorian education. Many early childhood classrooms have various Montessori materials (e.g., **nesting cubes**, wooden cylinder matching games), even if they are not necessarily a strict Montessori classroom by name. The first U.S. Montessori school was established and opened in 1912 in Tarrytown, New York.

nesting cubes
Blocks that fit inside one another which are used to support the understanding of size and sequence.

Arnold Gesell (1880–1961) was an American psychologist and pediatrician who developed a maturationist perspective on young children, in which development is seen as predetermined and intelligence as fixed. In this maturational model, the child is viewed as an organized whole—the laws controlling the growth of the mind and of the body are one and the same. Gesell's work held that child development takes place with the unfolding of innate dispositions. The environment does not generate the progression of development, but it does support it (Gesell, 1940). In Gesell's theoretical work, he suggested that development is continuous and likened to the growth of a plant: "The mind may be likened to a plant, but not to clay. For clay does not grow. Clay is molded entirely from without. A plant is primarily molded from within through the forces of growth" (1946, p. 20).

Gesell

Gesell started the Yale Child Study Clinic in 1911, where he used the words *child development* for the first time. He also was the first person to use observation windows and movie equipment to study children in detail. The focus in Gesell's clinic was on *how* children develop, not on how they are kept healthy, educated, or protected. His descriptive, normative studies influenced many other theorists (and research centers) into the advance study of the development of children. In the 1940s, Gesell's books were used as child development guides (Gesell, 1940).

The study of the "normal child" came to fruition as Gesell broke new ground in his use of careful observation of children's behavior as a method of studying the orderly sequence of their development. In his foundational work, Gesell proposed that psychological development followed a similar orderly sequence governed by what he termed *lawful growth processes*. Gesell was one of the first researchers to describe the expected maturational sequences in various domains of neuromotor development from early infancy through school age. Gesell believed that—similar to how the body develops in genetically encoded, sequenced patterns—behavioral patterns emerge in sequences that are reflective of differentiation in the central nervous system (Gesell, 1940).

As detailed in this chapter, ECE today has been positively affected by a rich, historical influence of concerned people who challenged societal conditions, theoretical understandings of those times, and themselves to make the world a better place for children and teachers and communities. Each of the individuals discussed in this section has left a lasting impression in ECE as it is practiced today. Beyond the scope of these significant people, the field of ECE also witnessed other significant events during the first half of the 20th century, which built on their work and assisted in the advancement of the field—some of which we briefly review next.

Significant Events

The establishment of laboratory schools during the early part of the 1900s was an instrumental way for different ECE professionals and practitioners to enhance the theories and thoughts of people like John Dewey and Maria Montessori in common educational settings, as well as make them into pedagogical practices for young children and communities. These early schools included the following:

- *Laboratory School at the University of Chicago:* The Laboratory School was founded by American educator John Dewey in 1896 in the Hyde Park neighborhood of Chicago. Building on Dewey's philosophical works, the school became a progressive institution that spanned nursery school through 12th grade.

- *Bank Street Nursery School:* The Bank Street College of Education began as a research group called the Bureau of Educational Experiments in 1916. During this time, people believed that children were to be seen and not heard, and education usually consisted of a teacher lecturing or conducting drills in front of the class. However, some educators and feminists in New York City, including Harriet Johnson, Caroline Pratt, Elizabeth Irwin, and Lucy Sprague Mitchell, questioned whether schools had to be that way (Cleverly & Phillips, 1986). The revolutionary educator John Dewey influenced these women, who also believed that a new and different approach to education could change society. Dewey believed that children could grow up to become accomplished thinkers and rational contributors to a democratic society if they were encouraged to inquire actively about experiences that related to the world outside the classroom. The initial pursuit of the Bureau of Educational Experiments was to formally study child development, discover ways that children learn best, and publish their findings.

- *Nursery School at Columbia University:* To meet the needs of young academic families, the Columbia Greenhouse Nursery School was founded in 1919 by the wife of a Columbia University zoology professor. It is one of America's oldest nursery schools.

Around the same time that the first laboratory schools were established, the White House held the first Conference on the Care of Dependent Children in 1909 under President Theodore Roosevelt. At this first conference, some of the recommendations called for the end of routine institutionalization of neglected or otherwise dependent children and the creation of the Federal Children's Bureau. This conference later became known as the White House Conference on Children and Youth.

Similar to the movement that led to the progression of the Conference on the Care of Dependent Children, in the 1920s, a group of professional researchers and educators began organizing nursery schools for young children. Patty Smith Hill identified a multidisciplinary group of 25 individuals—among them Arnold Gesell, Lois Meek (Stolz), and Abigail Eliot—who shared concerns about the quality of the proliferating programs for young children. They gathered together to consider the need for a new association, and in 1926, a public conference was held in Washington, DC. By 1929, the group was organized as the National Association for Nursery Education (NANE) and had published its first book—*Minimum Essentials for Nursery Education* (National Committee on Nursery School, 1929). The roots of the current NAEYC extend back to the NANE organization.

Several federal acts were inspired by socially and fiscally troubling times in the first half of the 20th century, which led to the creation of innovative assistance programs like the Work Projects Administration (WPA; originally named the Works Progress Administration). The WPA, established in 1935, was the largest New Deal agency, employing millions to carry out public works projects, including the construction of public buildings and roads. The WPA operated large arts, drama, media, and literacy projects; fed children; and redistributed food, clothing, and housing.

The Lanham Public War Housing Act (PL 76-849) was passed in 1940 to provide federal funding for states to pay for child care services for working mothers during World War II. The Lanham Act was implemented by California in 1943 through a statewide child care center program administered by the California Department of Education. Similarly, Kaiser Company's child care project provided child care centers for working mothers at the Kaiser shipyards. Kaiser needed to maintain a profit and meet war production deadlines, and through the U.S. Maritime Commission established and funded 24-hour child care centers. This landmark social experiment in American history served nearly 4,000 children, an effort unheard of before that time period (Cleverly & Phillips, 1986).

Another significant event of this time period was the publication of an important book that focused on critical ideas about child care. In 1946, Dr. Benjamin Spock published his book *The Common Sense Book of Baby and Child Care*, which became a bestseller. By 1998, the book had sold more than 50 million copies and had been translated into 39 languages. Spock influenced several generations of parents to be more flexible and affectionate with their children, and to treat them as individuals. His ideas about being flexible and affectionate with children and treating them as individuals went directly against previous conventional wisdom that child rearing should focus mainly on building discipline.

❋ ❋ ❋ Section Summary ❋ ❋ ❋

In this historical review of ECE during the first half of the 20th century, we discussed dramatic influences from a rich history of philosophers, theorists, and specialists whose work remains key in the field today. These historical figures—Freud, Dewey, Montessori, and Gesell—discussed and wrote about various aspects of the importance of the early years in a child's life. Their presence in the field of ECE was influential and expanded on during the next 50 years by similar theorists, discussed in the next section. Other significant actions took place during this time period to also enhance knowledge of early educational issues, from federal actions like the Lanham Act to more privatized actions such as Kaiser's child care project. These actions served children and families in numerous capacities and also increased the knowledge base of the field of ECE related to how we can best serve children and families.

Early Childhood Education in the Second Half of the 20th Century

ECE in the second half of the 20th century was built upon the ideas coming before it. The level of creation of new programs was very high during this period (see Figure 3.4), starting in the early 1960s when Head Start was launched, serving 560,000 children during the first summer program (Zigler & Styfco, 2010).

Major Theorists

The major theorists influencing ECE during the second half of the 20th century included Jean Piaget, Lev Vygotsky, Erik Erikson, B.F. Skinner, and Urie Bronfenbrenner. These theorists are discussed briefly here; see Chapters 5–9 for more details.

Piaget

Jean Piaget (1886–1980) was a constructivist theorist. His work had a tremendous impact on cognitive development, revealing that young children actively construct their own knowledge. Children integrate new learning into what they already know (assimilation) and modify what they already know to make sense of the new information (accommodation). With new learning, children are confronted with new information that conflicts with current understanding, which causes instability (disequilibrium) of the current understanding. New understandings are then constructed. Many Piagetian concepts have been of central importance to the NAEYC's proposal of developmentally appropriate practice, originally released in 1987 (Bredekamp, 1987).

Vygotsky

cultural transmission of information
Cultural information that is passed to children from adults, peers, and community.

In his short life, Lev Vygotsky (1896–1934) had a big impact on the field of ECE. Current reconstructions of NAEYC's proposal of developmentally appropriate practice have been influenced dramatically by Vygotsky's theories (Copple & Bredekamp, 2009). Vygotskian theory accounts for the impact of the social environment on children's construction of knowledge through interactions with significant adults and more advanced children (e.g., parents, teachers, classmates, siblings), as well as the historic development of higher mental functions within cultural groups (i.e., **cultural transmission of information**). Tools for development and learning consist of two types, external and internal (Lauria, 1979; Vygotsky, 1978). An external tool might be used for problem solving. For example, when completing a puzzle, a child might look at the picture of the puzzle on the box that it came in; this tool is external. It is a device for teachers to scaffold the placement of the puzzle pieces and thinking skills, such as by instructing students to look carefully before picking up a piece for the puzzle (Haywood, Brooks, & Burns, 1992). Internalization of these tools plays a role in the child's construction of mind, which influences the development of generalized thinking skills (Leong, Bodrova, & Henson, 2007).

Erikson

Erik Erikson's (1902–1994) ideas have affected ECE programs, especially on the social and emotional components of ECE during this time period. His stage-based ideas highlighted the psychosocial tension that preschool children face, such as the tension between initiative and guilt. He believed that preschool children need to explore, initiate, and develop curiosity, to even make mistakes and recover from them without guilt. Imaginative play opportunities should be provided, and teachers should take seriously the multiple *why* questions their young learners ask (Erikson, 1993).

Skinner

B.F. Skinner's (1904–1990) ideas are implemented in many ECE programs for children with disabilities, especially his verbal behavior theory. The theory posits that behavior is based on children's past and current environmental contingencies,

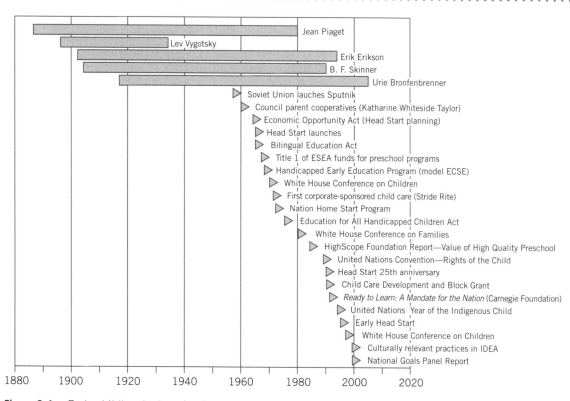

Figure 3.4. Early childhood education in the second half of the 20th century.

as well as heredity and biology. Skinner believed that behavior should be taught in small steps, with directions that are clear and repeated as necessary; reinforcement should be provided for accurate performance. Many of the behavior management programs seen in preschools during this time period were based on these types of behavioral principles (Skinner, 1957).

Urie Bronfenbrenner (1917–2005) addressed the needs of the young child in neighborhood, family, and community settings. His ideas have greatly affected Head Start programs. Bronfenbrenner's ecological theory helped in looking at the complexity of young children's lives, including the aspects (e.g., cultural, social, economic, political) that account for variability, and for richness to incorporate into classrooms. He identified aspects of young children's lives in microsystems (e.g., family, neighborhood, early childhood programs), mesosystems (e.g., links between microsystems such as shared cultural values), exosystems (e.g., a parent's loss of employment), macrosystems (e.g., broader values of society), and chronosystems (e.g., sociohistorical conditions of children and families over time, such as families who have been living in poverty generation after generation) (Bronfenbrenner, 1989).

Bronfenbrenner

Significant Events

As seen in Figure 3.4, the second half of the 20th century was rich in activity pertaining to ECE. This timeline begins with an event that was not specific to ECE—the Soviet Union launching Sputnik. However, this event concerned U.S. citizens about their country's progress in both space exploration and education. Soon after the launch of Sputnik, the Economic Opportunity Act of 1964 (PL 88-452) was passed, and formal plans for Head Start began. In 1965, Head Start was launched to serve children with low-income families, with goals of including 10% children with disabilities and 10% children from higher income families (although this latter goal was not realized). In 1972, Head Start began the National Home Start Program to expand parents' involvement in their young children's education. In 1984, the HighScope Educational Research Foundation released study results that supported the impact of such programs on children with low-income families (Berruta-Clement, Schweinhart, Barnett, Epstein, & Weikart, 1984).

In 1990, Head Start celebrated its 25th anniversary, with a major emphasis placed during this time period on renewed emphasis on high-quality programs. In 1995, Head Start added Early Head Start to its programs, which was a program for low-income pregnant women and families with infants and toddlers. At the end of the 20th century, Head Start advocated a renewed understanding that multilingual and multicultural knowledge was important for implementation of a high-quality program for young children and their families.

Goals of Head Start

The overall goal of Head Start was to improve children's social competence and school readiness. Through quality educational opportunities, it was initially believed that some of the impacts of poverty on young children could be remedied. Head Start also marked the beginning of including children with disabilities in ECE programs—long before the Individuals with Disabilities Education Improvement Act (IDEA) of 2004 (PL 108-446). Head Start mandates that 10% of children admitted to their programs have identified disabilities (Zigler & Styfco, 2010).

In 1967, the Elementary and Secondary Education Act (ESEA) Amendments (PL 90-247) included funds (Title 1) for preschool education and has continued to do so through the No Child Left Behind Act of 2001 (PL 107-110). In addition, the Bilingual Education Act was made a part of the ESEA Amendments of 1968 (PL 90-247) to address the needs of children learning English. Since then, the United States has had back-and-forth policies and interest in bilingual education, although there is evidence of the benefits of multilingualism (Bialystok, 2001; Genesee, Paradis, & Crago, 2011). Head Start has built on these findings and applies them to the programs, most recently using the terminology *dual-language learners* (Office of Head Start, 2008).

In 1968, the Handicapped Children's Early Education Program was developed to fund model preschool programs for young children with disabilities. In 1975, the Education for All Handicapped Children Act (PL 94-142) provided support for states to provide free and appropriate education for children with disabilities, including preschool children. IDEA 2004 (PL 108-446) also included infants and toddlers, followed by efforts to include appropriate education for children with disabilities who are also multilingual and multicultural.

Many of the previously mentioned programs have children's readiness for school as one of their goals. In the 1990s, the Carnegie Foundation (Boyer, 1991) and the National Education Goals Panel (1999) both issued reports on readiness. Also, there was (and still remains) a tremendous need to provide high-quality preschool experiences for children while in child care. In 1960, Katharine Whiteside Taylor started what is called Parent Cooperative Schools International for the exchange of ideas in preschool education. Stride Rite Corporation started the first **corporate-sponsored child care** in 1971. The federal government also created the Child Care Development and Block Grant in 1990, authorized under the Per-

corporate-sponsored child care *Child care or education that is provided by a parent's employer.*

United Nations Convention on the Rights of the Child

The United Nations established the following rights of each child (Office of the United Nations High Commissioner for Human Rights, 1989), summarized here briefly:

- To be without discrimination of any kind, irrespective of the child's or caregiver's race; color; sex; language; religion; political or other opinion; national, ethnic, or social origin; property; disability; or birth or other status

- To be protected against all forms of discrimination or punishment on the basis of the status, activities, expressed opinions, or beliefs of the child's caregivers or family members

- To rest and leisure, to engage in play and recreational activities appropriate to the age of the child, and to participate freely in cultural life and the arts

- To have the best interests of the child be a primary consideration with regard to public or private social welfare institutions, courts of law, administrative authorities, or legislative bodies

- To have economic, social, and cultural rights protected to the maximum extent of the government's available resources

- To have an inherent right to life, survival, and development

- To have the child's identity—including nationality, name, and family relations—preserved as recognized by law without unlawful interference

- To have freedom of thought, conscience, and religion

- To be protected from all forms of physical or mental violence, injury or abuse, neglect or negligent treatment, maltreatment or exploitation, including sexual abuse, while with caregivers

- To have access to the highest attainable standard of health and facilities for the treatment of illness and rehabilitation of health

- To have access to necessary medical assistance and health care with emphasis on the development of primary health care

- To have respect for the child's parents, cultural identity, language, and values; the national values of the country in which the child is living; the country from which he or she may originate; and civilizations different from his or her own

- For a child with disabilities to have enjoyment of a full and decent life, in conditions that ensure dignity, promote self-reliance, and facilitate the child's active participation in the community

- For a child with disabilities to have effective access to and receipt of education, training, health care services, rehabilitation services, preparation for employment, and recreation opportunities in a manner conducive to the child's achieving the fullest possible social integration and individual development, including his or her cultural and spiritual development

- For a child seeking refugee status or who is considered a refugee, to receive appropriate protection and humanitarian assistance in the enjoyment of applicable human rights

- For working parents to have the right to benefit from child care services and facilities for which they are eligible

sonal Responsibility and Work Opportunity Reconciliation Act of 1996 (PL 104-193). This program is intended not only to improve the quality of child care programs, but it also assists low-income families in finding child care so that parents can work or attend training/education (U.S. Department of Health and Human Services, 2010).

As was the case in the Roosevelt era, in the latter part of the 20th century, the White House took particular interest in the needs of young children and their families. In 1970, there was the White House Conference on Children and Youth, which brought these needs to the closer attention of society; this conference was re-established in 1997. The United Nations developed the Convention on the Rights of the Child in 1989; this was put into effect in 1990 with the signing by 20 nations—although the United States did not sign the treaty. The United States did not sign the treaty in part because some felt the language in the treaty undermined the rights of parents, for example, to punish their children as they saw fit (Mason, 2005).

❊ ❊ ❊ Section Summary ❊ ❊ ❊

In the second half of the 20th century, ECE was deeply influenced by major theorists with different views of the processes involved in the development and learning of young children. Consistent with those views were accompanying program models. During this period of time, great emphasis was placed on providing high-quality programs for all children (although there was controversy between programs addressing constructivist ideas and those focused on readiness for kindergarten). Additional themes in the provision of ECE included the availability of high-quality programs for children from low-income families and children with disabilities or multicultural and multilingual backgrounds, as well as quality child care for families with working parents. Finally, during this time, several White House conferences on children and the United Nations Convention on the Rights of the Child elevated the interests and needs of children in society.

KEY CONCEPTS

- Prior to the 19th century, historical figures such as Plato, Comenius, Locke, and Rousseau discussed and wrote about various aspects of the importance of the early years in a child's life. These philosophers, theorists, and specialists continue to have an impact on ECE theory in the 21st century.

- During the 19th century, thoughts about ECE were deeply influenced by the work of Pestalozzi and Froebel. Early childhood programs based on their ideas were opened in the United States, with some being taught in German.

- Nursery schools were started during the 19th century to meet the needs of factory workers, with some taking ideas from Owen, who proposed that day nurseries would improve the children's standing in society.

- The first efforts to professionalize ECE took place toward the end of the 19th century.

- During the first half of the 20th century, historical figures such as Freud, Dewey, Montessori, and Gesell discussed and wrote about various aspects of the importance of the early years in a child's life. Their work had a direct impact on ECE programs and was modeled in some.

- In the first half of the 20th century, public and private efforts in ECE (e.g., the federal Lanham Act, the private Kaiser child care project) served children and families in numerous capacities and also increased the knowledge base of the field of ECE related to how we can best serve children and families.

- During the second half of the 20th century, ECE was influenced by major theorists with different views of the processes involved in the development and learning of young children. Consistent with those views were accompanying program models.

- During the second half of the 20th century, emphasis was placed on providing high-quality programs for all children (although there was controversy among programs addressing constructivist ideas and those focused on readiness for kindergarten).

- During the second half of the 20th century, emphasis in ECE also took into account the availability of high-quality programs for children from low-income families, including child care for working parents, children with disabilities, and those with multicultural and multilingual backgrounds.

- White House conferences on children and the United Nations Convention on the Rights of the Child have elevated the interests and needs of children in society, including ECE concerns.

Integration of Information

You have just read the chapter on the history of ECE, which provides a sense of the richness and diversity of thought in this field. Does this chapter stand out to you as providing information that will help you understand the field of ECE?

Self-Reflective Guide

This self-reflective guide will help you assess whether you learned the information in this chapter. It also provides an opportunity to identify areas in which you want or need more information. Are there some new ideas learned that will affect your immediate practice with children?

1. Identify major philosophers, theorists, educators, and researchers who influenced ECE before and during the 19th century and during the 20th century. Does a particular person intrigue you? Why? Make a few notes.

2. Reflect on how these individuals changed the field during their time. Have they influenced how you will practice today? Name an individual and the influence you think you will find in practice today.

3. Know how the major U.S. laws and policies have influenced ECE and when they were introduced over the years. Write about one of these areas that you think will affect your practice.

4. Know how private sector actions affected ECE. Which action is interesting to you? What do you think are the long-term effects of the action? Make a few notes.

5. Identify major themes in the history of ECE. Write one down and note why it is interesting to you.

Helpful Web Sites

American Montessori Society

> www.amshq.org
> This site provides information on Montessori education, providing resources for families, school, and teachers, and discussing how Maria Montessori's influence lives on today.

The Center for Dewey Studies at Southern Illinois University Carbondale

> www.siuc.edu/~deweyctr
> This site provides information on past and current projects studying the life and work of John Dewey.

Froebel Web

> www.froebelweb.org/weblinks.html
> This site provides many links pertaining to the theories and works of Friedrich Froebel.

NAEYC Historical Overview

> www.naeyc.org/about/history
> This site provides information about the association's history.

Office of Head Start

www.acf.hhs.gov/programs/ohs/index.html
This site provides policy and research information regarding the Head Start program.

References

Berruta-Clement, J.R., Schweinhart, L.J., Barnett, W.S., Epstein, A.S., & Weikart, D.P. (1984). *Changed lives: The effects of the Perry Preschool Program on youths through age 19* (Monographs of the HighScope Educational Research Foundation, 8). Ypsilanti, MI: High/Scope Press.

Bialystok, E. (2001). *Bilingualism in development: Language, literacy, & cognition.* New York: Cambridge University Press.

Boyer, E. (1991). *Ready to learn: A mandate for the nation.* Princeton, NJ: Carnegie Foundation for the Advancement of Teaching.

Bredekamp, S. (Ed.). (1987). *Developmentally appropriate practice in early childhood programs serving children from birth through age 8.* Washington, DC: National Association for the Education of Young Children.

Bronfenbrenner, U. (1989). Ecological systems theory. *Annals of Child Development, 6,* 185–246.

Cleverly, J., & Phillips, D.C. (1986). *Visions of childhood: Influential models from Locke to Spock* (Rev. ed.). New York: Teachers College Press.

Comenius, J.A. (1956/1984). *School of infancy.* Chapel Hill: University of North Carolina.

Copple, C., & Bredekamp, S. (2009). *Developmentally appropriate practice in early childhood programs serving children from birth through age 8* (3rd ed.). Washington, DC: National Association for the Education of Young Children.

Dewey, J. (1938). *Experience and education.* New York: Touchstone.

Economic Opportunity Act of 1964, PL 88-452, 42 U.S.C. §§ 2701 et seq.

Education for All Handicapped Children Act of 1975, PL 94-142, 20 U.S.C. §§ 1400 et seq.

Elementary and Secondary Education Act Amendments of 1967, PL 90-247, 81 Stat. 783.

Elementary and Secondary Education Act Amendments of 1968, PL 90-247, 20 U.S.C. §§ 877b et seq.

Erikson, E.H. (1993). *Childhood and society.* New York: WW Norton.

Froebel, F. (1887). *The education of man* (W.N. Hailmann, Trans.). New York: Appleton. (Original work published 1826.)

Freud, S. (1949). *The ego and the id.* London: Hogarth Press. (Original work published 1923.)

Freud, S. (1961). *Beyond the pleasure principle* (J. Strachey, Trans.). New York: W.W. Norton. (Original work published 1920.)

Genesee, F., Paradis, J., & Crago, M.B. (2011). *Dual language development and disorders: A handbook on bilingualism and second language learning* (2nd ed.). Baltimore: Paul H. Brookes Publishing Co.

Gesell, A. (1940). *The first five years of life: A guide to the study of the preschool child, from the Yale Clinic of Child Development, parts 1–3.* New York: Harper & Brothers.

Gesell, A. (1946). *The child from five to ten.* New York: Harper & Brothers.

Haywood, H.C., Brooks, P., & Burns, S. (1992). *Bright start: Cognitive curriculum for young children.* Watertown, MA: Charlesbridge Publishers.

Hewes, D. (1995). *Sisterhood and sentimentality: America's earliest preschool centers.* Redmond, WA: Childcare Information Exchange.

Individuals with Disabilities Education Improvement Act (IDEA) of 2004, PL 108-446, 20 U.S.C. §§ 1400 et seq.

Lanham Public War Housing Act of 1940, PL 76-849, 42 U.S.C. §§ 1521 et seq.

Lauria, A. (1979). *The making of mind: A personal account of Soviet psychology.* Cambridge, MA: Harvard University Press.

Leong, D.J., Bodrova, E., & Hensen, R. (2007). *Tools of the Mind curriculum project preschool manual* (4th ed.). Denver, CO: Center for Improving Early Learning, Metropolitan State College of Denver.

Locke, J. (1979). In P.H. Nidditch (Ed.), *An essay concerning human understanding.* Oxford, England: Oxford University Press.

Mason, M.A. (2005). The U.S. and the International Children's Rights Crusade: Leader or laggard? *Journal of Social History, 38,* 955–963.

McDevitt, T.M., & Ormrod, J.E. (2004). *Child development: Educating and working with children and families.* Columbus, OH: Pearson.

Montessori, M. (1965). *Dr. Montessori's own handbook.* New York: Schocken.

National Committee on Nursery School. (1929). *Minimum essentials for nursery school education.* Washington, DC: National Association for Nursery Education.

National Education Goals Panel. (1999). *The National Education Goals report: Building a nation of learners.* Washington, DC: Author.

No Child Left Behind Act of 2001, PL 107-110, 115 Stat. 1425, 20 U.S.C. §§ 12501 et seq.

Nourot, P.M. (2005). Historical perspectives on early childhood education. In J.P. Roopnarine & J.E. Johnson (Eds.), *Approaches to early childhood education* (4th ed., pp. 3–43). Upper Saddle River, NJ: Merrill/Prentice Hall.

Office of Head Start. (2008). *Dual language: What does it take?* Washington, DC: U.S. Department of Health and Human Service.

Office of the United Nations High Commissioner for Human Rights. (1989). *Convention on the Rights of the Child.* Retrieved September 23, 2010, from http://www2.ohchr.org/english/law/crc.htm

Personal Responsibility and Work Opportunity Reconciliation Act of 1996, PL 104-193, 42 U.S.C. §§ 211 et seq.

Pettersson, R. (1993). *Visual information* (2nd ed.). Englewood Cliffs, NJ: Educational Technologies Publications.

Plato. (2003). *The republic* (D. Lee, Trans.). New York: Penguin.

Rousseau, J.J. (2007). *Emile: Or, on education.* Sioux Falls, SD: NuVision Publications. (Original work published 1762.)

Skinner, B.F. (1957). *Verbal behavior.* Acton, MA: Copley Publishing Group.

Spock, B. (1946). *The common sense book of baby and child care.* New York: Simon & Schuster.

Spodek, B., Sarachi, O.N., & Peters, D.L. (1998). *Professionalism and the early childhood practitioner.* New York: Teachers College Press.

U.S. Department of Health and Human Services. (2010). *About the Child Care and Development Fund.* Retrieved December 4, 2010, from http://www.acf.hhs.gov/programs/ccb/ccdf/index.htm

Vygotsky, L.S. (1978). In M. Cole, V. John-Steiner, S. Scribner, & E. Souberman (Eds.), *Mind in society: The development of high psychological processes.* Cambridge, MA: Harvard University Press.

Zigler, E., & Styfco, S.J. (2010). *The hidden history of Head Start.* New York: Oxford University Press.

Early Childhood Practice Today

with Myra Rogers

4

Learning Objectives

1. Understand the basics of setting up an ECE classroom environment, including learning centers and basic classroom design
2. Reflect on the types of daily schedules and what periods of time are needed for young children in different activities
3. Recognize the role of play in young children's learning and development
4. Identify the nature and key features of high-quality interactions between adults and children
5. Know the reasons for and basics of teamwork with families
6. Understand how to get started in your practice

How do I know how to set up tables, chairs, toys, and books? What do the children need outside when they play? How much time do preschool children spend in a large group? Is it true that play is the work of the preschool child? Do the children need a lot of time in learning centers? How many learning centers should I have in my room? When children are playing, is it best to leave them alone? How do I meet individual children's needs and interests? What does good teaching of preschool children look like? How do I make sure I teach them all they need to know? What about families? How do I include them? What are important things to know about starting up the year?

These are the types of questions being addressed in this chapter, which focuses on the basics of early childhood education (ECE), spanning across daily practice for teachers and caregivers. This chapter is not exhaustive, however. Chapters 5–9 provide additional information, as will your professional development, whether through preservice or in-service educational programs.

The Big Picture

ECE has been influenced by multiple philosophers, theorists, educational ideas, educational models, and government and private sector initiatives. Societal changes, such as households in which both parents work and equity concerns that all children achieve in school, further affect ECE. As noted in previous chapters, the availability of high-quality programs so that all children can receive rich **opportunities to learn** and develop is paramount. But what about the day-to-day basics and core practices of ECE? This chapter presents information on how to set up a preschool environment, the core aspects of early childhood practices, and some tips for beginning the year with new children.

opportunities to learn
Instruction and experiences provided in high-quality environments that support learning and development.

Setting Up the Environment

The preschool classroom should include centers that are visible to the teachers and that are safe for the children. For example, the centers should use age-appropriate furniture of the correct size that is sturdy and unable to tip over. Classroom space, materials, and toys should be organized and easily accessible and welcoming to children who have a variety of physical abilities and who may use adaptive equipment. It is important to introduce all materials and toys available to children in the classroom and have discussions about safety for various items (e.g., scissors, staplers, fasteners) throughout the school year. Some children might need one-to-one guidance on how to use tools in the different areas.

A label can be helpful in designating the different learning centers.

Throughout the classroom, photos and pictures should be clear; colorful; relevant; large enough; and clearly showing diversity in races, cultures, families, sexes, occupations, places, ages, and abilities. Some photos should be of students in the room modeling how they should be doing jobs, playing in centers, and interacting with each other. Pictures should be positioned at children's eye level. The environment should be labeled in the languages of children in the classroom, but labeling should not be overdone. Include labels that you will refer to and talk about. Labels that are not referred to or talked about are not functional in the children's lives and learning.

There are classroom spaces for unique and shared purposes such as **cubbies**, bathrooms, sinks, tables and chairs for eating (which can also be part of the learning centers), and a large-group area. The large-group area takes place in a space to accommodate all the children in the class and is set up in a way in which they can comfortably sit on the floor or dance without bumping into one another. Circle time, morning meeting, planning, sharing, singing, and music, for example, all take place in this space. Many of these same areas will be used for learning center time when working on such subjects as fine motor activities, literacy, math, and art. These learning centers are further described in the following sections.

cubbies
Private spaces in the classroom that are individually assigned to children, where they can hang their coats and keep other personal items.

Manipulative and Fine Motor Activities (Math)

In this area, you should include a wide range of interesting materials that facilitate fine motor development, such as puzzles, pegboards, markers, paper, play dough, cookie cutters, blocks, small **manipulative toys**, scissors, rulers, hole punchers, tape, washable paint, crayons, zippers, fasteners, snaps, beads, string, and small

manipulative toy
An educational toy that can be handled with a child's hands.

blocks. In addition, you might have bookshelves with the fine motor, perceptual, and math manipulatives; charting and graphing paper; and books on this topic.

Writing Center (Literacy)

In the writing center, you should include blank paper of different sizes and colors (preferably without lines), scissors, glue, markers, pencils, hole punchers, tape with a dispenser, stapler, stamps and stamp pads, books, blank greeting cards, stickers, envelopes, coupons, and computers with age-appropriate games.

The math area should include a wide range of interesting materials that promote active learning of math concepts.

Book Center (Literacy)

The book center is a quiet, comfortable area for language, reading, literacy, and social skills opportunities. It might have a rug, comfortable chairs, and an accessible shelving unit that displays the books. The selection should include age-appropriate, multicultural, multilingual, and multiability books with and without words. A variety of topics should be included, both fiction and nonfiction, and large-print books should be available. Some of the books should reflect upon and integrate current classroom themes.

Science Center

The science center should include a table for books on science and nature, discovery, and cause and effect, as well as pictures and photos. Other basic items may include magnifying glasses, living things (plants and/or pets; e.g., fish, lizard, worms, bugs, turtle), magnets, measuring containers, balancing device, ruler, tape measure, thermometers, container for storage of items (e.g., water, soil, sand), calculator, collections of plastic items (e.g., animals, insects, cars), collections of natural objects, paper and writing tools, safe mirror, and access to the outdoors for exploration and gathering real collections of materials. Paper and markers are available for "taking notes."

The literacy/book center is a quiet, comfortable area for language, reading, literacy, and social skills opportunities.

The science center should include basic items (e.g., magnifying glasses, magnets, measuring containers, calculators) and collections of natural objects.

The water/sand center should include a sand/water table or tub/bucket large enough for at least 2–3 kids to play in.

The water/sand center should also include items such as measuring cups, funnels, and scoops for filling and pouring.

Water and Sand Center

This center includes a sand and water table or tub large enough for at least two children to play in, as well as measuring cups, funnels, spoons, scoops, shovels, rakes, small containers with screw-on caps for filling and pouring, small toys for pretending, bubbles, plastic boats, sponges, shells, sea creatures, droppers, small people and animals, pictures, items relevant to possible classroom/**curriculum themes**, and books.

curriculum theme
A topic that defines a curriculum for a particular period of time.

Art Center

The art center should include easels, table, chairs, paint, markers, and crayons for the children to express their own ideas and experience using art materials; create three-dimensional art; and work on their fine motor, language, and social skills. Other items to include are pencils, chalk, chalkboard, dry-erase board and markers, play dough, paint brushes, glue, hole puncher, stamp pad and stamps, tape dispenser, sponges, cookie cutters, string, glitter, glue, magazine pages, cotton balls, construction paper, and cardboard. The inclusion of pictures, real photographs, and books with art-related themes is also important.

The art center should include a variety of materials to allow children to create and express themselves.

Items in the art center can be conveniently arranged in plastic tubs with photos and labels for type of material.

A good number of blocks of different sizes, shapes, and textures—wood, plastic, cardboard—should be on hand in the block center.

Examples of structures found in children's environments should be included for use in the block center.

Block Center

The block center is an area for children to develop imagination, critical thinking, social skills, cause and effect, and organization and teamwork skills. An uncluttered surface and space that holds at least three children who are able to build, balance, and create structures together or independently is needed. This area should also include a good number of various blocks of different sizes, shapes, and textures (e.g., hard smooth wood, plastic, cardboard); small objects, animals, people, vehicles, and road signs (including paper and markers to make new signs); books; pictures; pretend woodworking tools; and large plastic nuts and bolts. Sufficient storage shelves that are labeled and facing the block area for easy access and cleanup by children working in that area will support the effective use of the center.

Sociodramatic Play Center

This center is for pretending, make believe, practicing skills, developing social skills, language/communication, role play, and **parallel play**. You can set up the center in a variety of ways. One idea is a kitchen with a child sized table and chairs, refrigerator, stove, sink, storage shelves, cooking equipment (e.g., pots, pans, ladles, pitcher, different kinds of play foods, including ethnic foods), dolls of different races, doll clothes, shopping cart, cash register, play money, telephone (in styles children have experience with, e.g., old cell phones/cordless phones), mirror, stuffed animals, and a variety of hats and clothing. These basic materials can be transformed quickly into an actively used restaurant, grocery store, home setting,

parallel play
Occurs when children play alongside one another without interacting in any way.

The sociodramatic play center affords pretending, make believe, practicing skills, social skills, language/communication, role play, and parallel play.

The sociodramatic play center should contain a variety of clothing, hats, and other materials that can be quickly transformed into a make-believe scenario.

The woodworking center may contain real or plastic tools, chunks of Styrofoam or wood, and real or "pretend nails" (e.g., golf tees).

At least one area should be easily changed to make space for special projects associated with special activities, events, and seasonal themes.

fire station, or hospital. Writing materials and books on related topics also should be included.

Woodworking Center

The activities at the woodworking center can take many forms, such as working with chunks of foam or wood, using some plastic tools, or using real or even uncommon tools (e.g., using a meat tenderizer as a hammer and golf tees for nails). In all situations, some basics are needed, such as goggles, paper and pencil for making designs, books on making basic items, and glue as an alternative way to fasten items together. It is important to inform parents about the purpose of this center and the various materials with which the children will be working. Safety conversations when using real tools are essential.

Centers for Special Projects

At least one area should be easily changed to make space for special projects associated with special activities, events, and seasonal/curriculum themes. Consider, for example, transportation as a curriculum theme. During this theme, the class can transform the math center into a transportation center. They might create a mural that has roads, train tracks, an airport, and a lake on it, with an abundance of cars, buses, trains, airplanes, boats, and so forth. Incorporating the mural into the math center allows children to explore many math-related concepts (e.g., making patterns, counting like objects) as well as learn the curriculum theme.

A cot or mat, soft chairs, and enough space for each child are needed for resting, sleeping, and relaxed down time.

Outdoor Play

Outdoor play is a time for large (gross) motor activity, development and practice of social and language skills, and problem solving. Adequate supervision and interaction is a key component of outdoor play. Materials that can be included here are blocks, sand toys, balls, hula hoops, jump ropes, tricycles, and wagons, as well as safe climbing and balancing equipment that is anchored, accessible, and challenging and appropriate for preschoolers with different levels of ability.

Environment for Naps

Resting, sleeping, and relaxation time are a part of many early childhood programs. A cot or mat, soft chairs, clean surfaces, and enough space for each child is needed. Having children bring bedding from home can help make the children feel comfortable sleeping. Separate storage space for each mat and bedding is necessary.

Daily Schedule

There are many possible time frames for the ECE day. The following sample schedules can be used for guidance.

There are many time frames for the ECE day. A full-day schedule would include all activities from arrival to departure.

Example of Full-Day Schedule

8:30 a.m.	Arrival and breakfast
8:50 a.m.	Group meeting/planning/choice for center time
9:05 a.m.	Learning centers (includes cleanup)
10:05 a.m.	Review/recall of work
10:15 a.m.	Outdoor play
11:15 a.m.	Small-group time
11:30 a.m.	Large-group time
11:45 a.m.	Bathroom/lunch (includes preparation and cleanup)
12:15 p.m.	Rest
2:15 p.m.	Cleanup/bathroom/preparation for departure
2:30 p.m.	Dismissal
3:00 p.m.	Adult team planning

Example of Half-Day Morning Schedule

9:00 a.m.	Arrival and group meeting/planning
9:20 a.m.	Large-group art activity or teacher-directed reading
9:45 a.m.	Outdoor play
10:30 a.m.	Planning/choice for center time
10:45 a.m.	Learning centers (includes cleanup)
11:30 a.m.	Review/recall of work
	Bathroom/preparation for lunch
11:45 a.m.	Eat lunch (includes cleanup)
12:15 p.m.	Bathroom/preparation for departure
12:30 p.m.	Dismissal
1:00 p.m.	Adult team planning

Example of Half-Day Afternoon Schedule

12:00 p.m.   Arrival/group meeting

12:15 p.m.   Circle time

12:30 p.m.   Large-group, teacher-directed reading

12:45 p.m.   Planning/choice for center time

1:00 p.m.   Learning centers (includes cleanup)

1:45 p.m.   Review/recall of work

2:00 p.m.   Bathroom/preparation for snack time

2:15 p.m.   Snack

2:30 p.m.   Outdoor play

3:15 p.m.   Bathroom/preparation for departure

3:30 p.m.   Dismissal

4:00 p.m.   Adult team planning

Instructional Planning? Find a Friend

Through professional development, you will learn a great deal about ECE. Theories, instructional approaches, and specific activities will be presented, and you will be responsible for applying what you learn to provide a high-quality program for the young children in your classroom. You will learn how to assess what you implement in your classroom through evaluating whether you provide opportunities for *all* children in your class to develop and learn. Many of these ways to measure opportunities are presented in Chapters 5–9. You will also formally and informally observe your students' progress to assess if everyone is progressing. You will continuously reflect on the progress of your students as related to the opportunities you provide as well as your knowledge base regarding theory and effective early childhood practice. It is paramount, however, to find another ECE teacher (or two) with whom you can network. A **school mentor** might even fulfill this role when you are a beginning teacher. A friend can help you understand that the struggles you are experiencing are not yours alone but have been experienced by others. Hearing friends' solutions to common problems can be very helpful. You do not have to reinvent ECE practices. Your friends will be there to share!

school mentor
A school-based knowledgeable and trusted guide to help with difficulties related to teaching young children.

❋ ❋ ❋ Section Summary ❋ ❋ ❋

Effectively setting up the ECE classroom is central to providing a high-quality program for young children. The classroom learning environment includes public spaces (e.g., circle area, learning centers) and private spaces (e.g., cubbies, nap area). The furniture and decorations should be child-oriented in terms of size, location, and content. Learning centers should be welcoming and include an abundance of organized materials based on the learning goals of the center. Materials in the classroom can be rotated to keep the children's interest and should be respon-sive to their learning skills. A daily schedule helps to organize the ECE day.

The Core of Early Childhood Education Today

In the previous section, we addressed the environment and supplies needed for children's learning. In this section, we address the core of ECE: play, interactions, and building relationships with families. These concepts are introduced here and elaborated on in Chapters 5–9, especially as they relate to learning centers that ad-dress the whole child—including approaches to learning, social, emotional, cogni-tive, language, and physical development, as well as preschool content areas of creative arts, social studies, numeracy, science, and literacy. Treasuring every inter-action with the child and building relationships with families serve as the founda-tions of education in all early childhood programs.

Play

Research has demonstrated evidence of the strong connections between quality of play during the preschool years and children's readiness for school instruction (Bowman, Donovan, & Burns, 2000). Supportive, well-supplied classrooms are es-sential for development to take place. Stimulation from the environment changes the very physiology of the brain, interlocking nature and nurture (Shonkoff & Phillips, 2000). Further, research has directly linked play to children's ability to master academic content, such as literacy and numeracy (Hyson, 2008; Rogers & Sawyers, 1998).

In constructive play, materials are set up in a manner that promotes a specific goal or problem to explore through the play. Multiple types of materials should be available with which children can explore (e.g., sorting, classifying, looking at part/whole relationships, **equivalences**, experimenting with real-life number problems, making predictions and comparisons, seeing the impact of gravity, cause and effect). In a similar manner, materials and environments can focus on so-cioemotional development by having children act out scary concepts, frightening experiences, or something troubling they have seen on the news. Problem solving and different approaches to learning can be developed, as well as specific skills and concepts across all developmental areas.

Play promotes grounding of socially shared meaning for both physical and so-cial worlds (Bruner & Olsen, 1977). **Sociodramatic play** is a type of play in which language plays the central role; extensive language use is often viewed as a key feature of mature play (Bodrova & Leong, 2008; Smilansky, 1968; Smilansky & She-fatya, 1990). In sociodramatic play, children develop a scenario that they want to play out. This might be one chosen from a book that had been recently read in class or from events in the children's lives (e.g., going to the grocery store). The scenar-ios are often played out in the block center or sociodramatic play center with a number of children. Pretending is a central concept: Children pretend to be in cer-tain roles and use pretend objects and situations. Bodrova and Leong (2003) also pointed out how such sociodramatic play can be encouraged with fewer children or even with a child playing alone (e.g., in the sand table or art center). In these cases, toy people can be included in all learning centers so that a child can assign roles to figures and proceed to act out different play scenarios. Bodrova and Leong

equivalence
Two items with the same quantity.

sociodramatic play
A type of play in which a child or chil-dren assume roles and act out a familiar scene in play.

(2008) suggested that this type of play should be highly encouraged in all classroom learning centers.

Theory of Mind

Theory of mind (described in more detail in Chapter 5) is highlighted when children pretend during play. When children take on roles and assign roles to each other, they reflect on their thinking—specifically, on what is going on in their minds that others will not know about unless they say it out loud. When watching a scene develop in sociodramatic play, one can observe how this assignment of roles keeps the play scenario progressing.

Teachers are intentional in promoting play: They

> Purposefully plan and provide learning opportunities designed to meet the individual needs and interests of the various children in instructional settings. They use knowledge of effective practices and strategies when interacting with children in order to promote children's learning and development. (Burns et al., 2010, p. 6)

For children with disabilities, teachers might say part of the dialogue for a child and encourage the child to imitate it or provide assistive technology devices to help the child communicate. To encourage learning of new words, teachers name objects, actions, and events.

Peers also should be encouraged to get everyone involved to play their part. Teachers can help to negotiate the cultural differences present within the playgroup so that all children's diverse perspectives are taken into account. For children who are deaf or hard of hearing and children who are new to learning English, teachers should include enough visual and tactile cues or assistive technology devices so that these children can take part in the conversation. Play can provide an excellent opportunity for **prosocial behavior** because it allows children to choose their own level of social participation. Children can play near each other, in solitary or parallel fashion, or in a group situation that allows for interpersonal interaction. Blocks, for example, allow children to work in real situations where other children need help—or even sympathy because a building fell down (Rogers & Ross, 1986). All these experiences will enhance children's interpersonal skills.

prosocial behavior
Actions that demonstrate empathy for and awareness of the well-being of others.

To engage in quality play, children need time. To construct with materials and to explore their properties requires sufficient and supported time with the objects. Developing and acting out high-quality play scenarios requires at least 45 minutes. A long period of time allows the children to complete their play without worrying about cleaning up or rushing.

Interactions

In addition to multiple interactions with peers in play, similar interactions with adults and more advanced peers is a source for learning and development. The ways in which teachers interact with young children in classroom settings have important implications for children's developmental outcomes (Bowman et al.,

Play, Assessment, and Children with Disabilities

A classroom setup that facilitates considerable independent learning and free play is important. Play and peer interactions are instruction in a preschool classroom. Increasing attention is being given to the use of children's play as a form of assessment, prevention, and remediation, as well as something that can lessen developmental delays (Linder, 2008a, 2008b). The use of play for assessment purposes may produce a new view of the child for most clinical and school psychologists, who may be accustomed to the use of play only as a therapeutic tool. Free choice and natural creativity are often sacrificed in the interest of focusing on specific, high-sequenced instructional methods and criterion referenced assessments. It is up to the teachers to figure out how to assess where a child is performing when that child is performing typical play activities and interacting with peers. By creating a play environment with specific types of toys, the teachers can create an atmosphere where certain behaviors and skills can be formed, observed, and evaluated. Care must be taken in setting up the classroom for all levels of abilities to get the most out of the setup and content of each area of the classroom. Creating an environment where instruction and activities are perceived as fun and freely chosen by the children creates natural reinforcement and contingencies that promote more learning. It is an unobtrusive way of screening that can determine specific delays and help with a student's diagnosis.

The quality and amount of a child's play is influenced by the severity and type of disability. The differences that you see when young children are playing and interacting accounts for the importance of play as a means of assessment. Social play is one of the primary aspects of assessment in young children. Social play looks different for children with visual problems as well as motor, cognitive, and/or emotional needs. A speech therapist, occupational therapist, physical therapist, teacher, social worker, and psychologist may all be observing different aspects of one child's interactions in playtime activities. Valuable information can be obtained from watching how a child spontaneously interacts with peers, toys, objects, and the environment.

The teachers in the classroom should have a preplanned system of remembering, recording, and compiling data and occurrences of desired skills and levels of ability (e.g., checklists, charts, sticky notes). It may be necessary for ECE teachers to be more directive in the play process if children do not initiate interactions with objects and people in their environments. Be careful to interact with all children, even those who are not responsive. Social skills, fine and gross motor skills, self-care, sequencing, problem solving, behavior, language, and many other skills can be directly and indirectly monitored, assessed, and remediated during structured and nonstructured playtime activities with peers with and without disabilities. Addressing both the child's educational play and specific domains are possible and useful. Children can learn to constructively and appropriately interact with their environment, as well as objects and individuals in their environment, through a play-based curriculum. It is important that ECE professionals are clear about what play must involve and that they then maintain those elements as play is used in daily early interventions.

2000). These interactions happen as adults integrate into play and also throughout the day, such as at mealtimes, when adults can model more sophisticated thoughts and actions. Adults can describe ongoing actions taking place in the child's world. They can create opportunities for communication, making sure that children have time to talk and to get feedback from teachers. It is important that communication extends interactions. In extended interactions, all participants tend to interact in the conversation, and it is very important that the child have ample opportunity to talk during these conversations. In many situations, the children should have more time to talk. The adult should match the child's pace and style of talk, with the adult making sure that the child has the time and the ability to contribute to the interaction. The topic should stay close to the child's topic. Adults should ask questions that expand on that topic and confine these questions to ones that are real, illustrating that they are truly interested in the child's response.

scaffolding
Providing instruction that helps a child learn an activity but also requires that the child have as much responsibility for learning as possible (e.g., by including hints).

This process of supporting children's development and learning is a major part of what is referred to as *scaffolding* in teaching. A main point in scaffolding is to provide instruction that helps the child learn the activity but also requires that the child have as much responsibility for learning as possible. Children should not be shown how to complete activities that they are able to complete on their own. Even when teaching a difficult task, the adult should transfer the responsibility for completion to the learner as much as is possible.

zone of proximal development (ZPD)
A concept developed by Lev Vygotsky referring to the mental space between what a student can do independently and what that student can do with the assistance of a teacher or tutor.

Vygotsky's concept of the **zone of proximal development (ZPD)** can be used to conceptualize this approach (Vygotsky, 1978). Adults can provide a scaffold for children's learning that is within their ZPD, or the zone in which a difficult task can be completed with the help of a more competent peer or adult. When taught in this manner, children learn the activity or knowledge at hand and also increase their ZPD, thereby becoming receptive to more difficult challenges. As illustrated in Figure 4.1, scaffolding is a central process in children's learning through interactions.

Intentional teaching does not happen by chance. Epstein (2007) identified strategies for interacting intentionally with children. Teachers using intentional teaching plan and provide learning opportunities designed to meet the individual needs of the various children in instructional settings. Teachers should use children's abilities and prior knowledge, including their understanding of their students' cultural and ethnic backgrounds, to be responsive to their students' knowledge, feelings, and circumstances. Espinosa discussed teachers' intent in terms of curriculum: "Teachers have explicit instructional goals for children that guide all aspects of their interactions and classroom planning. Intentional teachers know their children, understand how to promote learning through individualized learning experiences, and reach out to families" (2009, p. 53).

Intentional Teaching

Teachers using intentional teaching purposefully plan and provide learning opportunities designed to meet the individual needs and interests of the various children in instructional settings. These teachers use knowledge of effective practices and strategies to implement those pedagogical approaches in order to promote children's learning and development (Burns et al., 2010; Kidd, Burns, Nasser, Assaf, & Muccio, 2009).

In the construct of intentional teaching, both children and teachers play active, deliberate roles in the processes that lead to children's learning and development (Burns, 2009). In many ways, this new construct reflects earlier work on effective teaching strategies proposed by those studying scaffolded teaching (Wood, 1980, 1998), mediated teaching (Feuerstein, Klein, & Tannenbaum, 1991; Karpov & Haywood, 1998), and content area teaching (Espinosa, 2009; Gelman & Brenneman, 2004; Ginsburg & Amit, 2008).

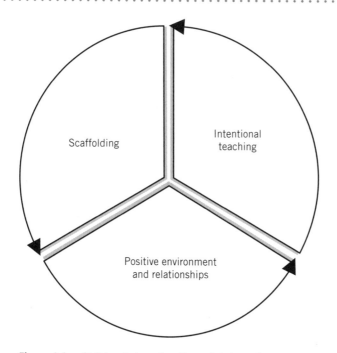

Figure 4.1. Children's learning through interactions.

Finally, intentional teaching and scaffolding cannot effectively take place unless the interactions with children are positive, authentic, heart-felt, and meant to build important relationships between children and adults. The interactions should begin with basic needs and socializing children into both the finer and larger world(s), being attentive and tuned into children's developmental levels, providing comfort and encouragement when and where needed, encouraging children to interact with the environment and the many aspects of those diverse settings, and promoting the fruition of children's broad social and emotional development (Morrison, 2009).

Building Relationships with Families

A wealth of historic research has illustrated the important relationship between the level of parental involvement and children's school success. Parents who are more involved with their children and their schooling are more likely to have children who are successful in school, from preschool through secondary education. Morrison spoke to this when he noted, "Education starts in the home and what happens there profoundly affects the trajectory of children's development and learning" (2009, p. 188).

The family is of primary importance in ECE. They are the source of your students' prior knowledge, cultural knowledge, and **family stories**. A significant quality factor in ECE is continuous interactions with the families served (Frank Porter Graham Child Development Center, 1999). As a teacher, knowing and tapping into the prior knowledge, cultural knowledge, and family strengths is extremely important. Having a concrete knowledge of these elements helps the teacher bridge the divide between home and school, plus provides a starting point for instruction that connects with the child. This connection allows children to see

family stories
Stories of an individual's family that have a meaningful impact on how he or she functions in the world.

the knowledge they already have as valuable and to then to build on it. This knowledge of the family and the child's prior knowledge often serves as the first rung of the scaffolding structure.

There are different venues for increasing parent involvement: the traditional back-to-school night, soliciting parent volunteers for field trips, or inviting parents to be involved in assessments (which typically makes parents and children more relaxed and comfortable with a process that can traditionally be highly emotional). Researchers have found that parents tended to feel more comfortable asking questions of the teacher during play-centered assessments and felt that they had a more collaborative role in their child's education during this important overview time (Linder, 2008a). When you effectively and consistently communicate with families, you can strengthen the respective partnerships. To accomplish this, you can also communicate with parents via face-to-face individual and group meetings, written communication, telephone conversations, e-mail and web-site communications, and parent discussion groups (McDevitt & Ormrod, 2004).

The preschool years mark the start of formal family relationships with educational systems. How you as a teacher initiate and build on these initial preschool experiences will potentially affect the family's future relationship with their child's educators, as well as the level of parental involvement that future schools will expect from the parents. A family's initial experience with you in preschool can become a model for how, what, and why parent involvement is so important. As a teacher, it is important to not assume that families know how to be involved with the school. Some parents may have had very negative experiences with their older children's education or culturally might not think it is appropriate to question a teacher. Therefore, it is important for you to model the types of relationships parents should have with school staff and teachers.

❋ ❋ ❋ Section Summary ❋ ❋ ❋

Play is central to young children's ECE experiences in that it supports their development across approaches to learning and development, including socioemotional, cognitive, language, and physical. Preschool content in areas such as creative arts, social studies, numeracy, science, and literacy are also learned through play. Research supports the view that teachers' strategies for interactions and for instructional purposes, along with their sensitivity to children's social and emotional development, are directly related to children's learning outcomes over the prekindergarten years (Pianta, Belsky, Vandergrift, Houts, & Morrison, 2008). Scaffolding and intentional teaching are two processes integral to young children's learning and development. Scaffolding and intentional teaching take place within positive exchanges between teachers and children, which build relationships between teachers and children. Families provide the primary relationships for children and are a major part of the team working in ECE. Without families, teachers cannot achieve intentional teaching because families provide the insight into the prior knowledge of the children, including information about language and culture and family stories.

The First Weeks of Preschool

How should you get ready for your first weeks of class? First, think of your goals for the first few weeks of school. Research has indicated that key factors to preschool success are building a positive, warm, trusting relationship with the children and their families; providing learning experiences that build upon the children's prior knowledge; having meaningful and interesting activities; and using effective assessment to plan group and individual children's learning opportunities (Bowman et al., 2000; Howes & Ritchie, 2002). In the first weeks of school, all of these goals should be met to varying degrees. First and foremost, the teacher should build a positive, warm, trusting relationship with the children and their families. However, this should not happen exclusive of the other goals. Many quality early childhood programs invest time and energy in these teacher, family, and child relationships. Home visits are encouraged to help form this relationship.

Your classroom will include children with many different characteristics. These children will represent a diverse range of cultural, lingual, ability, and socioeconomic backgrounds. Based on the type of children in your program, you should design an inviting activity agenda that considers the initial and ongoing transition into your school. You want your students to get to know and respect each other, as well as feel like a vital part of the classroom community of children, teachers, and families.

Therefore, during the first week of school, it is very important to establish daily routines and rituals, such as meeting and greeting children and their parents at the door, showing children where they put their backpacks or other gear upon entry into the room, and helping children separate from their caregivers and transition into your classroom.

The learning centers should include many group activities that allow all children to participate equally and collaboratively to get acquainted and establish friendships. During this first week, open a learning center or two so that children gradually and progressively learn about how and why you incorporate center-based practices into your daily routines. Be sure to clearly communicate your expectations of each of the learning centers. Expectations should include the use and purpose of materials and ways to safely use them. During the second week, you can open more of the learning centers. Children should demonstrate that they have a basic understanding of how to individually and collaboratively use the centers, so introduce an effective means by which children choose centers.

By the third week, all basic centers should be functioning effectively, and routines for choosing the centers can be established. A recall time should be added to the schedule and used after learning centers. The flow of the day should move away from strict teacher-guided management to a class-guided collaborative working environment. With this movement toward students' independence, there should be more self-regulation in their management of a center-based space. For example, the block center may have a sign posted to indicate that only five children are allowed in the center at one time. Therefore, when a student attempts to enter that space, he or she must count first and then move on to another center if no space is available. Some teachers disagree with the number limits on centers, and instead instruct children to assess whether a center is crowded. If there is nowhere to stand, the students should negotiate and make a different choice. However, in both of these processes, children independently regulate their behavior and actions with little feedback from the teacher or peers.

After the fourth week, most daily routines should move away from the large group to a more holistic small-group setting. In this environment, each of the centers will be occupied by small groups of children; these children control, with the teacher's assistance, the interactions within this environment. Many of the children may previously have needed detailed assistance from you because they have little experience regulating their own behavior, especially during their first school experience in a group of unfamiliar children. By the fourth week, they have witnessed the flow of the day and how readily you and their peers assist them. Therefore, by this point they should be growing continuously more comfortable in this setting, in which they will spend most of the academic year.

❊ ❊ ❊ Section Summary ❊ ❊ ❊

Launching the beginning of a 1-year or longer relationship with a new group of children and their families is a special time, and the steps in this section provide support for a gradual process for success. After the first few weeks of school, the children should be familiar and comfortable with the established routines. Children should be learning when they can share and speak in large-group meetings, as well as when and why they need to provide silence when their peers and teachers are talking.

KEY CONCEPTS

- The ECE classroom is central to providing a high-quality program for young children. The classroom learning environment includes public spaces (e.g., circle area, learning centers) and private spaces (e.g., cubbies, nap area).

- Furniture and decorations in ECE classrooms should be child oriented in terms of size, location, and content.

- There are a variety of learning centers and they should include an abundance of organized materials based on the learning goals of the center.

- A daily schedule helps to organize the ECE day.

- Play is central to young children's ECE experiences in that it supports their development across developmental areas—that is, approaches to learning and development, including socioemotional, cognitive, language, and physical, and content areas (e.g., creative arts, social studies, numeracy, science, and literacy) are also learned through play.

- Scaffolding and intentional teaching are two processes integral to young children's learning and development. Scaffolding and intentional teaching take place within positive exchanges between teachers and children, which build relationships between them.

- Families provide the primary relationships for children and are a major part of the team working in ECE. Without families, teachers cannot achieve intentional teaching because families provide the insight into the prior knowledge of the children, including information about language, culture, and family stories.

- When a new class is starting, this constitutes a special time for children. There are special steps needed to support a gradual transition for children to learn to know each other, the teachers, and the classroom activities and routines.

Integration of Information

You have just read the section on early education today, which introduced the basics of early childhood practice. This chapter serves as the groundwork for Chapters 5–9, which discuss approaches to learning, social-emotional, cognitive, language, and physical development.

Self-Reflective Guide

This self-reflective guide will help you assess whether you learned the information in this chapter. It also provides an opportunity to identify areas in which you want or need more information. Are there some new ideas learned that will affect your immediate practice with children?

1. A variety of materials (as well as duplicates of many) are needed within learning centers. Are there certain learning centers that have particular appeal to you? Name one center and why it appeals to you. Are there learning centers that you think should be opened at the beginning of the year and others that should be opened later in the year? Why?

2. Reflect on the types of daily schedules. What periods of time are needed for young children in learning centers so that play and constructive activities can take place? Why is this amount of time needed? How do these times flow with the needs of the children in the class? Make a few notes. How long should large group be? Why?

3. Recognize the role of play in young children's learning and development. What do you think is most important about play given the information provided? Why?

4. Identify the nature of high-quality interactions between adults and children. List some key features.

5. Know the reasons for and basics of forming partnerships with families. Note two reasons.

6. Understand how to get started with a new group of children. What is a main point to understand about the first day? What is a main point to understand about the first week? What is a main point to understand about the first month?

Helpful Web Sites

Cooperative Children's Book Center

www.education.wisc.edu/ccbc
The Cooperative Children's Book Center through the School of Education at the University of Wisconsin-Madison provides resources and booklists for children's books covering various topics.

Developmentally Appropriate Practice (DAP)

www.naeyc.org/DAP
This site provides information on the basics of setting up a quality early childhood education classroom within the DAP framework.

Florida Parental Information and Resource Center

www.floridapartnership.usf.edu/programs_services/earlychild/tip.htm
The Parental Information and Resource Center at the University of South
Florida provides many early childhood tips sheets (in English or Spanish) for
teachers and for teachers to share with parents.

HighScope

www.highscope.org/Content.asp?ContentId=264
This preschool section of the HighScope site provides information on activities
that are both specific to the HighScope program and can be used in other programs.

Teaching for Change

www.teachingforchange.org
This site provides multicultural book lists and resources.

References

Bodrova, E., & Leong, D. (2003, May). Chopsticks and counting chips: Do play and foundational skills need to compete for the teacher's attention in an early childhood classroom? *Beyond the Journal Young Children on the Web*.

Bodrova, E., & Leong, D. (2008). Developing self-regulation in kindergarten: Can we keep all the crickets in the basket? *Young Children, 63*(2), 56–58.

Bowman, B.T., Donovan, M.S., & Burns, M.S. (2000). *Eager to learn: Educating our preschoolers*. Washington, DC: National Academies Press.

Bruner, J., & Olsen, D. (1977). Symbols and texts as tools of intellect. *Interchange, 8*(4), 1–15.

Burns, M.S. (2009). Both/and thinking in early childhood education. *Focus on Pre-K&K, 22*(1), 1–3.

Burns, M.S., Stechuk, R.A., Assaf, M., Kidd, J.-K., Nasser, I., Aier, D., et al. (2010, June 21). *Intentional teaching in Head Start classrooms: Exploring construct definition and measurement*. Paper presented at the National Head Start Research Conference, Washington, DC.

Epstein, A. (2007). *The intentional teacher: Choosing the best strategies for young children's learning*. Washington, DC: National Association for the Education of Young Children.

Espinosa, L. (2009). *Getting it right for young children from diverse backgrounds: Applying research to improve practice*. Upper Saddle River, NJ: Pearson.

Feuerstein, R.F., Klein, P.S., & Tannenbaum, A.J. (1991). *Mediated learning experience (MLE): Theoretical, psychosocial, and learning implications*. London: Freund.

Frank Porter Graham Child Development Center. (1999). *Early learning, later success: The Abecedarian study*. Chapel Hill: The University of North Carolina.

Gelman, R., & Brenneman, K. (2004). Science learning pathways for young children. *Early Childhood Research Quarterly, 19*(1), 150–158.

Ginsburg, H.P., & Amit, M. (2008). What is teaching mathematics to young children? A theoretical perspective and case study. *Journal of Applied Developmental Psychology, 29*(4), 274–285.

Howes, C., & Ritchie, S. (2002). *A matter of trust: Connecting teachers and learners in the early childhood classroom*. New York: Teachers College Press.

Hyson, M. (2008). *Enthusiastic and engaged: Approaches to learning in the early childhood classroom*. New York: Teachers College Press.

Karpov, Y.V., & Haywood, H.C. (1998). Two ways to elaborate Vygotsky's concept of mediation: Implications for instruction. *American Psychologist, 53*(1), 27–36.

Kidd, J., Burns, M.S., Nasser, I., Assaf, M., & Muccio, L. (2009). *Sustaining teacher effective pedagogy (STEP): A model for professional development with Head Start teachers*. Paper presented at the American Educational Research Association Conference, San Diego, CA.

Linder, T.W. (2008a). *Transdisciplinary Play-Based Assessment, Second Edition (TPBA2)*. Baltimore: Paul H. Brookes Publishing Co.

Linder, T.W. (2008b). *Transdisciplinary Play-Based Intervention, Second Edition (TPBI2)*. Baltimore: Paul H. Brookes Publishing Co.

McDevitt, T.M., & Ormrod, J.E. (2004). *Child development: Educating and working with children and families*. Columbus, OH: Pearson.

Morrison, G.S. (2009). *Teaching in America* (5th ed.). Columbus, OH: Pearson.

Pianta, R.C., Belsky, J., Vandergrift, N., Houts, R., & Morrison, F.J. (2008). Classroom effects on children's achievement trajectories in elementary school. *American Educational Research Journal, 45*(2), 365–397.

Rogers, C.S., & Sawyers, J.K. (1998). *Play in the lives of children.* Washington, DC: National Association for the Education of Young Children.

Rogers, D.L., & Ross, D.D. (1986). Encouraging positive social interaction among young children. *Young Children, 41*(3), 12–17.

Shonkoff, J.P., & Phillips, D.A. (Eds.). (2000). *From neurons to neighborhoods: The science of early childhood development.* Washington, DC: National Academies Press.

Smilansky, S. (1968). *The effects of sociodramatic play on disadvantaged preschool children.* New York: Wiley.

Smilansky, S., & Shefatya, L. (1990). *Facilitating play: A medium for promoting cognitive, socio-emotional, and aca-* demic development in young children. Gaithersburg, MD: Psychological and Educational Publications.

Vygotsky, L.S. (1978). In M. Cole, V. John-Steiner, S. Scribner, & E. Souberman (Eds.), *Mind in society: The development of high psychological processes.* Cambridge, MA: Harvard University Press.

Wood, D. (1980). Teaching the young child: Some relationships between social interaction, language, and thought. In D.R. Olson (Ed.), *The social foundation of language and thought* (pp. 259–275). New York: W.W. Norton.

Wood, D. (1998). Aspects of teaching and learning. In M. Woodhead, D. Faulkner, & K. Littleton (Eds.), *Cultural worlds of early childhood* (pp. 157–177). New York: Taylor & Francis.

Approaches to Learning

1. Understand the theories presented to account for young children's approaches to learning, including social learning theory, information processing theory, social constructivist theory, and theory of mind

2. Recognize the features of the approaches to learning and identify where you have seen young children use these

3. Identify how the approaches to learning can be addressed across different learning centers and academic areas

4. Understand how and why engaging parents affects your understanding of the child's approaches to learning

5. Identify how a teacher can embrace and encourage the expression of approaches to learning in ways that may vary from her or his personal experience

6. Understand how children interact with teachers and peers as they develop effective approaches to learning

7. Understand how play affects approaches to learning

8. Identify how a teacher can assess whether he or she is providing quality opportunities for young children to learn effective approaches to learning

9. Determine how you would assess young children's approaches to learning so that you could adapt your curriculum based on findings and monitor the progress of your students

10. Understand how approaches to learning relate to other areas of development discussed in this book, such as socioemotional development, cognitive development and learning, using and understanding language, and physical and motor development

How do 3- to 5-year-old children learn to solve problems such as completing a puzzle, making a big box into a car, or kicking a soccer ball toward the net? How do they learn to find more than one way to achieve a goal, such as making a castle with clay or blocks, depending on the available materials? Do children's cultures and languages influence their approaches to learning? Why do some children seem to be overly dependent on adults to initiate learning? Why are some children curious about everything? Are they just born that way? What are approaches to learning and how are they important to teaching young children? Are approaches to learning really just a part of socioemotional or cognitive development? Can children with disabilities, especially attention-deficit/hyperactivity disorder (ADHD), learn effective approaches to learning? How can assessment be used to see if young students are learning effective approaches to learning? What are the correct activities to promote effective approaches to learning for all children?

These are the types of questions being addressed in this chapter on preschool children's approaches to learning. Approaches to learning are distinct ways that children become engaged in classroom interactions and learning activities (Fantuzzo et al., 2007; Hyson, 2008). Children's approaches to learning affect all other areas of their development, including language, social, emotional, cognitive, and physical development. This chapter addresses curiosity, engagement, initiative, persistence, problem solving, reasoning, and self-regulation, as well as the interrelationships between areas of development. This chapter also discusses the meaning of individual child, family, and community differences in providing early childhood education (ECE) that addresses young children's development of these approaches to learning.

As is evident from the opening questions, children in the early childhood years vary in terms of their approaches to learning and are affected greatly by both biological and environmental factors embedded in sociohistorical contexts. In the initial part of this chapter, key theories of ECE are highlighted, including social learning theory, information processing theory, social constructivist theory, and theory of mind. Building from that introduction, the chapter then discusses children's developing approaches to learning, as well as the associated skills and the role that interactions with adults and peers through play have in this development. Information is provided on how children's approaches to learning are addressed in typical curriculum areas included in ECE programs, such as literacy, numeracy, science, social studies, and creative arts. Further, the chapter reviews how teachers can use assessment practices to gauge whether they are providing young children with learning opportunities that will enhance their approaches to learning, how teachers can adapt curriculum to meet the needs of individual children, how teachers can ensure that the types of instruction and adaptations provide children with experiences that validate and affirm life experiences, and how teachers can evaluate whether children are making progress in this developmental area.

Theoretical Accounts: Approaches to Learning

Theoretical accounts of approaches to learning are presented in this chapter given the current understanding of ECE and care. Children's approaches to learning are central to development in the preschool years (Bronson, 2000) and predict later academic performance in school (Fantuzzo, Perry, & McDermott, 2004). Development across domains is dependent on children's acquisition and use of effective approaches to learning. Theoretical accounts range from behavioral, such as social learning theory (Bandura, 1977), to constructivist, such as the social constructivist theory (Vygotsky, 1978). Information processing theory is presented in relation to children's intake, elaboration, and output mechanisms important to approaches to learning (Atkinson & Schiffrin, 1968). Theory of mind (Siegler, DeLoache, & Eisenberg, 2003) is also presented because it provides important information about how young children understand their own mind and the minds of others, as well as how people experience things differently than others.

Social Learning Theory

Bandura (1977) proposed that children learn behaviors through observation, imitation, and reinforcement. Reinforcement is when something happens immediately after a behavior that makes the behavior more likely to happen again. For example, a young girl is more likely to ask more questions about the environment (e.g., birds) when her question about a woodpecker outside the window is answered:

Child: Why does he keep on knocking at the tree?

Adult: Oh, the woodpecker is knocking, called "pecking," for bugs.

Children's social environment is a main source for children to develop specific behaviors, attitudes, and emotions (Bandura, 1977). Although emphasis in this theory is on social-environmental impacts on children's learning, individual psychological and biological factors also affect effective approaches to young children's learning.

Social learning theory describes how adults and peers model behaviors in the various social contexts in which the child is familiar: home, school, and community. When a behavior is available in the environment, learners need to attend to the behavior, remember what was observed, and reproduce what was observed. Central to this process is the motivation to adopt a behavior (Bandura, 1991). Motivation is developed as children are reinforced for modeling the behaviors of others. Because motivation allows the child to internalize a behavior, understanding what drives the child is extremely important. Teachers often look to families for initial support in developing this understanding about young children.

Children's motivation can come just from using the modeled behavior with successful outcomes, such as when a child looks at the teacher's behavior. For example, when solving a puzzle, the child may observe how the teacher looks and sorts through all the puzzle pieces one by one, searching for just the right piece of the correct shape and color. The child then imitates this behavior to find the correct pieces and is thrilled at that success. Children can be reinforced by the person who is modeling; for example, the teacher may say, "Yes, that's the way you do it. You look for the puzzle piece with a pointy red part just like I did." Reinforcement can also come from an outside observer; for example, a teacher's assistant might say, "Great job, Michael. You looked carefully at the puzzle pieces to find the correct one." Reinforcement can also take place vicariously. For example, if Michael sees another child being praised for her systematic work in completing the puzzle, he might persist in the hard work as well to receive positive feedback.

Information Processing Theory

Information processing theory has been greatly influenced by the development of high-speed computers, which can handle complex information. Computers have been used to explore how information comes into children's mental processes, how it is elaborated, and how it is then applied. This theory can help one to understand mental processes such as attention, memory, and problem solving, as well as how information is integrated and used as a tool (Shonkoff & Phillips, 2000).

In this process, information is received from the environment, which can happen through direct experience from the social and physical world. These inputs are then put into working memory when problem solving and elaboration strategies

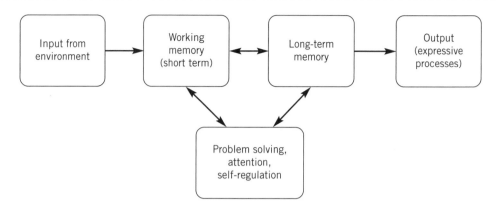

Figure 5.1.   Information processing theory. (*Source:* Atkinson & Shiffrin, 1968.)

are used with the information to move it into long-term memory. Once information is in long-term memory, it can then be expressed. Figure 5.1 illustrates a basic model of what happens to information after it is received by an individual (Atkinson & Schiffrin, 1968).

Social Constructivist Theory

Like social learning theory, social constructivist theory emphasizes the central role of the social environment in learning and development. However, rather than being based on modeling, imitation, and reinforcement, social constructivist theory has a broader definition of the social environment (Vygotsky, 1978). This definition includes the immediate impact of the social environment through interactions with significant adults and more competent children (e.g., parents, teachers, classmates, siblings), as well as the development of higher mental functions within cultural groups (i.e., cultural transmission of information). This information embodies a culture's approaches to learning (i.e., **mental tools**). With young children, it is important to remember that many of their social experiences have been within the family context. Therefore, it should be a main objective of the teacher to gain a deeper authentic understanding of how the family interacts with each other—especially with the child. For example, if a family creates songs and rhythms to interact with each other, the teacher should know this in order to support the child in the classroom.

mental tool
A way that an individual uses his or her mind to learn (e.g., visualizing something in order to remember it).

Children develop effective approaches to learning that might look different in various time periods and cultural contexts. For example, in the Sinagua region of northern Arizona in prehistoric times, very young children made ceramic figurines and pots alongside adults who were making larger items; by learning how to work with clay, these children also developed effective approaches to learning (Kamp, 2001). Similarly, the United States in the 1950s, young children learned how to make doll clothes alongside their mothers who were making clothes for the family; these children also developed effective approaches to learning. For social constructivist theorists, it is impossible to look only at the child in isolation without factoring in all the other elements that influence and ultimately create the human experience in a complex, intricate, and ever-changing world.

Social constructivist theorists address children's innate desire to make sense of their own environment by using mental tools to help regulate and direct them in new learning. Much like a physical tool, such as a spatula or a cellular phone, a mental tool provides a way to organize and control mental processes, such as controlling attention, solving problems, using **memory strategies**, organizing visually, and (especially for young children) using language as a tool. Consider the example of **private speech**, in which people talk to themselves while completing complex tasks. Private speech is thought to provide cognitive self-guidance. For example, when completing a puzzle, a child might say, "I need green. Where are you, green?" as he or she looks for the next piece. By doing this, the child is using speech to direct the search for the puzzle piece. This type of speech is believed to become internalized as the child develops a better understanding of the problem to be solved. Private speech should be encouraged and modeled for young children because it supports a child's effective approach to learning, and it can be used in whatever language the child prefers.

Vygotsky (1978, 1986) placed a great deal of emphasis on the role of language in development of self-regulation, symbolic thought, and use of symbols (see Chapter 8). How does this take place? Consider again the example of private speech. Because children learn through interactions with adults or more advanced peers, the content of private speech might actually be based on shared conversation. So in the previous example of the child searching for a green puzzle piece, the child's teacher earlier had suggested the following approach to solving a puzzle: "There are many clues we can get to figure out the next puzzle piece. One way is color. If the part of this hat is red and we are looking for the other half of the hat, we want to look for pieces that have red on them. So look for red. Red." Therefore, learning and development takes place first on a social plane (interpsychological), then within the child (intrapsychological; Vygotsky, 1978). Both externalized and internalized private speech take place on the intrapsychological plane.

Children's use of tools plays a specific role in Vygotsian theory. Tools for development and learning consist of two types: external and internal (Luria, Cole, & Cole, 1979; Vygotsky, 1978). An external tool might be used for problem solving. For example, when completing a puzzle, a child might look at the picture of the puzzle on the outside of the box; this tool is external and is a device for teachers to scaffold the placement of the puzzle pieces, as well as thinking skills (Haywood, Brooks, & Burns, 1992). Internalization of these tools plays a role in the child's construction of mind, which influences the development of generalized thinking skills (Leong, Bodrova, & Henson, 2007).

In ECE, adults and more advanced peers play important roles as scaffolds to support young children's learning. They guide children through demonstration, questions, and **verbal cues** when tasks appear insurmountable for the child using only the knowledge he or she possesses at that moment. The scaffolds provided are related to a child's zone of proximal development (Vygotsky, 1978). Young children complete easy activities with little or no scaffold. For a task that is somewhat difficult for the child, scaffolding is needed from a peer or an adult. Very difficult tasks are beyond a level where they can be successful even given peer or adult scaffolds. The easy tasks are considered children's independent level of performance and are usually measured when children's learning and development are assessed. The activities that can be completed with peer or adult scaffolding are those within the child's zone of proximal development. Many early childhood professionals suggest that it is important to include indica-

memory strategy
A strategy that can help an individual remember something, such as repeating or visualizing.

private speech
Oral communication directed toward oneself.

verbal cues
Hints from the teacher to assist the student in accomplishing a task, provided through speech rather than physical signals.

Puzzles are an important activity in which children learn problem-solving skills.

Young children begin to understand that others' minds don't always work in the same way as theirs.

tors of children's performance when they are given assistance (Burns, 1996; Burns, Delclos, Vye, & Sloan, 1992). Both these indicators and independent performance should be considered when planning instruction for individual children.

Theory of Mind

Theory of mind focuses on children's understanding of how the mind works and their understanding of how mental processes (e.g., remembering) can affect their own and others' behavior (Siegler et al., 2003). Children understand how the mind works; for example, they get insights into how they remember (e.g., "I got a picture in my head") or what gets them into a confused mental or emotional state (e.g., "All that talking is why I hit you"). Major changes take place in children's understanding of mind during the preschool years (Wellman, Cross, & Watson, 2001).

Young children begin to understand that others' minds (adults and other children) do not always work in the same way as their own. Children understand that others learn and think differently than they do. When children infer how other people think and learn, they learn new ways to solve problems and make decisions. This process serves as a means to learn more effective approaches to learning, as can be seen in the following example:

Ella, age 4, is impressed with how her sister Nina, age 7, could figure out how to remember all the movements to the chicken dance. Ella asks, "How do you do that?" Nina then tells Ella how she uses certain words in the song to give her a hint for an action, and that she listened a bunch of times until she got the dance right. By Ella asking this question, she indicates that she knows that Nina danced to the song quite well. It also shows that Ella knows Nina did something to learn how to do this. Ella understood that Nina had something to share about how she approached learning the actions to this dance. Ella starts to try out Nina's approach to learning. She pays closer attention to the words in the song, and she starts to remember the actions as she listens to the song over and over. Ella learns something about persistence.

Learning, remembering, and paying attention all involve doing something special with the mind. In a similar manner, young children also begin to learn about their own and others emotional states, as well as others' motives and intentions. Children learn that their feelings are different from other people's feelings, and that when an event makes them angry, for example, it does not mean that the event made other people angry. The basis of attention to others' behavior and imitation lies in theory of mind, by children knowing that other people might be doing something that could be helpful to imitate or learn. As children begin to understand how their mind works, they can use this information to guide the way they approach tasks. It also affects other areas of development, including socioemotional, cognitive, language, and physical development (Siegler et al., 2003; Wellman et al., 2001).

❊ ❊ ❊ Section Summary ❊ ❊ ❊

Young children's development of effective approaches to learning affects development across domains. Social learning theory and social constructivist theory are central to understanding young children's approaches to learning and are in use in ECE practice today. Social learning theory explains how children develop effective approaches to learning, such as by observing behavior modeled by adults and peers. Motivation is developed as children are reinforced for modeling the behaviors of others.

Information processing theory provides models of mental processes. Social learning theory is related to the social constructivist theory (Vygotsky, 1978), which also emphasizes the central role of the social environment in learning and development. Adults and more advanced children (e.g., parents, teachers, community members, classmates, siblings) transmit cultural information embodying the culture's approaches to learning, or mental tools; they scaffold new learning by providing help (instruction) within the learner's zone of proximal development (i.e., the zone within which the learner can make progress given the instruction). Theory of mind expands on this process as young children further understand how their own mind and the minds of others function. In this way, children develop a basis for comparing their mental functions to that of others and using that information as a basis for further development.

Features of Approaches to Learning

Approaches to learning are distinct ways by which children become engaged in classroom interactions and learning activities (Fantuzzo et al., 2007). Young children's approaches to learning are viewed as essential components of school readiness (National Education Goals Panel, 1999), although they are less understood or researched than other aspects of readiness (Fantuzzo et al., 2007). In Head Start's performance standards (U.S. Department of Health and Human Services, 2010), the following approaches to learning are identified:

- Initiative and curiosity

- Engagement and persistence

- Reasoning and problem solving

These features are discussed in this chapter (except for reasoning, which is discussed in Chapter 7).

A number of scholars have identified learning behaviors that are similar to these approaches to learning, such as cognitive functions that are used to find, elaborate, and report information effectively (Feuerstein, Rand, Hoffman, & Miller, 1980) and self-regulatory skills (Brown & DeLoache, 1978). The identified processes of these researchers overlap with and provide more detailed conceptualizations of the features of approaches to learning. This chapter uses a similar conceptualization to present young children's approaches to learning.

Children use multiple modalities (e.g., visual, auditory, tactile) to absorb, elaborate upon, and report new learning. Children's receptive processes identify and define new information or problems. In the elaboration processes, children engage with new information or problems, incorporating the new material with prior

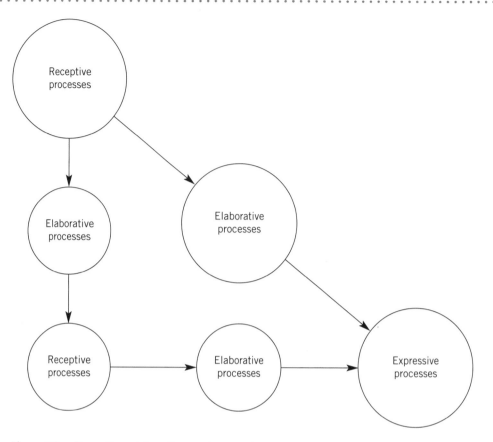

Figure 5.2. Receptive, elaborative, and expressive processes.

expressive processes
Language processes in which a person acts on the physical and social world through such things as action, speech, and writing.

knowledge. **Expressive processes** relate to how young children report new experiences and learn. Based on Figure 5.2, you might think that these processes occur in a linear fashion: First the child uses receptive processes, then elaboration processes, and ends with expressive processes. However, the processes do not happen in such a linear way; each process might happen for a very short period of time or be repeated many times in the course of one experience. These processes are elaborated in the following sections.

Receptive Processes

Young children are eager to learn (Bowman, Donovan, & Burns, 2000). They ask questions, interact with their environment, call upon their memory, define what they are exploring in multiple ways, take longer explorations to address complexity, and focus their exploration in light of the goals of the current experience. Features of receptive processes that have been identified with young children include initiative, curiosity, attention, and **impulse control**.

impulse control
The ability to regulate oneself and resist or delay an activity.

Initiative

Children are determined to participate in a variety of activities and gain information. They initiate questions about people, things, and the world around them, and

---

Houses Are Not All the Same

Consider the following incident, which occurred during class discussions and a presentation on the types of houses in which different students live. Bonnie and Carlos built two different types of houses. Bonnie looked through a book about the different types of houses near the school and built an apartment building like the one she lives in. Carlos copied a type of house from the LEGO chart—an igloo. While they were taking pictures of their buildings, Bonnie commented, "That house is not from around here. Where is that house?" Carlos and Bonnie then looked through all of the books, searching for an igloo to find out why they did not know "that house."

---

they discuss a growing range of topics and ideas, as well as completing activities. Mastery of their physical and social environment is the goal.

Curiosity

Many of the aspects mentioned for initiative (e.g., asking questions on a variety of topics and ideas) also apply to curiosity. Curiosity is sparked when current experiences do not meet expectations or when an experience is odd. For example, when a child playing with a toy car finds that it is curving off to one side and going slow, the child might then investigate to find that a wheel of the car is partially stuck.

Attention

Young children's attention spans expand during the preschool years. They can pay attention for longer periods of time when the situation meets their interests or motivation. With support, children can develop the ability to attend to information that is important to the current learning while eliminating details that are irrelevant. Over time and with increased experiences, young children begin to get a sense of the effort that it takes to regulate their attention (Ruff & Lawson, 1990).

Impulse Control

For children to take advantage of these receptive processes, they must be able to self-regulate their impulses. They should learn to stop and think. They should learn to listen to the full instructions before beginning an activity; then, they will know when to look for visual or other types of instructions and understand the various tools available to help them find the answers. They should learn to ask questions as needed to understand the current experience. Finally and possibly most importantly, they should learn to regulate their emotions; then, they will not get so excited that they cannot listen or so overwhelmed by the initial complexity of the activity that they get discouraged from trying (Kaiser & Rasminsky, 2011).

Elaborative Processes

In elaborative processes, children engage with new information or problems identified in receptive processes, incorporating the new material with prior knowledge and ways of thinking. They use memory to recall prior knowledge and organize this information with the new problem, often being creative to organize understandings in new ways. Features of elaborative processes that have been identified

Preschool children are more strategic when activities are embedded in a familiar context.

with young children include memory, organization, creativity, persistence, frustration tolerance, and private speech (Bodrova & Leong, 2008).

Memory

Scripts help preschool children to bring in their prior knowledge when figuring out problems or learning new information. The scripts—prior knowledge—were learned through experiences in physical, social, and cultural settings. For example, by going to the grocery store with their families, young children learn that parents make a list of needed items before going, then locate those items aisle by aisle at the grocery store and put the listed items into a cart. Children learn that the item is crossed off the list when it is found and in the cart. Finally, they learn that the items are paid for before they leave the store. This script can be used to play grocery store or plan a pretend picnic in the dramatic play learning center at school (Nguyen & Murphy, 2003).

As children develop during the preschool period, they start using various other memory strategies. Use of memory strategies becomes easier as they practice them and as they become more knowledgeable in a content area. Scripts access children's prior knowledge and lived experiences, which provides the link between what children already know and what school is teaching them. For knowledge to grow and expand in young children, it is necessary to see that they have had valuable experiences; those experiences may vary from what the teacher and school see as standards of knowledge. It is important to validate and ultimately integrate such scripts into the classroom.

I Know About Dinosaurs

Preschool children are more strategic when activities are embedded in a familiar context (Bjorklund & Douglas, 1997; Hyson, 2008). For example, consider a 4-year-old child who uses memory strategies when asked to remember the names of a group of dinosaurs. This child loves dinosaurs, plays with them often, visits museums where they are displayed, and is constantly asking her teacher and parents to read facts about dinosaurs from books and web sites. When asked to play a game about remembering the names of six dinosaurs in pictures that are to be taken away after a minute, the teacher notices that the child groups them by specific features, such as size. This strategy helps the child recall what dinosaurs were in the pictures and allows the child to name more dinosaurs than expected for a child of her age.

Organization

A central aspect of the elaborative process is the ability to organize information. Given memory and prior knowledge, young children learn to make plans and follow through on those plans. The ability to analyze all aspects of the necessary information is developed. As with every area of approaches to learning, asking questions to seek information and clarification helps the young child to learn the organizational skills to complete an activity. When young children are provided learning environments that are built on trust and community, they ask questions and take risks to extend and build knowledge (Burns, Haywood, & Delclos, 1987).

Creativity

Creativity helps children to organize what they see in different ways by using different approaches; that is, they can pursue alternative routes to problem solving. Flexibility and imagination are central to creativity. Creativity also provides children a way to see how other children think differently from themselves.

What Can It Be?

This activity by Leong, Bodrova, and Hensen (2007) was developed for children to practice symbolic thinking; children taking part in this activity learn creativity at the same time. The basic operation in the activity is having one item stand for more than one object. Consider a block from the block center. Initially the teacher might present some ideas and elicit from the children whether the block can be used as a particular object: Could this block be used as a phone? Could it be used as a blanket? Could it be used as a car? This can be quite a playful discussion. As children get used to this activity, the teacher shows an object such as a block and asks, "What can this be?" The children then generate ideas. After about 5 or 10 ideas, another object is shown and the activity repeated. You will be amazed at how creative young children can be.

Persistence, Frustration Tolerance, and Private Speech

Young children learn to maintain concentration over time and bring an activity to completion when the activities interest them. Part of persistence depends on children continuing an activity even in light of problems encountered—that is, being able to tolerate frustration. Young children often talk out loud when encountering problems with activities. This use of private speech helps them to self-regulate and persist in problem solving (Berk & Winsler, 1995).

A plain block can be many things in young children's play (e.g., a cell phone, an iron, a roast for dinner, a bus).

Expressive Processes

In expressive processes, young children report new experiences and learning. This is important because when children report new experiences and learning, they have incorporated this information in a different manner through telling others rather than by having experienced it alone; therefore, the information is more personally established and secure. Expressive processes represent what children have done or learned, including what may be intermediate understandings of a new experience. Children may also learn to take risks and to respond to a listener's clarification questions.

> ## HighScope's Plan-Do-Review Sequence
>
> **Plan-Do-Review** is a sequence that children may use when planning for learning centers (**planning time**), participating in those centers, and recalling what they did after participating in the centers. The first two parts of this process—planning and doing—help children learn and practice many receptive and elaborative approaches to learning. Reviewing helps children to learn and practice expressive processes. Children should recall and tell other adults and peers about what they did and learned (Hohmann, Weikart, & Epstein, 2008).

Plan-Do-Review
A method developed by HighScope to help children self-regulate and learn by planning what they want to achieve during learning center time and reviewing whether they achieved their goals afterwards.

planning time
A time during the preschool day when children have the opportunity to think about the play and activity they want to participate in that day.

representation
The expression of some person, group, or object by a separate entity or symbol.

Representation

Young children recall experiences through verbal explanation, visual **representation**, gestures, and full-body descriptions. It is important to respect all of these manners of recall, with the goal being to understand a child's experience or new learning. The listener's enthusiasm for understanding the new experience is integral to this process.

Familiarity with Clarification Questions

As young children provide explanations of their new learning and experiences, they take risks as they explain their experience—one that is not known to the listener. Children learn to become comfortable with listeners who ask clarification questions. Previously learned approaches to learning, such as persistence and frustration tolerance, also might come into play here.

❖ ❖ ❖ Section Summary ❖ ❖ ❖

Young children's approaches to learning are viewed as essential components of school readiness (National Education Goals Panel, 1999), although they are less understood or researched than other aspects of readiness (Fantuzzo et al., 2007). They include processes such as initiative, self-regulation, curiosity, engagement, organization, creativity, attention, persistence, recall, and explaining experiences and learning—many of which can be observed while children are engaged in their preschool day. Children use multiple modalities (e.g., visual, auditory, tactile) to absorb, elaborate on, and report new learning. When obtaining new information, children use receptive processes to identify and define new information or problems. In the elaboration processes, children engage with new information or problems, incorporating the new material with prior knowledge. Expressive processes deal with how young children report new experiences and learning. This process is not necessarily linear; each process might happen for a very short period of time or be repeated many times in the course of one experience.

Supporting Children's Effective and Diverse Approaches to Learning

Effective approaches to learning are promoted during learning centers through interactions in all academic areas, as well as through interactions with adults and more advanced peers, as presented in the previous sections. When you set up the physical environment and decide on related materials, the goal of promoting effective problem solving should be actively considered. However, the processes used to help children plan what they want to achieve during learning center time might be most central to developing effective approaches to learning. Through this process, young children should be taught how to ask for help when needed without limiting their curiosity and initiative. They should learn to make a plan, apply prior knowledge to completing that plan, and even how to talk themselves through a difficult part of an activity. An important piece of planning is reflecting on the process used to complete a plan, such as making a visual representation or verbally explaining how a plan was completed. As a new teacher, it might be useful to look at HighScope's materials, which provide a clear implementation of children's processes for developing a plan, enacting that plan, and reflecting on the plan (Hohmann et al., 2008).

Chapter 4 described different types of learning centers, such as the block center, dramatic play center, literacy centers for writing and reading, manipulatives center, science center, art center, and woodworking center. This section describes how academic content can be put together with approaches to learning and enacted in different learning centers. Figure 5.3 depicts the relationship between these components.

The described activities can be integrated across creative arts, social studies, numeracy, science, and literacy. However, note that these activities are only examples, provided as models; they are not necessarily the activities that you will be using, or those that are the most important to include as opportunities for your young children to develop effective approaches to learning. You will develop your own understanding of what activities to use and which centers to integrate as you get to know your individual children.

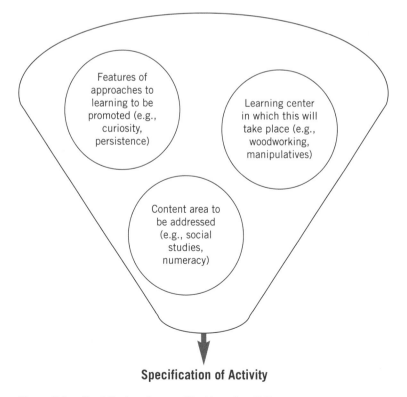

Specification of Activity

Figure 5.3. Contributors to specification of activity.

Again, the adult's role in these respective academic areas is to creatively arrange the environment and adjoining potential learning materials and activities. The adult then should encourage children to interact with the environment and the many aspects of those diverse settings in ways that best promote the fruition of children's approaches to learning. (Refer to pages 102–103 for details about teacher–child interactions.) Note that many of the centers are interconnected and related to each other.

Creative Arts

Every creative arts activity provides a context for developing effective approaches to learning. Suppose that you want children to listen to music and make a collage. Various types of paper, some pieces of yarn, buttons, and some fabric pieces can be made available to the children, as well as glue and a piece of cardboard on which to paste materials. This activity might take place at the art center. Music played in the background near that center might be a classical piece that includes fast and slow elements. Children can be asked to make a collage that depicts the music. The approaches to learning that can be emphasized might include creativity, impulse control, and organizing the collage space, as well as a verbal reflection on how the collage is related to the music. Creativity can be emphasized as children make their own unique collages, organizing the space and practicing impulse control by carefully using glue and not working too quickly when the music becomes fast. When children explain why the yarn, for example, zigzags in the collage because that is what the music did, they are reflecting on the collage and the music. In regard to Figure 5.3, this activity highlights the creative arts as the academic content area; creativity, impulse control, organizing space, and reflection as the features of approaches to learning; and the art area as the learning center.

Social Studies

Social studies activities provide opportunities for children to learn about their world, including their family, community, country, and other parts of the world where they have lived. Children can begin to think about how their experiences are the same as and different from those of others. Suppose, for example, that you want children to depict their neighborhood. The goal of the activity is to make a big map and insert landmarks such as the child care center, the police department, the grocery store, and multiple streets along which each child should add their home in a different activity.

The social studies content addressed in this activity is the neighborhood as well as community resources. The approaches to learning emphasized in the activity are planning, organizing space, following through on plans, and providing a completed visual representation. In regard to Figure 5.3, this activity highlights social studies as the academic content area; planning, organizing space, following through on plans, and providing a completed visual representation as the features of approaches to learning; and the center for special projects as the learning center.

Numeracy

Numeracy and approaches to learning are closely intertwined as children take systematic approaches to tasks such as counting, comparing sizes, sorting, and classifying, which lay the foundation for mathematics understanding. In the woodworking area, for example, a child who wants to make an airplane should determine how

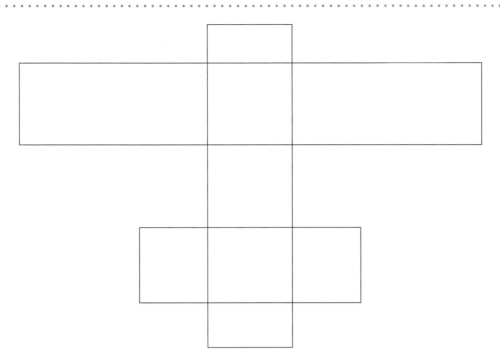

Figure 5.4.   Airplane template.

many pieces of wood are needed, as well as their approximate size (see Figure 5.4 for a sample template). All of this will take planning and follow through, as well as imagining what the airplane might look like. Numeracy will again come into play as the child decides how many nails are needed to complete the plane, how long the nails should be so that they do not come out the bottom of the plane, and how the pieces of wood should be laid out before hammering. In regard to Figure 5.3, this activity highlights numeracy as the academic content area, imagination and problem solving as features of approaches to learning, and woodworking as the learning center.

Science

Approaches to learning and science go hand in hand. As young children participate in science experiments, they observe the experiment, make hypotheses about the outcomes, attend to the processes involved in the experiment, ask questions to clarify directions, and report outcomes. One activity might be to explore whether light travels through certain materials. The science table should be placed in the darkest area of the classroom, along with several flashlights and materials to test (e.g., clear colored plastic, a block from the block table, a shirt made of thin material, a glass of water). Materials should be explored and hypotheses made about whether light would shine through them. In regard to Figure 5.3, this activity highlights science as the academic content area; observing, predicting, attending, and asking questions as the features of approaches to learning; and the science table as the learning center.

Literacy

Approaches to learning can be incorporated with literacy activities in numerous ways. For instance, you might set up a mailbox in the writing center and encourage children to write letters to each other. The approaches to learning addressed in this activity include initiative, persistence, and visual representation. Children can choose the recipient of the letter. They will spend time at the writing center using markers and papers to develop the message they want to convey. This creative process takes time and might include asking an adult in the room to help with getting the message down on paper—whether by using words or drawings. The completed letter then should be addressed and put in the mailbox. One of the children can deliver letters to cubbies, and teachers and authors will support recipients in reading their letter. In regard to Figure 5.3, literacy is the academic area being addressed; initiative, persistence, and visual representation are the features of approaches to learning being developed; and the writing center as the learning center.

Interaction and Play

The previous sample activities require a great deal of planning on the part of teachers. Just as important as planning these activities is planning how it is best to interact with students during these interactions. An important way for children to learn to use effective approaches to learning is to transfer prior learning to the situation at hand. By using the prior knowledge that the child possesses and relating it to the current problem, the child learns to see value in the things learned at home and in the community; he or she can actively use this prior knowledge to solve new problems effectively. For example, consider Roxy, a young girl who has spent many hours with her grandmother, a seamstress. In the art center, Roxy creates elaborate patterns with colored tape and letters. The teacher wonders how Roxy knows so much about patterns, so she asks Roxy's mom and finds out about Roxy's experience with her grandmother. This example required the teacher to observe and question Roxy's actions.

Teachers need to ask questions that move children forward in their development of approaches to learning. Teachers should be willing to investigate how children know what they know and should see such knowledge as valuable. Some questions to enhance children's effective approaches to learning include the following:

- How can you figure it out?

- How can you remember?

- What do you think is the problem?

- Where did you learn to do that?

- Do you think you have all the details?

- How did you do that?

Play and Memory

Research on young children's memory has shed light on the importance of play (Newman, 1990). In this experimental study, 4- and 5-year-old children were asked to remember or play with a set of 16 toys for 2 minutes; their recall of the items was then assessed. Asking the children to remember the toys led to less recall than when asked to play with them.

Teachers should ask these questions during conversations with children. These conversations also give the opportunity to create socially shared meaning. They happen as adults integrate into play, throughout the day, such as at mealtimes, and as relationships are formed among the teacher, children, and families. They give young children the opportunity to solve problems in social and learning contexts. Adults also can model sophisticated approaches to learning by describing ongoing actions taking place in the child's world. They can create opportunities for communication, making sure that children have time to talk and to get feedback from teachers.

Recall from Chapter 4 that it is important that communication extends interactions. In extended interactions, all participants tend to interact in the conversation, and it is very important that the child get ample and possibly even more opportunities to talk. The adult should match the child's pace and style of talk, with the adult intentionally making sure that the child has the time and ability to contribute to the interaction. The topic should stay close to the child's topic. Adults should ask questions that expand on the child's topic and confine these questions to ones that are real, revealing that they are truly interested in the child's response. Growth-enhancing conversations with young children should always stay positive in tone.

Chapter 4 also emphasized the importance of young children's play and providing extended time for play. Time devoted to play is needed to provide opportunities for teachers to ask the types of questions suggested previously and for young children to have opportunities to explore, discover, and construct their own understandings. A high-quality environment that supports ongoing explorations of approaches to learning is needed. This type of environment provides ample opportunities for problem solving and creativity. For example, items included in centers should not be exact replicas of real life items but ones that allow creative uses. It is amazing to see all the uses of Styrofoam pellets during play—they can be "soup" or "eggs" or "snow" or "rocks."

❋ ❋ ❋ Section Summary ❋ ❋ ❋

Approaches to learning are supported in the preschool years through rich learning centers that provide ample opportunities for play and conversation between adults and children and among peers. Learning centers should be well planned to have integrated effective approaches to learning so that children learn particular knowledge, skills, and strategies. It is important that a variety of learning centers provide a rich context for developing approaches to learning across curriculum areas. Conversation and extended interactions with adults and peers are central to passing along higher level thinking strategies.

Assessing Approaches to Learning

Assessing the availability of opportunities for developing effective approaches to learning can take place using the Early Childhood Classroom Observation Measure (ECCOM; Stipek & Byler, 2004) and the Classroom Assessment Scoring System™ (CLASS™; Pianta, LaParo, & Hamre, 2008).

The ECCOM focuses on teacher practices, including directed, constructivist, and child-centered teaching practices. The ECCOM can also be used to assess high-

---

Instructional Conversations that Develop Effective Approaches to Learning

Teacher and children participate equally in instructional conversations around clearly defined topics.

Teacher solicits children's questions, ideas, solutions, or interpretations around a clearly defined topic. *Example: "Can you tell me how you solved this problem?"*

Teacher listens attentively to children and allows them to complete their thoughts, but steers conversation back to topic if child's contribution is tangential. *Example: A child shares his experience about milking a cow and begins drifting into other topics. Teacher summarizes his story and brings the group back to discussion about farm animals (e.g., "So you were surprised at how hard it is to get the milk to come out. Who else has visited a farm or milked a cow?").*

Teacher asks probing questions or uses some other strategy to get children to engage in conversation or expand on their ideas. *Example: In a science lesson on five senses, teacher has children feel different textures in a bag and describe the sensations (e.g., "Daniel, you said it feels squishy. What other squishy things can you think of? ").*

Teacher uses inadequate solutions and/or children's underdeveloped understandings to enhance discussions. *Example: Teacher begins a discussion of the moon by making a list of what the children already "know" (e.g., it's made of cheese, a man lives inside, etc.) and uses this "knowledge" to initiate group discussion.*

Teacher encourages children to ask questions, and respond to or elaborate upon classmates' comments. *Example: Teacher encourages others to ask a child questions to determine what he has brought in the Surprise Box.*

Figure 5.5. Early Childhood Classroom Observation Measure assessment example. (From Stipek, D.J., & Byler, P. [2004]. The Early Childhood Classroom Observation Measure. *Early Childhood Research Quarterly, 19*[3], 375–397; reprinted by permission).

quality opportunities that teachers offer young children. Quality instructional conversations are assessed, which develop young children's uses of effective approaches to learning. Such indicators are presented in Figure 5.5.

The CLASS™ focuses on preschool quality. It also includes areas to assess whether a teacher is providing quality opportunities for children to develop approaches to learning. Keys to this can be observed in the area of measurement called concept development. Figure 5.6 lists indicators of high levels of quality in this area.

Adapting Curriculum and Monitoring Progress

Criterion-referenced assessments or **curriculum-based assessments** can be used to meet individual children's learning needs and monitor their progress. Children are observed, asked questions, and even audio and video recorded. The focus here can be on an assessment system enclosed with a curriculum model. Figure 5.7 presents some of the preschool expectations that are particularly important when addressing young children's approaches to learning, that is, talking to one's self, explaining and seeking information, and getting things done. These are from *Speaking and Listening for Preschool Through Third Grade, Revised Edition* (Resnick & Snow, 2009).

criterion-referenced assessment
Children are measured on whether or not they have a particular skill using a tool that includes skills across developmental or academic areas.

curriculum-based assessments
An assessment in which a child is measured on whether or not they have mastered an activity or skill that is part of a particular curriculum.

Concept Development[8]

Measures the teacher's use of instructional discussions and activities to promote students' higher-order thinking skills and cognition and the teacher's focus on understanding rather than on rote instruction

	Low (1,2)	Mid (3,4,5)	High (6,7)
Analysis and reasoning • *Why* and/or *how* questions • Problem solving • Prediction/experimentation • Classification/comparison • Evaluation	The teacher rarely uses discussions and activities that encourage analysis and reasoning.	The teacher occasionally uses discussions and activities that encourage analysis and reasoning.	The teacher often uses discussions and activities that encourage analysis and reasoning.
Creating • Brainstorming • Planning • Producing	The teacher rarely provides opportunities for students to be creative and/or generate their own ideas and products.	The teacher sometimes provides opportunities for students to be creative and/or generate their own ideas and products.	The teacher often provides opportunities for students to be creative and/or generate their own ideas and products.
Integration • Connects concepts • Integrates with previous knowledge	Concepts and activities are presented independent of one another, and students are not asked to apply previous learning.	The teacher sometimes links concepts and activities to one another and to previous learning.	The teacher consistently links concepts and activities to one another and to previous learning.
Connections to the real world • Real-world applications • Related to students' lives	The teacher does not relate concepts to the students' actual lives.	The teacher makes some attempts to relate concepts to the students' actual lives.	The teacher consistently relates concepts to the students' actual lives.

---

[8]The Concept Development dimension is not just about the development of a specific concept (e.g., seasons, subtraction) but about teachers' use of strategies to encourage understanding and thinking skills.

Figure 5.6. Classroom Assessment Scoring System™ assessment example. (From Pianta, R.C., La Paro, K.M., & Hamre, B.K. [2008]. *Classroom Assessment Scoring System™ [CLASS™]*. Baltimore: Paul H. Brookes Publishing Co.; reprinted by permission.)

Talking to One's Self

Preschoolers begin to use language to monitor their social behavior, verbalize goals, talk themselves through a task, remember steps in a newly learned skill or emphasize their intentions. This behavior is a precursor to the valuable self-monitoring skills used later in reading and should be encouraged. Specifically, we expect preschool children to:

- begin to make spontaneous and audible corrections to their own behavior, actions or language (for example, "Hoppy, I mean happy!" or "I said, 'two,' I meant, three!'"); and
- talk to themselves out loud to make plans, guide behavior and actions, or monitoring thinking.

Explaining and Seeking Information

Children who experience daily read-alouds and conversation with peers and adults are likely to turn to books to seek information. In later years, children are expected to organize information in essays and reports, the preschool version of which is explanatory talk. Though preschoolers still may use personal narratives to provide information, explanatory talk should begin to appear. Specifically, we expect preschool children to:

- seek or provide information by observing; looking at books; or asking teachers, parents, and peers;
- request or provide explanations of their own or others' actions, speech or feelings;
- explain their own or others' intentions and thinking when asked (for example, Q: "Why is the milk out?" A: "For cereal. I want some cereal.");
- give simple, one-sentence explanations, with supporting details or evidence (for example; "I cut my knee because I fell.");
- request or provide explanations of word meanings (for example, "What's 'your highness'?");
- use all their senses to describe physical characteristics of objects, self and others;
- describe objects, self and others in terms of location and position; and
- use gestures and sounds when they don't have descriptive words (for example, describing an accident scene, "They took him in that . . . that . . . RRRR-RRRR. It was LOUD!").

Getting Things Done

At the preschool level, children are able to give and follow directions on simple tasks that are visible, familiar or close at hand. Their ability to plan step by step is limited; however, they may articulate future goals or actions. And, with assistance, they can complete projects that span several days. Their sharing and negotiating skills are just beginning to mature. Specifically, we expect preschool children to:

- listen to, comprehend and carry out directions with three to four simple steps (for example, "Go to the cubby, hang up your sweater and bring your lunch back.");
- give directions that include several sequenced steps;
- ask for clarification to carry out more complicated directions (for example, while baking, "What comes next?");
- use actions or pictures to augment language (for example, demonstrating how to cut the paper or open a container); and
- engage in brief conversation (three or four exchanges) to negotiate sharing, planning, and problem solving.

Figure 5.7. *Speaking and Listening for Preschool Through Third Grade* assessment example. (From Resnick, L.B. & Snow, C.E. [2009]. *Speaking and Listening for Preschool Through Third Grade* [Rev. ed.]. Newark, DE: International Reading Association; Copyright © 2011 by the International Reading Association [www.reading.org]; reprinted by permission.)

❉ ❉ ❉ Section Summary ❉ ❉ ❉

This section discussed some assessments that teachers can use to determine the quality of the approaches to learning they are providing in their classrooms. Examples from several of these measures were described but others are available. A main purpose for teachers using these instruments is to assess whether they are providing their young learners with the opportunities to develop effective approaches to learning in a responsive manner. In addition, teachers need to be familiar with measures used to determine whether they are adapting curricula to meet individual children's learning needs and monitoring if children are making progress (Copple & Bredekamp, 2009). Several examples of these types of measures that are relevant to approaches to learning are provided.

KEY CONCEPTS

- Theory and research about approaches to learning have an impact on ECE teacher practice. Both social learning and social constructivist theories highlight the effect of adults and peers on approaches to learning.

- Social learning theory explains how children develop effective approaches to learning, such as by observing behavior modeled by adults and peers.

- Social constructivist theory elaborates on how adults and more advanced children transmit cultural information that embodies the culture's approaches to learning, or mental tools; they scaffold new learning by providing help (instruction) within the learner's zone of proximal development (i.e., the zone within which the learner can make progress given the instruction).

- Theory of mind expands on this process as young children further understand how their own mind and the minds of others function. In this way, children develop a basis for comparing their mental functions to that of others and for using that information as a basis for further development.

- Information processing theory provides models of mental processes appropriate to approaches to learning, especially thinking of processes at input, elaboration, and output.

- Young children's development of effective approaches to learning affects development across domains.

- Teachers need to understand features of approaches to learning to provide appropriate ECE. These include processes such as initiative, self-regulation, curiosity, impulse control, organization, creativity, persistence, and explaining/representing experiences and learning—many of which can be observed while children are engaged in their preschool day.

- Children use multiple modalities (e.g., visual, auditory, tactile) to absorb, elaborate on, and report new learning. Young children's approaches to learning are viewed as essential components of school readiness.

- Approaches to learning are supported in the preschool years through rich learning centers that provide ample opportunities for play and conversation between adults and children and among peers. Learning centers should be well planned and integrate effective approaches to learning so that children learn particular knowledge, skills, and strategies across curriculum areas.

(continued)

KEY CONCEPTS *(continued)*

- Conversations and extended interactions with adults and peers are central to passing along higher level thinking strategies across activities, curriculum, and developmental areas.

- Play is a particularly rich context for observing, learning, and practicing appropriate approaches to learning. Important is ample time for play, including play that is rich in the possibilities for adult and peer involvement. Materials that impact creativity are central.

- Teachers should use assessments that measure the quality of the education in the area of approaches to learning. Teachers need to assess whether they are providing their young learners with the opportunities to develop effective approaches to learning in a responsive manner.

- Ongoing child-oriented assessments provide teachers with information necessary to reflect on and adapt their instruction in the areas of approaches to learning to be responsive to each individual child's needs and monitor the children's progress for the purposes of curriculum planning.

- Teachers should constantly reflect on the effectiveness of supporting children's approaches to learning and understand how this area of development has an impact on all other areas of development—that is, socioemotional development, cognitive development, language development, and physical development.

Integration of Information

You have just read the section on approaches to learning, which introduced different areas of development and associated ECE practices. What do you think? Do these approaches to learning stand out to you as extremely important for early childhood educators to be familiar with? Do you think you will enjoy teaching young children to use effective approaches to learning? Why are approaches to learning seen as such an integral part of teaching young children?

Self-Reflective Guide

This self-reflective guide will help you assess whether you learned the information in this chapter. It also provides an opportunity to identify areas in which you want or need more information. Are there some new ideas learned that will affect your immediate practice with children?

1. Reflect on the theories presented to account for young children's approaches to learning—social learning theory, information processing theory, social constructivist theory, theory of mind. Are there aspects of these theories that align with your observations of young children's learning? Does a particular theory resonate with you? Why? Make a few notes.

2. Recognize the features of approaches to learning. Have you seen young children use these? List one approach to learning that you think is extremely important for young children to learn and why. List another, and again describe why this is important for young children to learn.

3. Identify how approaches to learning can be addressed across different learning centers and academic areas. List one center and one academic area in which you can develop approaches to learning. Elaborate on why these are important contexts.

4. Consider how and why engaging parents affects your understanding of the child's approaches to learning. List at least one example of how this takes place.

5. Identify how a teacher can embrace and encourage the expression of approaches to learning in ways that may vary from her or his personal experiences. Elaborate on such an experience and why knowing so is important for teachers.

6. Understand how children interact with teachers and peers as they develop effective approaches to learning. Describe a type of interaction that you want to develop as an early ECE teacher. Elaborate on why this type of interaction is important and how it relates to approaches to learning.

7. Reflect on how play affects approaches to learning. Elaborate on why play is important in children's learning and development in this area.

8. Describe how a teacher can assess whether he or she is providing quality opportunities for young children to learn effective approaches to learning.

9. Connect what and how you would assess young children's approaches to learning so that you are able to adapt your curriculum based on findings and also monitor the progress of your students. Identify a child with a disability (note the specific disability) and describe how such assessment information could help you adapt your instruction (learning center) to meet this child's needs.

10. Reflect on approaches to learning and how this area of development relates to others discussed in this book—social and emotional development, cognitive development and learning, using and understanding language, and physical and motor development.

11. Identify other information learned that can have an immediate impact on your current practice if you are a practicing teacher or caregiver at this time.

12. List areas you need to explore further. Who can help you learn about your concerns?

Helpful Web Sites

Head Start Activity QuickSource

www.teacherquicksource.com/headstart/domain.aspx?contentID=2
This site provides important information on approaches to learning and related activities.

HighScope Plan-Do-Review

www.highscope.org/Content.asp?ContentId=182
This site provides information on HighScope's Plan-Do-Review process.

International Association for Cognitive Education and Psychology

www.iacep-coged.org/displaycommon.cfm?an=1&subarticlenbr=30
This site provides access to research and programs addressing approaches to learning for young children.

Key to Learning

www.keytolearning.com/cm.html
This is a site for a specific program, Key to Learning, that addresses how to teach approaches to learning. Although this site is for a specific program, the information provides insight to and sample activities for teaching approaches to learning.

PBS Child Development Tracker

www.pbs.org/parents/childdevelopmenttracker/five/approachestolearning.html
This Public Broadcasting Service site discusses approaches to learning and provides excellent examples of activities and ways to modify teaching practices to be more aligned with current research in child development.

Tools of the Mind

www.mscd.edu/extendedcampus/toolsofthemind
Tools of the Mind is a program that addresses approaches to learning in a comprehensive manner in the United States. The background information provides insight into early education, which provides opportunities to develop young children's approaches to learning.

References

Atkinson, R.C., & Shiffrin, R.M. (1968). Human memory: A proposed system and its control processes. In K.W. Spence & J.T. Spence (Eds.), *The psychology of learning and motivation: Advances in research and theory* (Vol. 2, pp. 89–195). New York: Academic Press.

Bandura, A. (1977). *Social learning theory.* Englewood Cliffs, NJ: Prentice Hall.

Bandura, A. (1991). Self-regulation of motivation through anticipatory and self-reactive mechanisms. In R.A. Dienstbier (Ed.), *Nebraska symposium on motivation: Perspectives on motivation.* (Vol. 38, pp. 69–164). Lincoln: University of Nebraska Press.

Berk, L., & Winsler, A. (1995). *Scaffolding children's learning: Vygotsky and early childhood education.* Washington, DC: National Association for the Education of Young Children.

Bjorklund, D.F., & Douglas, R.N. (1997). The development of memory strategies. In N. Cowan (Ed.), *The development of memory in childhood* (pp. 201–246). New York: Psychology Press.

Bodrova, E., & Leong, D. (2008). Developing self-regulation in kindergarten: Can we keep all the crickets in the basket? *Young Children, 63*(2), 56–58.

Bowman, B., Donovan, S., & Burns, M.S. (Eds.). (2000). *Eager to learn: Educating our preschoolers.* Washington, DC: National Academies Press.

Bronson, D.E. (2000). Progress and problems in social work research. *Journal of Social Work Research and Evaluation, 1*(2), 125–137.

Brown, A.L., & DeLoache, J.S. (1978). Skills, plans, and self-regulation. In R. Siegler (Ed.), *Children's thinking:*

What develops? (pp. 3–35). Mahwah, NJ: Lawrence Erlbaum Associates.

Burns, M.S. (1996). Dynamic assessment: Easier said than done. In M. Luther, E. Cole, & P. Gamlin (Eds.), *Dynamic assessment for instruction: From theory to application* (pp.182–190). North York, ON, Canada: Captus Press.

Burns, M.S., Delclos, V.R., Vye, N., & Sloan, K. (1992). Changes in cognitive strategies in dynamic testing. *International Journal of Dynamic Testing and Instruction, 2,* 45–54.

Burns, M.S., Haywood, H.C., & Delclos, V.R. (1987). Young children's problem solving strategies: An observational study. *Journal of Applied Developmental Psychology, 8,* 113–121.

Copple, C., & Bredekamp, S. (2009). *Developmentally appropriate practice in early childhood programs serving children from birth through age 8.* Washington, DC: National Association for the Education of Young Children.

Fantuzzo, J., Bulotsky-Shearer, R., McDermott, P.A., McWayne, C., Frye, D., & Perlman, S. (2007). Investigations of dimensions of social-emotional classroom behavior and school readiness for low-income urban preschool children. *School Psychology Review, 36*(1), 44–62.

Fantuzzo, J., Perry, M.A., & McDermott, P. (2004). Preschool approaches to learning and their relationship to other relevant classroom competencies for low-income children. *School Psychology Quarterly, 19,* 212–230.

Feuerstein, R., Rand, Y., Hoffman, M., & Miller, R. (1980). *Instrumental enrichment: An intervention program for cognitive modifiability.* Baltimore: University Park Press.

Haywood, H.C., Brooks, P.B., & Burns, M.S. (1992). *Bright start: Cognitive curriculum for young children.* Watertown, MA: Charlesbridge Press.

Hohmann, M., Weikart, D.P., & Epstein, A.S. (2008). *Educating young children: Active learning practices for preschool and child care programs* (3rd ed.). Ypsilanti, MI: HighScope.

Hyson, M. (2008). *Enthusiastic and engaged learners: Approaches to learning in the early childhood classroom.* New York: Teachers College Press.

Kaiser, B., & Rasminsky, J.S., (2011). *Challenging behavior in young children: Understanding, preventing and responding effectively* (3rd ed.). Upper Saddle River, NJ: Allyn & Bacon.

Kamp, K. (2001). Prehistoric children working and playing: A southwestern case study in learning ceramics. *Journal of Anthropological Research, 57,* 427–450.

Luria, A.R., Cole, M., & Cole, S. (1979). *The making of mind: A personal account of soviet psychology.* Cambridge, MA: Harvard University Press.

Leong, D.J., Bodrova, E., & Hensen, R. (2007). *Tools of the mind curriculum project preschool manual* (4th ed.). Denver, CO: Center for Improving Early Learning, Metropolitan State College of Denver.

National Education Goals Panel. (1999). *Building a nation of learners.* Washington, DC: Author.

Newman, L.S. (1990). Intentional and unintentional memory in young children: Remembering vs. playing. *Journal of Experimental Child Psychology, 50*(2), 243–258.

Nguyen, S.P., & Murphy, G.L. (2003). An apple is more than just a fruit: Cross-classification in children's concepts. *Child Development, 74,* 1783–1806.

Pianta, R.C., La Paro, K.M., & Hamre, B.K. (2008). *Classroom Assessment Scoring System™ (CLASS™).* Baltimore: Paul H. Brookes Publishing Co.

Resnick, L.B., & Snow, C.E. (2009). *Speaking and listening for preschool through third grade* (Rev. ed.). Newark, DE: International Reading Association.

Ruff, H.A., & Lawson, K.R. (1990). Development of sustained, focused attention in young children during free play. *Developmental Psychology, 26,* 85–93.

Shonkoff, J., & Phillips, D. (Eds.). (2000). *From neurons to neighborhoods : The science of early childhood development.* Washington, DC: National Academies Press.

Siegler, R., DeLoache, J., & Eisenberg, N. (2003). *How children develop.* New York: Worth.

Stipek, D.J., & Byler, P. (2004). The Early Childhood Classroom Observation Measure. *Early Childhood Research Quarterly, 19*(3), 375–397.

U.S. Department of Health and Human Services. (2010). *The Head Start child development and early learning framework.* Retrieved March 12, 2011, from http://eclkc.ohs.acf.hhs.gov/hslc/tta-system/teaching/eecd/Assessment/Child%20Outcomes/revised-child-outcomes.html

Vygotsky, L.S. (1978). In M. Cole, V. John-Steiner, S. Scribner, & E. Souberman (Eds.), *Mind in society: The development of high psychological processes.* Cambridge, MA: Harvard University Press.

Vygotsky, L.S. (1986). In A. Kozulin (Ed.), *Thought and language* (Rev. ed.). Cambridge, MA: The MIT Press.

Wellman, H.M., Cross, D., & Watson, J. (2001). Meta-analysis of theory-of-mind development: The truth about false belief. *Child Development, 72*(3), 655–684.

Social and Emotional Development

Learning Objectives

1. Understand the theories presented to account for young children's social and emotional development, including ecological theory and psychosocial theory

2. Recognize the features of social and emotional development

3. Identify how social and emotional development can be addressed across different learning centers and academic areas

4. Understand how children interact with teachers and peers as they develop socially and emotionally

5. Understand how play affects social and emotional development

6. Identify assessments that teachers can use to provide quality opportunities for young children to develop and learn in social and emotional areas

7. Determine how teachers can assess young children's social and emotional development so that teachers can adapt curricula and monitor the progress of students

8. Identify how social and emotional development relates to other types of development discussed in this book, including approaches to learning, cognitive development, language development, using and understanding language, and physical and motor development

9. Explain how and why social and emotional development is the foundation of learning

10. Understand the role that families have in their children's social and emotional development, as well as how teachers can support this healthy development

11. Describe how the classroom community and overall relationships among children, teachers, parents, and community members affect children's social and emotional development

H ow should my classroom feel to the children who play, learn, and interact in it? How do 3- to 5-year-old children learn to socially handle problems such as bullying by a peer? How do those continued interactions potentially affect them emotionally and academically? Should I set up learning centers in a special way so that children are more likely to play with each other, especially with class-mates they do not usually interact with? What is the relationship between social and emotional develop-ment? Should I provide children who are exhibiting behaviors that hinder their development with highly socially challenging activities? How can I challenge young learners without frustrating them? When children are frustrated how can my understandings of socioemotional development influence my inter-actions with them? How can I help children develop healthy social and emotional skills in the class-room community? Mina is the only child who speaks Arabic; how can I support her in the class? I have a child whose father recently died; should I have different emotional and social goals for her? Can the class talk about it? One of my children has Down syndrome and the other children do not play with him; how can I encourage the class to see him as an equal part of the classroom community?

These are the types of questions addressed in this chapter on preschool children's social and emo-tional development. As with other chapters, we start with theoretical discussions on socioemotional de-velopment in young children. The impact of children's life experiences cannot be overstated, especially in socioemotional development. These life experiences fall within a wide-ranging scope of developmen-tal bounds affecting all areas of development, including language, cognition, physical, and overall will-ingness to engage in learning behaviors (see Chapter 5). This chapter also provides supports for refining curricula and instruction to meet children's social and emotional needs.

Theoretical Accounts: Social and Emotional Development

The theoretical accounts of approaches to social and emotional development dis-cussed in this chapter were chosen in light of current early childhood education (ECE) and care. Clearly, the theoretical accounts presented in Chapter 5 on ap-proaches to learning are central in ECE and care. Social learning theory and social constructivist theory affect how ECE programs view the role of teachers and peers in young children's social and emotional development. As proposed in social learning theory, observing and imitating behavior modeled by adults and peers is an everyday occurrence. In addition, as proposed in social constructivist theory, adults and more advanced peers (e.g., parents, teachers, classmates, siblings) transmit cultural information that embodies the social and emotional goals of pre-school classrooms. Theory of mind adds additional clarity to what is happening as young children understand their own feelings and the feelings of others, which again contributes to social and emotional goals in early childhood programs. In this chapter, we discuss two additional theories that are particularly relevant to current ECE practice—ecological theory and psychosocial theory.

Ecological Theory

ecosystems
Independent aspects of an individual's life that interact with each other and affect each other.

To examine the development of children within and across a broad spectrum of systems, Uri Bronfenbrenner, one of the cofounders of Head Start, studied and devel-oped ecological theory. The theoretical underpinnings of his ecological theory (Bron-fenbrenner, 1989) include the following structural items: microsystems, meso-systems, exosystems, macrosystems, and chronosystems. These **ecosystems** work together to help explain the complex socioemotional worlds of young children.

The microsystem includes the child's family, friends, peers, child care center, schools, community, and neighborhood. The mesosystem is composed of the important links between the various microsystems. Schools that form immediate links between the two systems encourage, advocate, and support family involvement to promote success for the child. For example, schools that work to connect parents who are recent immigrants may provide meetings, policies, and programs that are responsive to the specific needs of such families. Such schools encourage family involvement while remaining cognizant of the populations they serve. Through the links formed between children's microsystems and mesosystems, a child is more likely to connect with the school and see it as a place where he or she is accepted, safe, and included.

Schools should encourage, advocate, and support family involvement in order to promote success for the child.

The exosystem includes issues outside of the child's immediate environmental context that are highly involved in the child's success in school and life. For instance, when a decision is made to discontinue after-school programs and sports, it can have immediate and long-lasting effects on children who were using these services. Similarly, if a new school policy is implemented that requires all visitors to provide valid identification, this decision might discourage the involvement of families (especially immigrant/minority families) who perceive the policy as unwelcoming. Such issues are extremely important in ECE settings, where families should be involved as much as possible.

Macrosystems involve larger cultural and social norms, customs, and values. For example, parents who believe it is first and foremost the school's job to educate their children might appear to be uninvolved in their child's education when compared to other parents. For other cultures, especially some South American cultures, it is important for teachers to show love toward their students. In this case, it is important that the teacher communicate that he or she also loves the child but in a different way from the parents. With this type of understanding and communication, all members of the relationship continue to do what is best for the child while validating the larger macrosystem norms of the parents and the school.

Finally, the chronosystem includes the sociohistorical contexts within which children, families, and teachers live on a day-to-day basis, which are developed over long periods of time. For parents who had personal negative school experiences, their willingness to trust and connect with the school and the staff is compromised. Understanding and gaining knowledge of these parents' experiences can help to lessen the impact of these sociohistorical experiences. Teachers should recognize the multiple systems in place and reflect on the impact they have on families and children; this can go a long way to contributing to children's overall potential academic success. Figure 6.1 shows how the main systems are connected.

Ecological theory looks broadly and specifically at historical and current issues affecting children across a broad range of community settings (Bronfenbrenner, 1989). Even though young children typically experience the everyday world of adults, they are often not provided an opportunity to process and reflect on things they hear or see. Imagine, for example, a very trusting and loving discussion in a Head Start classroom between students and teachers, which can demonstrate how children move between each level of the theory to form a deeper understanding of their worlds. The conversation began on a microsystem level, with discussions between the children about one child's father being stopped for a minor traffic incident, which caused him to face possible deportation because he was an immigrant without proper documentation. A few of the children became very emotional and concerned about this issue and the related consequences for their classmate. On a

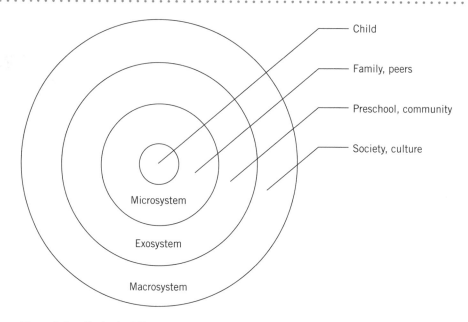

Figure 6.1. Ecological theory.

mesosystem level, links were formed between the class as a group and the child suffering the potential loss of her father. The children's heightened sense of the exosystem issues increased around immigration, a political factor that was out of their control.

Because they were part of a supportive and loving classroom community, the teacher was comfortable discussing issues of concern to the children. The class was able to problem-solve and process a chronosystem that they did not understand. The children could voice their fears about their own parents being sent away because they did not have "papers," as well as the idea that not having "papers" was not a reason to go to jail. Ecological theory shows how being a part of such a supportive, encouraging, and caring environment helps young children understand the social worlds in which they live.

As each of these subcomponents of a larger system stress, the socioemotional development of children is heavily affected in both positive and negative ways, depending on individual and group experiential factors and the interaction of these factors (Cicchetti & Rogosch, 1996; Goodman & Gotlib, 1999; Halberstadt, Denham, & Dunsmore, 2001). The quality of educational experiences—whether in the home, community, or school—significantly affects children's overall development (Bronfenbrenner & Morris, 1998; Sroufe, 2005). The quality of interactions has a significant impact on the current and future development of children, regardless of the quantity of time spent in the various settings (Bronfenbrenner & Morris, 1998). A parent may only be able to spend a half-hour with the child because of a hectic work schedule to support the family. However, if that half-hour is high-quality, responsive, loving, caring, and trusting time, it can be much more valuable and have a more significant impact than a parent who spends all day disciplining, reprimanding, and dismissing a child.

Many issues in the ECE field have a profound effect on children's socioemotional development, such as government-mandated staff–child ratios, caregiver expertise, parental relationships with children, parental mental health, **ethnic identity**, neighborhoods, and access to quality healthcare (Weisner, 2001; Wentzel & Asher, 1995). Ecological theory serves to demonstrate how each of these and numerous other issues stand to affect the social and emotional development of all young children.

ethnic identity
An individual's identity with his or her ethnic group, which affects emotions, thoughts, and behavior.

Susie

Susie, a 4-year-old child, has a working mother. Her mother puts out Susie's breakfast every morning before she leaves for work at 5:30 a.m. Susie does not have the opportunity to talk with her mother in the morning, to tell her mother how she feels or whether she is looking forward to her day at school. Susie's 13-year-old brother assists her in waking up, getting breakfast, readying for school, and then getting her safely to preschool on a city bus. You feel uncomfortable treating Susie's brother as a parent; however, you rarely get to speak with Susie's mother. Sometimes you even wonder if Susie's mother cares about how Susie is doing in school, about whether she respects that you have important information to share about Susie, and indeed whether she really cares at all about Susie. However, you realize that Susie's mother does care when you formally visit her in the evening on a home visit and you both get to share your thoughts.

As Bronfenbrenner's conceptual work (1989) so prolifically revealed, a wide variety of different aspects of a constellation of interconnected forces (e.g., cultural, social, economic, political) affect child development patterns in a multitude of different ways (Larson, Russ, Crall, & Halfon, 2008). A child's interactions and experiences—both positive and negative—in the home and school settings have a direct impact on current and future socioemotional, cognitive, and neurobiological developmental patterns (Maughan, Cicchetti, Toth, & Rogosch, 2007). Within and across these various settings, a host of other relevant background factors enter into the daily experiences for individual children, including socioeconomic status, parental marital status, parental education, quality-of-care settings, and exposure to violence (Belsky, 2009).

Psychosocial Theory

Erik Erikson's psychosocial theory (1993) has had a strong impact on ECE today. After studying childhood and childrearing within the Lakota and Yurok Native American tribes, as well as training as a cultural anthropologist and working as a psychoanalyst, Erikson began to construct a theory of social and emotional development centered on successful completion of typical experiences. During the early childhood years, children want to further their independence in activities (industry); however, they may be hindered by doubts about whether they should complete an activity independently (guilt). Erikson proposed that successful resolution at this time leads to children developing "purpose" and "courage." If children are unsuccessful at this stage, they might be ruthless or inhibited. Immediately before this early childhood stage when children are addressing independence, they are exploring autonomy versus shame and doubt, figuring out whether they should hold on to or let go of parental figures in a developmentally appropriate manner. Erikson proposed that successful resolution at this time leads to children developing "will" and "determination." If children are unsuccessful at this stage, they might be impulsive or compulsive.

Children in the early childhood years need ongoing socioemotional, learning, and developmental support, while still being allowed to be curious, make mistakes, and recover from them. Imaginative play opportunities should be provided. In this context, teachers should take seriously the multiple *why* questions their young learners ask.

Critical Theory and Early Education

Many of the theories just discussed have provided essential constructs through which we understand child development. They have provided a foundation on which the field has built current theory. In deliberations about these processes, it is important to also consider the current and future critical trends that question the established norms (i.e., continued agreement) within which so much of ECE traditionally operates (Dahlberg & Moss, 1999; Harry & Klinger, 2005; Nieto, 2010). Within this structure, theorists and practitioners critically engage age-old theories, critiquing them as normative structures, asking different questions, and establishing alternative notions that reveal alternate discourses about children and child development (Brookfield, 1995; Harry, 1992).

❋ ❋ ❋ Section Summary ❋ ❋ ❋

As with the approaches to learning that were discussed in Chapter 5, children's social and emotional development affects development across domains. Ecological theory plays a central role in our understanding of young children's social and emotional development—that the multiple systems within which the child functions (e.g., microsystems, macrosystems) affect social and emotional learning and development. Psychosocial theory plays an important role as teachers consider opportunities to provide for young children to support their social and emotional development. Social learning theory, social constructivist theory, and theory of mind are important in understanding social and emotional development and should be taken into account when providing education and care in early childhood. As children learn through observing behavior modeled by adults and peers, they are affected by more advanced adults and peers who transmit cultural information that embodies the culture's social and emotional content. Further, young children begin to understand how their own emotions and social behavior and that of others might be similar but also quite different. Therefore, they learn to function by taking into account the complexities of others.

Features of Social and Emotional Development

As Bronfenbrenner (1989), Erikson (1993), and other theorists (e.g., Bowlby, 1973) provided the foundational establishment of important theoretical knowledge, their contributions to our further understandings today reveal that the complexities of socioemotional development are an integral part of viewing the child as a whole person functioning in a complex social world.

Temperament and Personality

Temperament helps children to organize their understanding and approach to the world around them. The inherent traits of children influence how they learn about the greater world and how they negotiate their learning environments and day-to-day experiences. While learning to understand their emotions and social worlds, young children rely on their parents' and caregivers' abilities to communicate and help them integrate these traits. Because young children spend a large amount of their time with their families, home is where they first learn social and emotional functioning of other people in their lives. Therefore, it is important for teachers to connect with families of young children in order to understand and develop a deeper understanding of what inherent traits each child might have. Parents have deeper understandings and more accessible firsthand knowledge of how and possibly why their own children respond to specific situations in certain ways. Teachers and other experienced caregivers obtain these understandings after increased interactions with parents in the classroom, in the family home, or during community activities. Seeing children in their various social worlds is imperative to understanding all of their complex dimensions.

Tony

Tony, a 3-year-old boy, tends to be fussy following a long nap, likes to cuddle before going to bed, and gets apprehensive (e.g., stiffens up and clings) during transitions. Healthy, well-connected caregivers are able to apply this knowledge and adjust their behaviors to be responsive to Tony's individual needs. This adjustment allows Tony to see the caregivers in his life as caring and emotionally available to him.

Attachment

Young children must feel safe and secure in order to develop. Attachment to adults in their lives plays a significant role in forming such emotions. This deep emotional bond that forms between a young child and his or her parents forms the basis for the child's development of a sense of security (Bowlby, 1990). Not only must this attachment occur between child and parent but also between child and other caregivers. When children feel connected to the adults in their lives, they are better able to explore, interact, and learn from the world around them. The connection formed does more than fulfill daily needs; it must be a soul-to-soul link between the child and important adults in his or her life. At times, children cannot form appropriate attachments to adults because of various environmental and biological issues such as neglect, abuse, or certain types of disabilities.

Gina

Gina is 3 years old. At the beginning of the year, Gina was very independent, often ignoring the teacher's advice on ways to complete activities. For example, when Gina was learning how to use glue, she refused to stop pouring the glue out; she went around the room collecting glue containers and emptying them. When the teacher asked her to stop, she started screaming and having a tantrum. Gina would not calm down and continued to focus on the glue. This happened several times in the class. The only way the teacher could resolve the problem was to completely remove the item.

Gina's teacher sees her behavior as noncompliant and believes her to be a "spoiled brat." The special education teacher is called in to observe Gina, and she asks about the child's home life: When she is hurt does she seek out an adult? How is she with her peers? The special education teacher hypothesized that there might be attachment issues with Gina, not special education concerns.

Identity

Young children, even at 3 years of age, have started to develop personal identity characteristics. Over the course of a child's lifetime, the various parts of who he or she is and what he or she believes in—and why—will continue to evolve. Identity in young children is just as complex as it is in adults; yet, in young children, their limited life experiences and understanding of the larger world affects how and what they are able to process. Young children have racial, ethnic, cultural, socio-economic, sexual, ability, and social identities. Many well-respected theorists have investigated children's understanding of race and personal identity (e.g., Clark & Clark, 1940; Van Ausdale & Feagin, 2001). This formation of ethnic identity has critical implications for how children view themselves, as well as their own personalized strengths and weaknesses based on their racial and ethnic backgrounds.

Young Children and Race

Two important social experiences in the 20th century helped to form our understanding of how children perceive race. First, the Clark experiment of the 1940s was a famous psychological experiment that showed black and white baby dolls to young African American children. The children were asked various questions to demonstrate their understanding of race, including which doll was good and clean and which doll was dirty and bad. The African American children said they did not want the black doll because it was bad and dirty. Kenneth and Mamie Clark reported their findings as evidence of the impacts of segregated education (Clark, 1953).

In 1968, Jane Elliott, a classroom teacher in Iowa, separated her third-grade class by brown-eyed and blue-eyed children. She did this as a lesson after Martin Luther King's assassination. She modeled and acted out segregation with the class. The brown-eyed children were praised and allowed extra recess. The blue-eyed children had to wear special collars, could not play with the brown-eyed children, and were constantly reprimanded. The children's change in attitude and behavior toward their blue-eyed friends was marked. In follow-up meetings, the students discussed how much their lives and perspectives about race changed after this activity. (For more information, visit http://janeelliott.com.)

Several studies have been conducted that reveal the importance of Native American and African American parents actively emphasizing cultural heritage and pride in their young children when they knowingly and instrumentally place a greater emphasis on "socializing ethnic pride over mistrust and bias" (Cole, Cole, & Lightfoot, 2005, p. 371). These findings speak to positive development from childhood into adolescence and across developmental areas. When parents actively address these issues in childhood, their children have "stronger cognitive abilities and problem solving skills, and fewer behavior problems compared with children whose parents provided other forms of racial socialization" (Cole et al., 2005, p. 371). The positive awareness of and active attention to identity themes like sex roles and ethnic identity by adult caregivers and children themselves has important implications for positive developmental progression throughout childhood.

Resiliency and Protective Factors

In the early years of a child's life, an enormous amount of opportunities present themselves to both children and caregivers for the potential promotion of effective socioemotional development. Each of these opportunities helps children form healthy and productive ways to deal with changes in their lives. Resiliency is the child's ability to acknowledge a change in his or her daily routine without losing total control of his or her emotions. With understanding and caring, teachers can refine and further develop healthy **resiliency skills**.

Protective factors support and are a key part of a child's resiliency skills. Resilient children's life experiences may have taught them that disappointments and changes happen. More importantly, resilient children have learned that they can trust the adults in their lives, who will do their best to follow through. However, the life experiences of children who lack resilience may have taught them that pain and suffering come from sudden change and that adults seldom follow through with them.

Given what we know of the deep connections between emotion and cognition (Phelps, 2006) and how they are intertwined in the brain (Izard, 2009), teachers and caregivers of young children should include considerate, developmentally effective promotion of these interactive phenomena (Andreassen & West, 2007). Izard's work illustrated that how children interact with their siblings, peers, classmates, parents, and teachers, as well as how these significant others repeatedly interact or react to these varied discrete and nondiscrete initiations, "influence neural systems and mental processes involved in emotion feelings, perception, and cognition" (2009, p. 3).

Bronfenbrenner's and Erikson's theoretical works and the influence of those foundational theories in ECE continue to affect a wide array of socioemotional developmental practices (Copple & Bredekamp, 2009). Children's learning opportunities and experiential background around socioemotional development contribute to their growth in this area (Fredrickson & Tugade, 2004). Adults play a pivotal role in this development as they have the potential to provide children with the necessary experiences that will assist in the provisioning of constructive ways to express oneself (Aikens, Coleman, & Barbarin, 2008; Spagnola & Fiese, 2007) in effective ways. Not recognizing and taking advantage of the possible positive growth opportunities here can lead to a "cascade of psychological, neurobiological, and genetic processes that interfere with the acquisition of adaptive **self-regulatory capacities** in youngsters and increase children's risk for future emotion regulation" (Maughan et al., 2007, p. 699).

resiliency skills
Strategies used to bounce back or recover from difficult situations.

self-regulatory capacities
The abilities of individuals to govern or be in command of themselves.

Although the home is where children learn and interact the most in their lifetimes, the classroom is also a place where they can form a sense of community, support, love, and deep caring for each other (Howes & Ritchie, 2002). As a teacher, many children who have had significant traumas at very young ages will enter your life, which should inspire and ignite your willingness to help and support all children.

✻ ✻ ✻ Section Summary ✻ ✻ ✻

Many different features of young children's social and emotional development are viewed as essential components of healthy child developmental processes, such as temperament and personality, attachment, identity, resiliency, and protective factors. The multitude of different interactions that children have with their siblings, peers, classmates, parents, teachers, and other community members affect the healthy or unhealthy trajectory of these features, as well as influence children's social and emotional developmental patterns in childhood and potentially over their lifetimes.

Supporting Children's Effective and Diverse Social and Emotional Development

Social and emotional development is promoted during learning centers through interactions in all academic areas, as well as through interactions with adults and more advanced peers, as presented in the section on theories and research earlier in this chapter. When you set up the physical environment and decide on related materials for learning centers, you should take into account the goal of promoting effective social and emotional development. This section describes how academic content should be put together with social and emotional development and enacted in different learning centers. Figure 6.2 depicts the relationship between these three components.

In this section, we specify activities that are integrated across literacy, numeracy, science, social studies, and creative arts using the model in Figure 6.2. However, note that these activities are only examples, provided as models; they are not necessarily the activities that you will be using, nor those that are the most important to include as opportunities for your young children to develop effective social and emotional development. You will develop your own understanding of what activities to use and which centers to integrate as you get to know your individual children.

Set up learning centers so that children are more likely to play together—especially with classmates with whom they do not usually interact.

Literacy

Being able to express emotions and emotional state must be learned. By forming a community of learners and providing dramatic play scenarios, children begin to learn the language needed to express themselves: "[The] ability to symbolize feelings and put them into words provides a powerful tool for emotion regulation, influencing emotion-cognition relations, and developing high-level social skills" (Izard, 2009, p. 20).

For example, a wide array of children's books focus on socioemotional aspects of life. These books can be vital components of a literacy center in a preschool, as well as an engaging aspect of the overall curricula and specific curricular unit plans over the course of the year. In regard to Figure 6.2, this activity highlights literacy as the academic con-

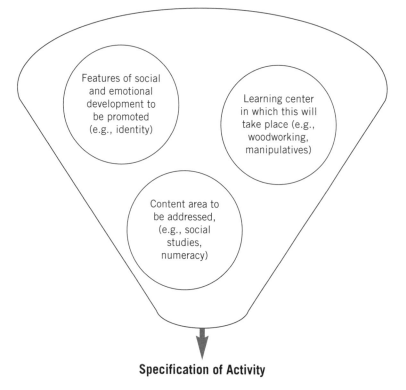

Specification of Activity

Figure 6.2.   Contributors to specification of activity.

tent area, emotional expression as the aspect of social and emotional development being emphasized, and the book and dramatic play areas as the learning centers.

Numeracy

Healthy experiences in numeracy provide opportunities to develop and enhance children's understanding of mathematical principles, which lay the foundation for increased mathematical understanding throughout their lifetimes. For example, when children have ample opportunities for free play and block play, they are potentially involved in conceptualizing principles such as comparison, shape, pattern, number, measurement, space, geometry, **symmetry**, order, width, height, and area. These concepts are explored and measured in relation to each child's identity, for example, his or her height or hair length. In regard to Figure 6.2, this activity highlights numeracy as the academic content area, identity development as the aspect of social and emotional development being emphasized, and the block center as the learning center.

symmetry
The congruence of form or shape across a line dividing the object into two parts.

Science

So many of the traditional early childhood science activities and experiences involve group work and active manipulation of the environment (e.g., working with machines, experimenting firsthand with **found materials**) alone and collectively with peers. Traditional early childhood science experiences provide opportunities for children to foster prosocial behavior as they work with another peer or in small

found materials
Materials for children that were not necessarily intended for use in a play activity (e.g., a cardboard box).

groups. These types of group work create opportunities for sharing, negotiating, learning to get along with others, taking turns, and developing cognitive competencies. All of these provide enhanced opportunities to work through socio-emotional development as children learn and acquire important skills that will serve them immediately, throughout childhood, and well into adulthood. In regard to Figure 6.2, this activity highlights science as the academic content area, prosocial behavior as the aspect of social and emotional development being emphasized, and the water table or science table as the learning center.

Social Studies

Active experiences in social studies assist children in developing and enhancing their broad understandings of the world. Knowing about their communities and neighborhoods helps children begin to develop an interest in the world outside their own lives. Through social studies, young children discuss, analyze, and reflect on topics of importance to them, such as family dynamics, friendships, social and political issues affecting their families, and community violence. When young children are members of a responsive and respectful classroom community, many of these issues can be discussed. For example, in Mary Cowhey's (2006) work *Black Ants and Buddhists,* children in her classroom investigated religious views of the classroom members and brought in people from the community to discuss whether the class should kill ants living in the classroom. Young children are more than willing to discuss topics that some adults think are too controversial or think children do not have opinions about, such as abuse, race, immigration, or homelessness. In regard to Figure 6.2, this activity highlights social studies as the academic content area, acceptance of various social views as the aspect of social and emotional development being emphasized, and the book center as the learning center for addressing these issues in books and having extended conversation.

Creative Arts

The creative arts allow for freedom of expression and wide-ranging opportunities for children to express their emotions and feelings as they see fit. Through their work in the creative arts, children can exhibit a wide range of diverse work that creatively allows them to be open, playful, experimental, and expressive, as well as to take chances and therapeutically work through life challenges. In our interactions with preschool children, we have observed a wide range of artistic work that illustrated firsthand experiences that these children were working through. Through creative expression, young children may be able to bring forth ideas and have open socioemotional expression that is not otherwise possible for them. Participating in the creative arts creates possibilities for open-ended group work; sharing, negotiating, and learning to get along with others; taking turns; and developing cognitive competencies—all of which are important parts of healthy child development. In regard to Figure 6.2, this activity highlights creative arts as the academic content area, emotional expression as the aspect of social and emotional development being emphasized, and the art area as the learning center.

Interaction and Play

Adults and more competent peers play a significant role in forming and developing classrooms and relationships that support children's socioemotional development (Hyson, 2003). Young children learn in socially complex worlds. Building,

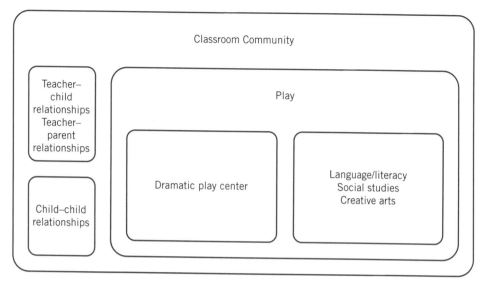

Figure 6.3. Classroom community.

supporting, and encouraging the formation of a classroom community (see Figure 6.3) is one way teachers develop spaces where young children can explore, learn coping strategies, and form healthy social/emotional skills. McCaleb (1994) outlined a process for seeing all members of the child's world, the school community, and the teacher's world as part of the elements necessary to build a community of learners. A central element of a classroom community is relationships. Relationships include not just the one between teacher and child but also the relationships between teacher and parent and between the children.

In supportive classroom communities, children are willing to take risks in the topics they discuss and emotions they express. They are taught how to resolve conflicts. Without a supportive and encouraging classroom community, children are very unlikely to discuss emotional topics because they do not feel that they will be respected and heard by the adults and peers in the classroom.

Conflict Resolution

A problem-solving approach to conflict resolution helps children solve problems without resorting to aggression or retreating into avoidance. For instance, teachers can use the following six steps (Evans, 2002) to help children resolve conflicts:

1. Approach calmly, stopping any hurtful actions
2. Acknowledge children's feelings
3. Gather information
4. Restate the problem
5. Ask for solutions and choose one together
6. Be prepared to give follow-up support

Children can often independently implement sequences like these six steps after using them consistently.

Play is a child's way of knowing and learning about the world. It is through play that the young child can recreate the world and come to understand it. Play is serious to children, so the opportunity to play freely is vital to healthy child development. Play fills up most of the waking life in a child's early years, and children work as hard at it as many adults do at learning, teaching, or working. This ability to play, have fun, and enjoy oneself establishes a very important life pattern—one that says happiness and security can be created from within and are not given to you by someone else. All high-quality ECE environments have some type of play-based philosophy about how children learn.

Dramatic play is the most popular type of play, especially in the way it helps to develop and support socioemotional development. Dramatic play involves the substitution of an imaginary situation for real-life experiences. Children can use **mental representations** of objects, situations, and behaviors to coordinate the roles of themselves and others in various scenarios, from cooking food for a doll to going on an emergency call about a house on fire in the block learning center.

mental representation
How objects and concepts are represented in an individual's mind.

Dramatic play provides a wealth of opportunities to practice perspective taking, such as taking on the role of a hospitalized child or an angry parent. When young children are members of a supportive and responsive classroom community, they feel capable of exploring incidents from their home lives. Dramatic play is a central type of play for young children and has been researched as to the very positive effects it has on young children's socioemotional development (Copple & Bredekamp, 2009). This type of play can be of a social nature or it can be cognitively complex. Most of the activities in dramatic play are social, including others in complex interactions. There are times and incidents in which interactions are also solitary, such as talking on the pretend phone or needing to do one's "work" alone. When play is cognitively complex, children represent complex themes and take on various roles.

❊ ❊ ❊ Section Summary ❊ ❊ ❊

Social and emotional development are supported in the preschool years through contextually rich learning experiences in which there is ample opportunity for play and conversation between adults and children and among peers. Experiences in learning centers should be well planned and provide ample opportunities to develop effective social and emotional skills as children interact with significant others and with rich curricular materials that address this development. It is important that a variety of learning centers provide a meaningful context for enhancing emotional and social development across curriculum areas. Conversations and extended interactions with adults and peers are central to passing along higher level social skills.

After assessing young children's social-emotional development, adapt your curriculum based on findings and monitor the progress of your students.

Assessing Social and Emotional Development

When professionals think about assessment of social and emotional development, psychological assessment often comes to mind (Snow & Van Hemel, 2008). In this current framework of providing early educational opportunities for young children, we focus on assessing whether we are providing instructional activities for young children, adapting curricula to meet individual children's learning needs, and monitoring if children are making progress (Copple & Bredekamp, 2009).

Positive Climate

Reflects the emotional connection between the teacher and students and among students and the warmth, respect, and enjoyment communicated by verbal and nonverbal interactions

	Low (1,2)	Mid (3,4,5)	High (6,7)
Relationships • Physical proximity • Shared activities • Peer assistance • Matched affect • Social conversation	There are few, if any, indications that the teacher and students enjoy warm, supportive relationships with one another.	There are some indications that the teacher and students enjoy warm, supportive relationships with one another.	There are many indications that the teacher and students enjoy warm, supportive relationships with one another.
Positive affect • Smiling • Laughter • Enthusiasm	There are no or few displays of positive affect by the teacher and/or students.	There are sometimes displays of positive affect by the teacher and/or students.	There are frequent displays of positive affect by the teacher and/or students.
Positive communication • Verbal affection • Physical affection • Positive expectations	There are rarely positive communications, verbal or physical, among teachers and students.	There are sometimes positive communications, verbal or physical, among teachers and students.	There are frequently positive communications, verbal or physical, among teachers and students.
Respect • Eye contact • Warm, calm voice • Respectful language • Cooperation and/or sharing	The teacher and students rarely, if ever, demonstrate respect for one another.	The teacher and students sometimes demonstrate respect for one another.	The teacher and students consistently demonstrate respect for one another.

Figure 6.4. Example items from the Classroom Assessment Scoring System™ in the socioemotional domain. (From Pianta, R.C., La Paro, K.M., & Hamre, B.K. [2008]. *Classroom Assessment Scoring System™ [CLASS™]*. Baltimore: Paul H. Brookes Publishing Co.; reprinted by permission.)

It is helpful to consult observational instruments developed to assess the early childhood environment, such as the Classroom Assessment Scoring System™ (CLASS™; Pianta, LaParo, & Hamre, 2008) and the Early Childhood Classroom Observation Measure (ECCOM; Stipek & Byler, 2004) to focus on teacher practices and constructivist, child-centered practices. In the social and emotional areas, ratings for positive climate on the CLASS™ provides indicators of whether opportunities for growth are being provided (see Figure 6.4).

The ECCOM assesses additional areas of social and emotional development from a different perspective. Several scenarios may occur in a classroom:

1. The teacher takes full responsibility for maintaining an orderly classroom, not allowing children to take (or learn how to take) any responsibility.

2. The teacher does not take any responsibility for maintaining an orderly, predictable environment.

3. The teacher and children share responsibility, with children being allowed to take responsibility to the degree that they are able.

Figure 6.5 provides an example of an ECCOM item that assesses how children are given opportunities to develop responsibility, as in the third scenario.

Adapting Curriculum and Monitoring Progress

Given what we know about social and emotional development from our practical and theoretical experiences, it is vitally important to consider the multitude of different, diverse paths that children travel down from birth, through childhood, and into adolescence. Criterion-referenced or curriculum-based assessments can be used to meet individual children's learning needs and monitor their progress. Children can be observed, asked questions, and have their work collected and photographed. The focus here should be on an assessment system enclosed with a curriculum model. Such assessment is part of the HighScope curriculum, a renowned ECE model that was found to have an impact on children's social and emotional

- Children have specific roles and jobs that they carry out as part of a classroom community. *Examples: attendance monitor, table washer, closet monitor, plant monitor*
- Children get, take care of, and put away their own materials in the classroom.
- Children follow through with instructions without more than occasional teacher reminders.
- The teacher monitors children's work but does not offer unnecessary help or reminders. *Example: Teacher does not cut or glue things for child unless safety is an issue.*
- Teacher provides opportunities for children to have leadership roles. *Example: During share time, children are allowed to choose and/or call on peers with questions; child is in charge of explaining a center activity.*
- Children try to solve problems on their own before coming to the teacher.
- Teacher facilitates conflict resolution and rarely imposes adult solutions. *Example: Teacher encourages children to "use their words" to solve problems; teacher solicits ideas from children on how to solve conflict and assists them in making an effective decision.*

Figure 6.5. Example items from the Early Childhood Classroom Observation Measure in the socioemotional domain. (From Stipek, D.J., & Byler, P. [2004]. The Early Childhood Classroom Observation Measure. *Early Childhood Research Quarterly, 19*[3], 375–397; reprinted by permission.)

Objective 2 Establishes and sustains positive relationships

c. Interacts with peers

Not Yet	1	2	3	4	5	6	7	8	9
		Plays near other children; uses similar materials or actions • Sits next to child playing an instrument • Imitates other children building with blocks • Looks at other child's painting and chooses the same color		**Uses successful strategies for entering groups** • Watches what other children are doing for a few minutes and then contributes an idea • Asks, "Can I run with you?"		**Initiates, joins in, and sustains positive interactions with a small group of two to three children** • Sees group pretending to ride a bus and says, "Let's go to the zoo on the bus." • Enters easily into ongoing group play and plays cooperatively		**Interacts cooperatively in groups of four or five children** • Works on tasks with others toward a common goal • Plays and works together for extended periods of time	
red		orange yellow		green	blue		purple		

Objective 3 Participates cooperatively and constructively in group situations

b. Solves social problems

Not Yet	1	2	3	4	5	6	7	8	9
		Expresses feelings during a conflict • Screams when another child touches his crackers • Gets quiet and looks down when another child pushes her		**Seeks adult help to resolve social problems** • Goes to adult crying when someone takes the princess dress she wanted to wear • Calls for the teacher when another child grabs the play dough at the same time he does		**Suggests solutions to social problems** • Says, "You ride around the track one time, then I'll take a turn." • Says, "Let's make a sign to keep people from kicking our sand castle like we did in the block area." • Asks teacher to make a waiting list to use the new toy		**Resolves social problems through negotiation and compromise** • Says, "If I let you use the ruler, will you let me use the hole-punch?" • Responds, "Hey, I know! You two can be the drivers to deliver pizza."	
red		orange		yellow	green	blue	purple		

Figure 6.6. Example items from the Teaching Strategies GOLD® tool in the socioemotional domain. (From Heroman, C., Burts, D.C., Berke, K., & Bickart, T. [2010]. *Teaching Strategies GOLD® Objectives for Development & Learning: Birth Through Kindergarten*. Washington, DC: Teaching Strategies; adapted by permission. *Key to colors in Teaching Strategies GOLD*: red, birth to 1 year; orange, 1 to 2 years; yellow, 2 to 3 years; green, preschool 3 class; blue, pre-K 4 class; purple, kindergarten.)

127

development as well as a decrease in behavioral problems as children get older (Consortium for Longitudinal Studies, 1983; Hohmann, Weikart, & Epstein, 2008).

Teaching Strategies GOLD Objectives for Development & Learning (Heroman, Burts, Berke, & Bickart, 2010) is an assessment tool that can be used across curriculum models, as it provides a comprehensive means of monitoring children's social, emotional, physical, language, cognitive, and academic progress. Teachers document and observe children's development to help adapt curricula and provide differentiated instruction and support. Figure 6.6 provides a few examples of socioemotional development from the Teaching Strategies GOLD tool. In the examples, the green band refers to expectations for children in a preschool 3 class, and the blue band refers to expectations for children in a pre-K 4 class. Please refer to the full assessment document for more information.

❋ ❋ ❋ Section Summary ❋ ❋ ❋

This section discussed assessments that teachers can use to determine the quality of the social and emotional experiences they are providing in their classrooms and addressing in their curricular offerings. Examples from several of these measures were described but others are available. A main purpose for teachers using these instruments is to assess whether they are providing young learners with the opportunity to develop socially and emotionally in an effective and responsive manner. In addition, teachers need to be familiar with measures used to determine whether they are adapting curricula to meet individual children's learning needs and monitoring if children are making progress (Copple & Bredekamp, 2009).

KEY CONCEPTS

- Theory and research about socioemotional development have an impact on ECE teacher practice.
- Ecological theory plays a central role in our understanding of young children's socioemotional development.
- Psychosocial theory is important as teachers consider social and emotional opportunities to provide for young children.
- Social learning theory, social constructivist theory, and theory of mind are important in understanding socioemotional development and should be taken seriously when providing education and care in early childhood.
- Children's social and emotional development affects development across domains.
- Teachers need to understand features of socioemotional development to provide appropriate ECE. Temperament and personality, attachment, identity, resiliency, and protective factors serve as essential components of a healthy child development process.
- Socioemotional development is supported in the preschool years through contextually rich learning experiences in which there is ample opportunity

for play and conversation between adults and children and among peers. Learning and academic centers are set up specifically to support these op-portunities.

- The classroom community and environment fulfills an important role in a child's socioemotional development. Through supportive, respectful, and loving relationships with teachers and peers, children are more capable of discussing emotional topics and are more likely to take learning risks in the classroom.

- Conversations and extended interactions with adults and peers are central to passing along social skills and a healthy trajectory for socioemotional skills such as identify formation, attachment, and resiliency.

- Play is a particularly rich context for observing, learning, and practicing ap-propriate socioemotional behavior. Adults and more advanced peers in this area transmit cultural information that embodies the culture's socioemo-tional content. Further, young children begin to understand how their own emotions and social behavior might be similar but also quite different than that of others. Therefore, they learn to function by taking into account the complexities of others.

- Teachers should use assessments that measure the quality of the education in the area of socioemotional development. A main purpose for teachers using these instruments is to assess whether they are providing young learners with the opportunity to develop socially and emotionally in an ef-fective and responsive manner.

- Ongoing child-oriented assessments provide teachers with information nec-essary to reflect on and adapt their socioemotional curriculum to be re-sponsive to each individual child's needs.

- Teachers should constantly reflect on their education and care of children in the area of socioemotional development and understand how this area of development has an impact on all other areas of development—that is, ap-proaches to learning, cognitive development, language development, and physical development.

Integration of Information

You have just read the chapter on social and emotional development, which intro-duced different areas of development and associated ECE practices. As is the case in all areas of development, the information included in this chapter overlaps with all other areas of development, including approaches to learning, cognitive devel-opment, language development, and physical and motor development. What kinds of things from this chapter were of interest to you? Does the importance of social and emotional development seem important for early childhood educators to be familiar with? Do you think you will enjoy interacting with young children as they develop in this area?

Self-Reflective Guide

This self-reflective guide will help you assess whether you learned the information in this chapter. It also provides an opportunity to identify areas in which you want or need more information. Are there some new ideas learned that will affect your immediate practice with children?

1. Reflect on the theories presented to account for young children's social and emotional development, including ecological and psychosocial theories. Are there aspects of these theories that align with your observations of young children's learning? Does a particular theory resonate with you? Make a few notes.

2. Recognize the features of social and emotional development. Have you witnessed young children incorporating these into interactions with other children or adults? List two aspects of social and emotional development that you think are extremely important for young children to learn and why.

3. Consider what potential benefits would come from forming a classroom community. What would you need to do to form this type of classroom?

4. Understand how children interact with teachers and peers as they learn and develop socially and emotionally. Describe a type of related interaction that you want to develop as an ECE teacher. Elaborate on why this type of interaction is important.

5. Identify how social and emotional development can be addressed across different learning centers and academic areas. List one center and one academic area that are fruitful contexts for enhancing social and emotional development. Elaborate on why these are important contexts.

6. Reflect on how play affects socioemotional development. Elaborate on why play is important in children's learning and development in this area.

7. Describe how a teacher can assess whether he or she is providing quality opportunities for young children to develop and learn in the socioemotional area.

8. Connect what and how you would assess young children's socioemotional development so that you are able to adapt your curricula based on findings and also monitor the progress of your students. Identify a child with a disability (note the specific disability) and describe how such assessment information could help you adapt your instruction to meet this child's needs.

9. Reflect on socioemotional development and how this area of development influences and is influenced by other developmental areas discussed in this book, such as approaches to learning, cognitive development, using and understanding language, and physical and motor development.

10. Identify other information learned that can have an immediate impact on your current practices if you are a practicing teacher or caregiver at this time.

11. List areas you need to explore further. Who can help you learn about your concerns?

Helpful Web Sites

A Place of Our Own

> http://aplaceofourown.org/topic.php?id=4
> A Place of Our Own is a nonprofit organization that provides topic discussions for teachers and families of young children. This particular part of the site addresses social and emotional development.

Center for Early Childhood Mental Health Consultation

> www.ecmhc.org
> This site, which is supported by Georgetown University, offers information on challenging behaviors, emotional development, and ways to discuss peer conflict with young children.

Center on the Social and Emotional Foundations for Early Learning

> http://csefel.vanderbilt.edu
> This site is supported by Vanderbilt University and provides information about socioemotional development, with resources for teachers and parents in English and Spanish. It also hosts online chat sessions regarding strategies for supporting young children.

Kaboom!

> http://kaboom.org/help_save_play/play_research/studies_and_research
> This site works with the Gesell Institute and provides links to high-quality research articles related to social and emotional development.

Teaching Tolerance

> www.tolerance.org
> A project of the Southern Poverty Law Center, this site provides information geared towards teachers. Lesson plans and activities are categorized by grade level and help guide conservations about race, class, fairness, and other social issues in ways that are appropriate for young children.

Technical Assistance Center on Social Emotional Intervention for Young Children

> www.challengingbehavior.org/communities/teachers.htm
> This site is supported by the U.S. Department of Education and the IDEA Works Network, and it provides resources, practical information, and strategies to address young children's challenging behavior.

References

Aikens, N.L., Coleman, C.P., & Barbarin, O.A. (2008). Ethnic differences in the effects of parental depression on preschool children's socioemotional functioning. *Social Development, 17*(1), 137–160.

Andreassen, C., & West, J. (2007). Measuring socioemotional functioning in a national birth cohort study. *Infant Mental Health Journal, 28,* 627–646.

Belsky, J. (2009). Classroom composition, childcare history and social development: Are childcare effects disappearing or spreading? *Social Development, 18*(1), 230–238.

Bowlby, J. (1973). *Attachment and loss: Volume 1.* New York: Basic Books.

Bowlby, J. (1990). *A secure base: Parent-child attachment and healthy human development.* London: Routledge.

Bronfenbrenner, U. (1989). Ecological systems theory. *Annals of Child Development, 6,* 185–246.

Bronfenbrenner, U., & Morris, P.A. (1998). The ecology of developmental processes. In W. Damon & R.M. Lerner (Eds.), *Handbook of child psychology: Vol. 1: Theoretical models of human development* (pp. 993–1028). New York: Wiley.

Brookfield, S.D. (1995). *Becoming a critically reflective teacher*. San Francisco: Jossey-Bass.

Cicchetti, D., & Rogosch, F.A. (1996). Equifinality and multifinality in developmental psychopathology. *Development and Psychopathology, 8,* 597–600.

Clark, K. (1953). The effects of segregation and the consequences of desegregation: A social science statement. Appendix to appellants' brief: Brown v. Board of Education of Topeka (1953). *Minnesota Law Review, 37,* 427–439.

Clark, K.B., & Clark, M.K. (1940). Skin color as a factor in racial identification of negro preschool children. *The Journal of Social Psychology, 11*(1), 159–169.

Cole, M., Cole, S.R., & Lightfoot, S. (2005). *The development of children* (5th ed.). New York: Worth Publishers.

Consortium for Longitudinal Studies. (1983). *As the twig is bent . . . Lasting effects of preschool programs.* Mahwah, NJ: Lawrence Erlbaum Associates.

Copple, C., & Bredekamp, S. (2009). *Developmentally appropriate practice in early childhood programs serving children from birth through age 8* (3rd ed.). Washington, DC: National Association for the Education of Young Children.

Cowhey, M. (2006). *Black ants and Buddhists: Thinking critically and teaching differently in the primary grades.* Portland, ME: Stenhouse.

Dahlberg, G., & Moss, P. (1999). *Beyond quality in early childhood education.* Philadelphia: Falmer.

Erikson, E.H. (1993). *Childhood and society.* New York: WW Norton & Company.

Evans, B. (2002). *You can't come to my birthday party! Conflict resolution with young children.* Ypsilanti, MI: HighScope.

Frederickson, B., & Tugade, M. (2004). Resilient individuals use positive emotions to bounce back from negative emotional experiences. *Journal of Personality and Social Psychology, 86*(2), 320–333.

Goodman, S.H., & Gotlib, I.H. (1999). Risk for psychopathology in the children of depressed mothers: A developmental model for understanding mechanisms of transmission. *Psychological Review, 106*(3), 458–490.

Halberstadt, A.G., Denham, S.A., & Dunsmore, J.C. (2001). Affective social competence. *Social Development, 10*(1), 79–119.

Harry, B. (1992). *Cultural diversity, families, and the special education system: Communication and empowerment.* New York: Teachers College Press.

Harry, B., & Klinger, J. (2005). *Why are so many minority students in special education: Understanding race and disability.* New York: Teachers College Press.

Heroman, C., Burts, D.C., Berke, K., & Bickart, T. (2010). *Teaching Strategies GOLD®: Objectives for Development & Learning: Birth Through Kindergarten.* Washington, DC: Teaching Strategies.

Hohmann, M., Weikart, D.P., & Epstein, A.S. (2008). *Educating young children: Active learning practices for preschool and child care programs* (3rd ed.). Ypsilanti, MI: HighScope.

Howes, C., & Ritchie, S. (2002). *A matter of trust: Connecting teachers and learners in the early childhood classroom.* New York: Teachers College Press.

Hyson, M. (2003). Putting early academics in their place. *Educational Leadership, 60*(7), 20–23.

Izard, C.E. (2009). Emotion theory and research: Highlights, unanswered questions, and emerging issues. *Annual Review of Psychology, 60,* 1–25.

Larson, K., Russ, S.A., Crall, J.J., & Halfon, N. (2008). Influence of multiple social risks on children's health. *Pediatrics, 121,* 337–334.

Maughan, A., Cicchetti, D., Toth, S.L., & Rogosch, F.A. (2007). Early-occurring maternal depression and maternal negativity in predicting young children's emotion regulation and socioemotional difficulties. *Journal of Abnormal Child Psychology, 35*(5), 685–703.

McCaleb, S.P. (1994). *Building communities of learners. A collaboration among teachers, students, families, and community.* New York: St. Martin's Press.

Nieto, S. (2010). *The light in their eyes: Creating multicultural learning communities* (10th anniversary ed.). New York: Teachers College Press.

Phelps, E.A. (2006). Emotion and cognition: Insights from studies of the human amygdala. *Annual Review of Psychology, 57,* 27–53.

Pianta, R.C., La Paro, K.M., & Hamre, B.K. (2008). *Classroom Assessment Scoring System™ (CLASS™).* Baltimore: Paul H. Brookes Publishing Co.

Snow, C.E., & Van Hemel, S.B. (2008). *Early childhood assessment: Why, what, and how.* Washington, DC: National Academies Press.

Spagnola, M., & Fiese, B.H. (2007). Family routines and rituals: A context for development in the lives of young children. *Infants & Young Children, 20*(4), 284–299.

Sroufe, L.A. (2005). *Emotional development: The organization of emotional life in the early years.* New York: Cambridge University Press.

Stipek, D.J., & Byler, P. (2004). The Early Childhood Classroom Observation Measure. *Early Childhood Research Quarterly, 19*(3), 375–397.

Van Ausdale, D., & Feagin, J.R. (2001). *The first R: How children learn race and racism.* Lanham, MD: Rowman & Littlefield.

Weisner, T.S. (2001). Children investing in their families: The importance of child obligation in successful development. *New Directions for Child and Adolescent Development, 94,* 77–83.

Wentzel, K.R., & Asher, S.R. (1995). The academic lives of neglected, rejected, popular, and controversial children. *Child Development, 66*(3), 754–763.

Cognitive Development and Learning

How do 3- to 5-year-old children learn to sequence items from small to large, recognize patterns, and understand cause and effect? Can cognitive development be addressed in all areas of early childhood education (ECE) curricula? How can I provide children from homes that speak a language other than English with cognitively challenging activities? What can young children reason about? I have a child with autism in my room; do I have to have different reasoning and problem-solving goals for him? What is the relationship between cognition and language? How can I challenge young learners without frustrating them?

These are the types of questions addressed in this chapter on preschool children's cognitive development and learning. First, it is important to know that children cannot be split into areas of development. You will notice that young children's cognitive development is interwoven with their more general approaches to learning, as well as into their language, social, emotional, cultural, and physical development. This chapter presents theories of cognitive development that affect current practices in ECE and care, and it discusses how cognition is an integral part of curricula in literacy, numeracy, science, social studies, and creative arts. We review how assessment can be used by teachers to determine whether they are providing young children with opportunities that will enhance their cognitive development, how teachers can adapt curricula to meet the needs of individual children, and how they can evaluate whether children are making progress in this developmental area.

Theoretical Accounts: Cognitive Development and Learning

The theoretical accounts of cognitive development presented in this section were chosen in light of current ECE practices. The theoretical accounts presented in Chapters 5 and 6 also are relevant in this discussion of cognitive development. For example, ecological theory plays an important role in the understanding of young children's cognitive development, as microsystems and macrosystems are taken into account (Bronfenbrenner, 1989). Social constructivist theory (Vygotsky, 1986) is also central in the discussion of cognitive development, as it takes into account the sociocultural factors that affect cognitive development. Social learning theory (Bandura, 1977) and theory of mind (Siegler, DeLoache, & Eisenberg, 2003) are important in understanding cognitive development as children learn through observing behavior modeled by adults and peers. As children understand that their reasoning is both similar to and different from other children's, this information can be used to promote their cognitive development. In addition, some new theories are introduced in this chapter: **constructivist theory**, narrative construction of reality theory (and its intersection with social constructivist theory), the dynamic skills perspective, and theories about brain development.

constructivist theory
A perspective on children's development and learning that highlights how children construct their own knowledge through interaction with the environment, both physical and social.

Constructivist Theory

Jean Piaget is an important theorist who has affected our understanding of young children's cognitive development. Piaget had a major effect in the field of ECE as his observations and theory about young children demanded a constructive view of learners—that young children actively construct their own knowledge. According to constructivist theory (Piaget, 1977), children integrate new learning into what they already know (assimilation) and modify what they already know to make sense of the new information (accommodation). With new learning, children are confronted with new information that conflicts with current understanding, which causes instability (disequilibrium) of the current understanding. New understandings are then constructed. Piaget conceptualized development as being in **stages of cognition**: sensorimotor, preoperational, concrete operational, and formal operational thought. These stages are conceptualized as universals—that is, they occur across individuals, families, communities, and cultures.

stages of cognition
Distinct levels of mental abilities along the process of child development.

According to Piaget (1977), the stage that preschool children function within is the period of preoperational thought. During this time, children's thinking is perception based and unidimensional; it is limited by irreversibility, transductive reasoning, and egocentrism. One example of the preoperational child is illustrated when the child is asked to estimate numbers. For example, two lines of seven coins are placed in front of the child, clearly showing that the lines contain the same number of objects. Then one line of coins is lengthened. When asked which line has more coins, the preoperational child will point to the longer line. This child relies on the perceptual feature of the task—length—to solve the problem. The child's thinking is one-dimensional in that the child only focuses on one feature of the items (length) rather than also considering the number of items.

The preoperational child also has difficulty reversing an action that has taken place. For example, if a child leaves a Popsicle on the counter in a plastic container overnight so that it melts, the child might conclude that the melted Popsicle is ruined rather than realizing that it can be "fixed" by refreezing it. In transductive reasoning, the preoperational child thinks that when one event follows another, there is a causal relationship between the two events, which is often erroneous. An example of this might be when a child rides in a red car before getting a stomach bug and therefore concludes that she got the stomach bug from the red car and begins to refuse to ride in the red car.

With egocentrism, the preoperational child only thinks of her or his viewpoint and lacks the ability to consider the viewpoints of other people in a given situation. Children's use of private speech is considered by Piagetians as an example of the preoperational child's egocentrism. Private speech is spoken aloud but not addressed to anyone other than the child; it needs no audience other than the child. According to Piaget (1977), private speech is egocentric and is an indication of the preoperational child's inability to differentiate his or her world from the world of others. This speech is viewed as having no communicative (social) or cognitive value.

Vygotskian theorists, on the other hand, view private speech as having an important self-regulatory function for preschool-age children (see Chapter 5). This concept is one that is illustrative of the difference between Piagetian and Vygotskian theory and practice. According to Vygotsky (1986), private speech has a function in providing cognitive self-guidance (Berk & Winsler, 1995; Kohlberg, Yaeger, & Hjertholm, 1999). Recall the example mentioned in Chapter 5 about a preschool child talking out loud when completing a cognitively challenging puzzle. The child used speech to direct the search for the green puzzle piece. This type of speech is believed to become internalized as a child develops a better understanding of the problem to be solved. Private speech should be encouraged and modeled for young children because it supports the child's cognitive development.

Narrative Construction of Reality Theory

Bruner (1996), like Vygotsky (1978), proposed that a child's environment (both social and physical) provides support, such as scaffolding within a child's zone of development for the child's learning and development to take place. Bruner added emphasis on the role of culture. Young children develop within their cultural context, learning in a similar manner because of the way a particular culture sets up the young child's physical and social environments. Within this cultural milieu, children actively construct their knowledge through active engagement in the environment; therefore, the quality of these environments is central to development and learning. Although Bruner's theory of development is similar to Vygotsky's, the focus on culture (including the cultural variation embedded in language) helps to further explain the impact of culture on development (Bruner, 1996).

Narratives are a way for children to structure their worlds, understanding logic, and understand abstract concepts. Features particularly important in narrative and cognitive development in ECE are that they teach children about reality as constructed by their mind and the physical environment; they occur over time and actually give a sense of time; and they are cumulative, with one story building on another. Play—especially sociodramatic play in which narratives can be developed and acted out—is central in narrative construction of reality theory.

Bruner's theory (1996) ultimately rejected the notion of stages, although they were presented in an earlier child development theory he proposed (Bruner, 1956). A formulated set of children's developmental stages was excluded because children do not develop in the same way, nor do their families have the same expectations for their children. Therefore, development according to Bruner is more fluid and flexible.

Dynamics Skills Perspective

developmental trajectory
A developmental course followed by an individual as determined by child development milestones for typical development; multiple developmental trajectories acknowledge that there are variations in development (e.g., a child with a specific language impairment will develop in a different way and rate).

Dynamic skills perspective was developed substantially by Fischer (2009). It adds a great deal to the ideas of fluid and flexible trajectories of development using diverse developmental pathways. This theory is quite a diversion from decades of universals of cognitive development, in which cognitive **developmental trajectories** were the same for all children. Dynamic skills perspective questions the assumption of one common pathway of development. For example, Fischer (2009) proposed that there are a number of different pathways children can take to develop abstract concepts and logic. Therefore, when a child does not complete the cognitive pathway, dynamic skills perspective addresses the distinct pathway taken by the child—the viewpoint from the child's own circumstance. Cognitive behavior is therefore viewed as distinctive rather than primitive, regressed, or delayed.

Brain Development

Although maturationalists' viewpoints (e.g., Gesell, 1940) have not recently been placed in central roles in providing information about pedagogical approaches to cognitive learning and development, they reflect the need for us to consider and address the interaction between biology and experience in cognitive development and learning. Brain development is central in cognitive development. Children's brains need to be stimulated for the network of connections to grow (Nelson & Bloom, 1997). Although there has been great emphasis on brain development in the first 3 years of life, continued attention in the area is warranted for children ages 3 and older (Shonkoff & Phillips, 2000). In many ways, the brain develops satisfactorily given basic childhood experiences, intact senses, and lack of toxins, whether from the physical or social environment. These basic childhood experiences foster new brain growth and refinement of existing brain structures. However, unique life experiences make for individual differences in brain development. These experiences are linked to increases in synapses or increases in the connectedness between neurons. The new synapses are not created before these new experiences but in response to the experiences (Shonkoff & Phillips, 2000).

❊ ❊ ❊ Section Summary ❊ ❊ ❊

Cognitive development and learning has been studied from a number of different perspectives; the theories presented in this chapter were chosen in light of current ECE practices. The theoretical accounts presented in Chapters 5 and 6 also are important in a discussion of cognitive development. Ecological theory plays an important role in the understanding of young children's cognitive development. Social constructivist theory is also central in the discussion of cognitive development as it highlights the role of the social and cultural factors on development. Social learning theory and theory of mind are important in the further understanding of cognitive development as children learn through observing behaviors modeled by adults and peers. In addition, when children understand that their reasoning and that of other children is similar and different, this information can be used to promote their cognitive development.

New theories were also introduced in this chapter, including constructivist theory, which highlights the importance of children constructing their own knowledge. Narrative construction of reality theory highlights the importance of culture and the relationship between learning and social experiences. Dynamic skills perspective focuses on how diverse pathways of development can be addressed, while other research has investigated physiological brain development. Each theoretical approach sees cognitive development through a different lens; the observations and dynamics of each approach are true within the framework of their own particular lens. Crucial to understanding cognitive learning and development is that there is not one theory that is absolute truth. Also, by nature, all theories are in the process of refinement, specification, and growth.

Features of Cognitive Development and Learning

Major aspects of cognitive development were presented in Chapter 5—attention, problem solving, thinking skills, self-regulation, memory, and impulse control. This chapter focuses on concept formation, understanding, relationships, and generalizations of knowledge.

ECE professionals promote development that helps children learn concepts from specific to abstract; establish relationships; determine associations and describe how items compare in functions, characteristics, and **attributes**; make generalizations; draw conclusions from relationships and concepts; and group items into classes by finding common elements. Many concepts learned can be seen concretely, but abstractions are also made as children become more familiar with items.

attribute
A construct associated with characteristics of items (e.g., color, shape, size).

Sets

Important contributors to the ECE field have expressed the features of cognition in different ways. In the HighScope curriculum (Hohmann, Weikart, & Epstein, 2008), classification is addressed by active involvement in activities examining objects that do or do not belong in a set, objects that are identical, objects that are the same in some ways and different in other ways, and objects that are different in most ways. Sets are made of these objects and labels (concepts) are attributed to them. Similar sets are taken in seriation, number, space, and time. In the Head Start Child Outcomes Framework (U.S. Department of Health and Human Services, 2000), these same concepts are addressed within outcomes in the area of mathematics.

Geometry and Spatial Sense

In the preschool years, children are beginning to perceive the relationships between objects in space and in two-dimensional form. They are learning the components needed to think spatially on a mental level and to recreate visual images from memory. On a day-to-day basis, children recognize, describe, compare, and name common shapes (e.g., square), their parts (e.g., four sides), and their attributes (e.g., sides look the same). Children also begin comparing shapes to each other.

> Young children learn to sort by more refined special attributes, grouping and regrouping according to more than one feature at a time.

As with sets mentioned in the previous section, young children start sorting by more refined special attributes (Copley, 2009). Given that color or texture can be added to the mix of attributes, children then learn to group and regroup according to more than one feature at a time (e.g., one pile of red rectangles and another pile of yellow rectangles). In a similar manner, features of objects can be explored when making patterns with objects. In this way, more than one feature can be varied and complexity increased.

An important feature to be learned during this period of time is size—that is, big and little, long and short, as well as being able to match items and two-dimensional visual representations according to size. Children should further understand that this is a concept that depends on relative size. For example, children should understand that a rectangular cereal box is big compared to a rectangular box of candy, and that the cereal box is small compared to the box that contained their new bicycle.

Numbers

Integral to early cognitive development is the beginning understanding of numeracy. It is important that children recognize the numbers 1–10 and begin counting to 10. However, more important is for children to be able to count with one-to-one correspondence (Ginsburg & Amit, 2008). For example, when counting out cups for snack time, it is helpful for a young child to count as he puts a cup at the spot for each child, which allows the number symbol to be mapped to the number concept. In a similar manner, counting can be used with the concepts of *more* and *less*, which moves the young learners from a concept based on perceptual features alone to the realization that a higher number symbol is related.

Vocabulary

Chapter 8 addresses concepts in relation to language development, but it is important to note that vocabulary words are tremendously important in cognitive development and learning (Copley, 2009). Words for position and direction (e.g., *up* and *down*, *in* and *out*, *front* and *back*) are important to learn for conceptual meaning, as are the concepts of *more* and *less*. Other words related to time are also important (e.g., *fast* and *slow*, *day* and *night*).

Patterns and Measurement

Patterns can be used to further explore different attributes of objects. In addition, young children can recognize, duplicate, and extend patterns. For example, when given a design of beads in a specified pattern (e.g., red square, purple square, red square, purple square), the child should be able to add additional beads continuing the same pattern. This type of activity can move quickly into issues of measurement as children compare their bead patterns, indicating whose pattern is longer or shorter.

Measurement can be explored in many parts of the child's life. Children first start noticing differences between themselves and others (e.g., "I am bigger than my sister," "Your shoe is bigger than mine"). Nonstandard forms of measurement help children move toward a better understanding of standard forms of measurement as they mature.

In general, intellectual processes are used and children gain knowledge and ideas from their perception. However, content knowledge and culture play roles in all of the previously mentioned processes, including pattern recognition. For example, if a child's early childhood was spent with his mother who worked as a seamstress, the child's seriation, spatial relationships, sorting, and pattern recognition abilities can be very flexible in the context of sequins on a fancy gown or wedding dress. A child who spent the early years working with shapes in preschool might be more flexible in using primary-colored objects of different shapes and sizes. There is strong evidence that when children have accumulated substantial knowledge, they have the ability to think abstractly at levels well beyond what is ordinarily observed (Bowman, Donovan, & Burns, 2000).

Young children are able to recognize, duplicate, and extend patterns.

✳ ✳ ✳ Section Summary ✳ ✳ ✳

Discussion of cognitive development and learning overlaps with approaches to learning (e.g., reasoning). In some ways, the concepts addressed in this chapter supply rich contexts to practice effective approaches to learning (e.g., making sets, measuring the length of a beaded necklace). Features specific to cognitive development and learning include making sets, patterns, and groupings, and using these and seriation to measure attributes of objects. Concepts related to numeracy, time, and space are learned in this time period. In specific cases such as numeracy, the symbolic representation (number) is learned in terms of its corresponding concept. As will be elaborated in Chapter 8, shared language is needed for instruction in cognitive development to take place. In many situations a child's home language needs to be used to communicate about the complex features of cognition. Picture and symbol systems can also serve a communicative function for children for whom a teacher does not know the home language and for children with autism and other language-based disabilities.

Supporting Children's Effective and Diverse Cognitive Development

This section relates our understanding of ECE theories to how teachers can set up the physical environment and decide on materials with the goal of promoting cognitive development. Academic content can be combined with the goal of promoting cognitive development and enacted in different learning centers. The following sections specify activities that are integrated across creative arts, social studies, numeracy, science, and literacy using the model in Figure 7.1. However, note that these activities are only examples, provided as models; they are not nec-

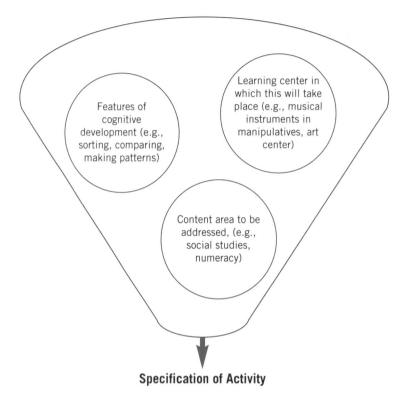

Specification of Activity

Figure 7.1. Contributors to specification of activity.

essarily the activities that you will be using, nor those that are the most important to include as opportunities for your young children's cognitive development. You will develop your own understanding of what activities to use and which centers to integrate as you get to know your individual children.

Creative Arts

Music is a creative context in which to address patterns as a feature of cognitive development.

Music is an excellent context in which to address patterns as a feature of cognitive development. Musical instruments can be made available in the listening center; be sure that the instruments can be used independently by children, are relatively quiet, and are safe. An audio recording of sound patterns can be played; the children can listen to the recording first and then match the pattern with the instruments. Start with simple patterns, such as a quick shake followed by a longer shake. Children also can be asked to make up their own rhythms and represent them on a whiteboard for other children to match. Experimenting with what it sounds like for one child to play short rhythms and another simultaneously playing longer rhythms is a good demonstration to compare and contrast.

The expansion of this activity in terms of the audio support, use of a whiteboard, and addition of various instruments makes this activity more complex. In regard to Figure 7.1, this activity highlights the creative arts as the academic content area; development, matching, and expansion of patterns as the aspects of cognitive development being emphasized; and the listening center as the learning center.

Social Studies

As mentioned in previous chapters, social studies provide young children with opportunities to learn about the world around them and how it functions. At the dramatic play center, children may open a grocery store after the class visits the local grocery store to learn how it contributes to the community. The grocery store is easy to stock when parents are asked to send items such as empty cereal boxes and egg cartons.

A cognitive skill that can be addressed in the grocery store is the classification of foods, such as placing all the cereal in one area and making sure the same kinds of cereal are next to each other. In regard to Figure 7.1, this activity highlights social studies as the academic content area, classification and its complexities as the cognitive development feature being addressed, and the dramatic play area as the learning center.

Numeracy

The grocery store also provides a great context for numeracy, especially in the checkout area where the shoppers and cashiers should have pretend money (both bills and coins). Cognitive processes involved include identifying characteristics of the groceries and drawing conclusions about their cost (e.g., "You got a lot of groceries, so that is going to cost a lot! I need 10 of your dollars," "You got four boxes of cereal, so that will cost \$4"). One-to-one correspondence might also be part of the process as each item is moved over the scanner and the child makes a beep sound with each item. In regard to Figure 7.1, this activity highlights numeracy as the academic content area, identifying the characteristics of physical items and one-to-one correspondence as the cognitive development features being addressed, and the dramatic play area as the learning center.

Science

Collecting rocks and having them available for examination at the science learning center provides a great context for looking at the characteristics of nature, as well as putting items into collections and sets. The science learning center should already have numerous supplies for examining the rocks, such as magnifying glasses, containers of various sizes for sorting, measures, egg cartons, and clear bowls of water. Children should examine the rocks in terms of such things as size, color, shape, texture, and what happens to them when they are put in water. The rocks can then be sorted and resorted by these characteristics in the various containers. Egg cartons can be used to set up a child's individual collection for display, possibly including an audio or written description of why they included the rock. In regard to Figure 7.1, this activity highlights science as the academic content area, examining and identifying the characteristics of physical items and sorting them as the cognitive development features being addressed, and science as the learning center.

Literacy

Part of cognitive development is learning about concepts denoting locations (e.g., *top, side, front, inside, next to, down, under, through*) and time characteristics (e.g., *day, night, week, month*). These concepts are included in children's books that can be included in the literacy center. Children can explore on their own or ask for teachers to read and discuss with them. Having multiple books on the same topic grouped together at the book center can build on and expand young children's understanding of concepts of location and time. In regard to Figure 7.1, this activity highlights literacy as the academic content area, concepts related to location and time as the cognitive development features being addressed, and the book center as the learning center.

Interaction and Play

Research from a variety of theoretical perspectives suggests that a defining feature of a supportive environment is a responsible and responsive adult (Hyson, 2008). Parents, teachers, and caregivers promote development when they create learning experiences that build on and extend the child's competence—experiences that are challenging but within reach. Three different areas of importance for cognitive development are interactions with adults, interactions with peers, and play.

For cognitive development, adult interactions involving conversation and intentional teaching are important. Intentional teaching requires a rich learning environment as described previously to provide opportunities for cognitive development (Epstein, 2007). In addition, teachers should have a warm, caring, and positive relationship with the students in their classes (Pianta, Belsky, Vandergrift, Houts & Morrison, 2008). These components provide the necessary support for young children's learning, but are not enough to promote their cognitive development and learning. For this to take place, teachers also need to provide interactions with children that are coherent, are related to children's prior knowledge, are focused on identifiable concepts and children's understanding, and have clearly articulated goals (Espinosa, 2009). In these interactions, teachers should alter activities according to children's interests and abilities, while at the same time promoting higher level thinking in children.

Both children and teachers should be active in the processes that lead to children's learning and development (Burns, 2009). In many ways, intentional teaching reflects earlier work on effective teaching strategies proposed by those studying scaffolded teaching (Wood, 1980, 1998) and mediated teaching (Feuerstein, Klein, & Tannenbaum, 1991; Karpov & Haywood, 1998).

Play is an additional area that promotes children's cognitive development and learning. Research has provided evidence of the strong connections between the quality of play during the preschool years and children's readiness for school instruction (Bowman et al., 2000). Further, research has directly linked play to children's ability to master such academic content as literacy and numeracy (Hanline, Milton, & Phelps, 2008).

A supportive context for cognitive development to occur is essential as stimulation from the environment changes the very physiology of the brain, interlocking nature and nurture (Shonkoff & Phillips, 2000). For constructive play that enhances cognitive development, materials should be set up in a manner that promotes a specific goal or problem to explore in the play. Multiple types of materials with which children can explore cognitive concepts are needed, including materials for sorting, classifying, looking at part/ whole relationships, determining equivalences, experimenting with real-life number problems, making predictions and comparisons, and seeing the impact of such things as gravity. Blocks are an excellent material to use for constructive play. The theme of block play can vary tremendously, but throughout the whole process, cognitive development and learning should be actively promoted.

To engage in this type of constructive play, children need time. To construct with materials and explore their properties requires a long period of supportive time with the necessary objects—at least 45 minutes. This long period of time allows the children to complete their structure and play with it without worrying about cleaning up or rushing.

Many young children are intrigued with the function and characteristics of trains and train tracks and learn math concepts through this play.

❊ ❊ ❊ Section Summary ❊ ❊ ❊

Cognitive development and learning is supported in the preschool years in rich learning centers that provide ample opportunities for play and conversation between adults and children and among peers. Learning centers should be well planned and include many manipulative materials geared toward teaching features of cognition.

Assessing Cognition

When professionals think about assessment of cognitive development, psychological assessment of cognitive functioning often comes to mind (Snow & Van Hemel, 2008). In this current framework, teachers should focus on assessing whether they are providing instructional activities for young children, adapting curricula to meet individual children's learning needs, and monitoring if children are making progress (Copple & Bredekamp, 2009).

It may be helpful to consult observational instruments developed to assess the ECE environment, such as the Early Childhood Environment Rating Scale (ECERS; Harms, Clifford, & Cryer, 2005) and the Early Childhood Classroom Observation Measure (ECCOM; Stipek & Byler, 2004), to focus on teacher practices and constructivist, child-centered practices. For cognitive development, the criteria for math/number and nature/science environments on the ECERS are indicators of whether opportunities for growth are being provided (see Figure 7.2). In a similar manner, a particular subject area can be evaluated as related to cognitive development. In Figure 7.3, using the example of math instruction, the ECCOM can assess whether teachers actively guide and support children's learning efforts in a manner that promotes shared responsibility for understanding the concepts being learned.

Adapting Curriculum and Monitoring Progress

Criterion-referenced or curriculum-based assessments are used to meet individual children's learning needs and monitor their progress. Children are observed, asked

Inadequate 1	2	Minimal 3	4	Good 5	6	Excellent 7
25. Nature/science						
1.1 No games, materials, or activities for nature/science accessible.		3.1 Some developmentally appropriate games, materials, or activities from two nature/science categories accessible. 3.2 Materials accessible daily. 3.3 Children encouraged to bring in natural things to share with others or add to collections (Ex. bring fall leaves in from playground; bring in pet).		5.1 Many developmentally appropriate games, materials, and activities from three categories accessible. 5.2 Materials are accessible for a substantial portion of the day. 5.3 Nature/science materials are well organized and in good condition (Ex. collections stored in separate containers; animals' cages clean). 5.4 Everyday events used as a basis for learning about nature/science (Ex. talking about the weather, observing insects or birds, discussing the change of seasons, blowing bubbles or flying kites on a windy day, watching snow melt and freeze).		7.1 Nature/science activities requiring more input from staff are offered at least once every 2 weeks (Ex. cooking, simple experiments like measuring rainfall, field trips.) 7.2 Books, pictures, and/or audio/visual materials used to add information and extend children's hands-on experiences.
26. Math/number						
1.1 No math/number materials accessible. 1.2 Math/number taught primarily through rote counting or worksheets.		3.1 Some developmentally appropriate math/number materials accessible. 3.2 Materials accessible daily.		5.1 Many developmentally appropriate materials of various types accessible (Ex. materials for counting, measuring, learning shape and size). 5.2 Materials are accessible for a substantial portion of the day. 5.3 Materials are well organized and in good condition (Ex. sorted by type, all pieces needed for games stored together). 5.4 Daily activities used to promote math/number learning (Ex. setting table, counting while climbing steps, using timers to take turns).		7.1 Math/number activities requiring more input from staff are offered at least every 2 weeks (Ex. making a chart to compare children's height, counting and recording number of birds at bird feeder). 7.2 Materials are rotated to maintain interest (Ex. teddy bear counters replaced by dinosaur counters, objects to weigh).

Figure 7.2. Example items from the Early Childhood Environment Rating Scale in the cognitive domain. (Reprinted by permission of the Publisher. From Thelma Harms, Richard M. Clifford, and Debby Cryer, *Early Childhood Environment Rating Scale, Revised Edition*, New York: Teachers College Press. Copyright © 2005 by Thelma Harms, Richard M. Clifford, & Debby Cryer. All rights reserved.)

Math instruction emphasizes developing understanding

Teacher emphasizes mathematical processes and models appropriate strategies for solving problems.
> *Examples: Asks children to show different strategies to solve the same problems or there is evidence of children using different strategies*

Teacher encourages children to use manipulatives to solve or check math problems or children are seen using manipulatives.
> *Example: Counters, fingers*

Teacher engages children in mathematical conversations.
> *Example: Asks children to explain their strategies, propose alternative strategies, and build on each other's comments*

Teacher integrates math into other instructional areas as well as having a specified math time.
> *Examples: Children use paper patterns to make quilt squares after reading story about quilts; children sort and graph fall leaves; children count stairs as they climb them*

Teacher provides children with authentic math activities.
> *Example: Counting number of children present during attendance; dividing food into equal parts for snack*

Teacher may use rote counting activities, but their use is balanced with more conceptual activities as described above.

Figure 7.3.   Example items from the Early Childhood Classroom Observation Measure in the cognitive domain. (From Stipek, D., & Byler, P. [2004]. The Early Childhood Classroom Observation Measure. *Early Childhood Research Quarterly, 19*[3], 375–397; adapted by permission.)

questions, and have their work collected and photographed. For cognitive development, the focus can be on an assessment system enclosed within a curriculum model, such as the mathematics-related assessments associated with the *Tools of the Mind* curriculum (Leong, Bodrova, & Hensen, 2007) or the Teaching Strategies GOLD Objectives for Development & Learning assessment tool that is used across curriculum models.

The *Tools of the Mind* curriculum includes multiple areas of cognitive development and learning. When using *Tools of the Mind,* teachers have multiple opportunities to address areas such as math across circle time (e.g., graphing weather, attendance), small group (e.g., student's performance when given help), and progress throughout the year in the content areas of number and operation, geometry and spatial, measurement, pattern/algebra, and displaying and analyzing data.

Teaching Strategies GOLD Objectives for Development & Learning (Heroman, Burts, Berke, & Bickart, 2010) is an assessment tool that can be used across curriculum models as it provides a comprehensive means of monitoring children's development as well as academic progress. Teachers document and observe children's development to help adapt curriculum and provide differentiated instruction and support. Figure 7.4 provides a few example areas in which children are assessed for cognitive development with Teaching Strategies GOLD tool. In the examples, the green band refers to expectations for children in a preschool 3 class, and the blue band refers to expectations for children in a pre-K 4 class. Please refer to the full assessment document for more information.

Objective 13 Uses classification skills

Not Yet	1	2	3	4	5	6	7	8	9
		Matches similar objects • Puts one sock with another sock • Gathers all the vehicles from a shelf • Picks out and eats only the animal crackers • Puts only blue pegs in pegboard; leaves red and yellow pegs to the side		**Places objects in two or more groups based on differences in a single characteristic, e.g., color, size, or shape** • Puts all the red beads together and all the blue beads together • Pulls out all the trucks from the vehicle bin • Identifies fabric pieces as being scratchy or soft • Puts pictures into piles of babies, older children, and grown-ups		**Groups objects by one characteristic; then regroups them using a different characteristic and indicates the reason** • Says, "These buttons are blue, and these are red"; then resorts buttons into big and little • Points to groups of animals and says, "These are zoo animals and these are farm animals"; then sorts the zoo animals into those with stripes and those without stripes		**Groups objects by more than one characteristic at the same time; switches sorting rules when asked, and explains the reasons** • Organizes a sticker collection into groups and subgroups and explains why and how; then creates a new grouping when the teacher makes a suggestion • Creates four piles of shapes: big red triangles, small red triangles, big blue triangles, small blue triangles. Switches when asked to form two groups of all the big and small triangles	

Figure 7.4. Example items from the Teaching Strategies GOLD® tool in the cognitive domain. (From Heroman, C., Burts, D.C., Berke, K., & Bickart, T. [2010]. *Teaching Strategies GOLD® Objectives for Development & Learning: Birth Through Kindergarten.* Washington, DC: Teaching Strategies; adapted by permission. *Key to colors in Teaching Strategies GOLD:* red, birth to 1 year; orange, 1 to 2 years; yellow, 2 to 3 years; green, preschool 3 class; blue, pre-K 4 class; purple, kindergarten.)

✼ ✼ ✼ Section Summary ✼ ✼ ✼

This section discussed assessments that teachers use to determine the quality of the cognitive learning experiences they provide in their classrooms. Examples from several of these measures were described, but others are available. Teachers can use these instruments to assess whether they are providing young learners with the opportunities to develop and learn in areas related to cognition. In addition, teachers need to know the measures used to determine whether they are adapting curricula to meet individual children's learning needs, as well as monitor whether children are making progress (Copple & Bredekamp, 2009). Several examples of measures that are relevant to cognitive development and learning were provided.

KEY CONCEPTS

- Theory and research about cognitive development have an impact on ECE teacher practice.

- Constructivist theory highlights the importance of children constructing their own knowledge.

- Narrative construction of reality theory highlights the importance of culture and the relationship between learning and social experiences.

- Social constructivist theory is also central in the discussion of cognitive development, highlighting the role of the social and cultural factors on development.

- Dynamic skills perspective focuses on how diverse pathways of development can be addressed, whereas other research has investigated physiological brain development.

- Crucial to understanding cognitive learning and development is that there is not one theory that is absolute truth.

- Teachers need to understand features of cognitive development in order to provide appropriate ECE. Features specific to cognitive development and learning include making sets, patterns, and groupings, and using these and seriation to measure attributes of objects. Concepts related to numeracy, time, and space are learned in this time period. In specific cases such as numeracy, the symbolic representation (number) is learned in terms of its corresponding concept.

- Learning and academic centers provide ample opportunities for cognitive development, especially when they encourage opportunities for play and conversation between adults and children and among peers. Learning centers should be well planned and include many manipulative materials geared toward teaching features of cognition (e.g., beads of different colors and shapes to make necklaces with interesting patterns).

(continued)

KEY CONCEPTS *(continued)*

- Play that is structured to include features of cognitive development does not only include manipulatives but also includes using materials in other play areas geared toward addressing cognitive development (e.g., having grocery store items of different sizes in the dramatic play area or ice cubes in the water play area).

- Throughout the day the teacher's extended conversations with children provide a scaffold to promote clearer understanding of the various features of cognitive development, for example, by highlighting the patterns seen in setting up the table for lunch or how the lunch items (e.g., napkins, forks, plates) are stored in categories.

- Teachers should use assessments that measure the quality of the education in the area of cognitive development. The goal is to be sure that high-quality ECE learning opportunities are available in this specific area of children's development and learning.

- Ongoing classroom assessments provide teachers with information necessary to reflect on and adapt cognitive curriculum to be responsive to each individual child's needs.

- Teachers should constantly reflect on their education and care of children in the area of cognitive development and understand how this area of development has an impact on all other areas of development—approaches to learning, social and emotional development, language development, and physical development.

Integration of Information

You just read the chapter on cognitive development and learning, which introduced different areas of development and associated ECE practices. As is the case in all areas of development, the information included in this chapter overlaps with all other areas of development—approaches to learning, social and emotional development, language development, and physical and motor development. What do you think? Does the importance of cognitive development and learning seem important for early childhood educators to be familiar with? Do you think you will enjoy teaching young children as they develop in this area?

Self-Reflective Guide

This self-reflective guide will help you assess whether you learned the information in this chapter. It also provides an opportunity to identify areas in which you want or need more information. Are there some new ideas learned that will affect your immediate practice with children?

1. Reflect on the theories presented to account for young children's cognitive development and learning—constructivist theory, narrative construction of reality, dynamic skills perspective, and brain development. Are there aspects of these theories that align with your observations of young children's learning? Does a particular theory resonate with you? Make a few notes.

2. Recognize the features of cognitive development and learning. Have you seen young children use these? List two approaches to learning that you think are extremely important for young children to learn and why.

3. Identify how cognitive development and learning can be addressed across different learning centers and academic areas. List one center and one academic area that are fruitful contexts for enhancing cognitive development. Elaborate on why these are important contexts.

4. Understand how children interact with teachers and peers as they develop cognition and learning. Describe a type of interaction that you want to develop as an ECE teacher. Elaborate on why this type of interaction is important.

5. Reflect on how play affects cognitive development and learning. Elaborate on why play is important in children's learning and development in this area.

6. Describe how teachers can assess whether they are providing quality opportunities for young children to develop and learn in the cognitive area.

7. Determine how you would assess young children's cognitive development and learning so that you are able to adapt your curriculum based on findings and also monitor the progress of your students. Identify a child with a disability (note the specific disability) and describe how such assessment information could help you adapt your instruction to meet this child's needs.

8. Reflect on cognitive development and learning and how this area of development relates to others discussed in this book—approaches to learning, social and emotional development, using and understanding language, and physical and motor development.

9. Identify other information learned that can have an immediate impact on your current practice if you are a practicing teacher or caregiver at this time.

10. List areas you need to explore further. Who can help you learn about your concerns?

Helpful Web Sites

HighScope Math

> www.highscope.org/Content.asp?ContentId=293
> This section of the HighScope site on math and science provides an overview of concepts that apply to a variety of curriculum models.

Museum of Science, Boston

> www.mos.org/discoverycenter/livinglab/mlc/list
> This section of the Museum of Science, Boston site provides information and activities on math and cognition.

National Council of Teachers of Mathematics

> www.nctm.org/resources/default.aspx?id=230
> This site provides lessons, research, and articles on cognitive processes.

PBS Teachers PreK Math Resources

> www.pbs.org/teachers/classroom/prek/math/resources
> This Public Broadcasting Service site provides math resources for prekindergarten teachers and includes information on creating inquiry-based lessons.

ScienceStart!

> www.rochester.edu/warner/ScienceStart
> This site provides an overview of the ScienceStart! preschool science program, as well as information about using science in preschool classrooms across different curriculum models.

Smithsonian Education

> http://smithsonianeducation.org/educators/lesson_plans/science_technology.html
> This Smithsonian Institute site for educators provides important discussions and professional development activities, including items addressing prekindergarten.

References

Bandura, A. (1977). *Social learning theory.* Englewood Cliffs, NJ: Prentice Hall.

Berk, L.E., & Winsler, A. (1995). *Scaffolding children's learning: Vygotsky and early childhood education.* Washington, DC: National Association for the Education of Young Children.

Bowman, B.T., Donovan, M.S., & Burns, M.S. (2000). *Eager to learn: Educating our preschoolers.* Washington, DC: National Academies Press.

Bronfenbrenner, U. (1989). Ecological systems theory. *Annals of Child Development, 6,* 185–246.

Bruner, J. (1956). *A study of thinking.* New York: Wiley.

Bruner, J. (1996). *The culture of education.* Cambridge, MA: Harvard University Press.

Burns, M.S. (2009). Both/and thinking in early childhood education. *Focus on Pre-K&K, 22*(1), 1–3.

Copley, J.V. (2009). *The young child and mathematics* (2nd ed.). Washington, DC: National Association for the Education of Young Children.

Copple, C., & Bredekamp, S. (2009). *Developmentally appropriate practice in early childhood programs serving children from birth through age 8.* Washington, DC: National Association for the Education of Young Children.

Epstein, J.L. (2007). Connections count. Improving family and community involvement in secondary schools. *Principle Leadership, 8*(2), 16–22.

Espinosa, L. (2009). *Getting it right for young children from diverse backgrounds: Applying research to improve practice.* Upper Saddle River, NJ: Pearson.

Feuerstein, R.F., Klein, P.S., & Tannenbaum, A.J. (1991). *Mediated learning experience (MLE): Theoretical, psychosocial, and learning implications.* London: Freund.

Fischer, K.W. (2009). Mind, brain, and education: Building a scientific groundwork for learning and teaching. *Mind, Brain, and Education, 3,* 2–15.

Gesell, A. (1940). *The first five years of life: A guide to the study of the preschool child, from the Yale Clinic of Child Development, parts 1–3.* New York: Harper & Brothers.

Ginsburg, P.H., & Amit, M. (2008). What is teaching mathematics to young children? A theoretical and case study. *Journal of Applied Developmental Psychology, 29,* 274–285.

Hanline, M., Milton, S., & Phelps, P. (2008). A longitudinal study exploring the representational levels of three aspects of preschool sociodramatic play and early academic skills. *Journal of Research in Childhood Education, 23*(1), 19–29.

Harms, T., Clifford, R., & Cryer, D. (2005). *Early Childhood Environment Rating Scale* (Rev. Ed.). New York: Teachers College Press.

Heroman, C., Burts, D.C., Berke, K., & Bickart, T. (2010). *Teaching Strategies GOLD®: Objectives for Development & Learning: Birth Through Kindergarten.* Washington, DC: Teaching Strategies.

Hohmann, M., Weikart, D.P., & Epstein, A.S. (2008). *Educating young children: Active learning practices for preschool and child care programs* (3rd ed.). Ypsilanti, MI: HighScope.

Hyson, M. (2008). *Enthusiastic and engaged learners: Approaches to learning in the early childhood classroom.* New York: Teachers College Press.

Karpov, Y.V., & Haywood, H.C. (1998). Two ways to elaborate Vygotsky's concept of mediation: Implications for instruction. *American Psychologist, 53*(1), 27–36.

Kohlberg, L., Yaeger, J., & Hjertholm, E. (1999). Private speech: four studies and a review of theories. In P. Lloyd & C. Fernyhough (Eds.), *Lev Vygotsky: Critical assessments* (Vol. 2; pp. 185–225). New York: Routledge.

Leong, D.J., Bodrova, E., & Hensen, R. (2007). *Tools of the Mind curriculum project preschool manual* (4th ed.). Denver, CO: Center for Improving Early Learning, Metropolitan State College of Denver.

Nelson, C.A., & Bloom, F.E. (1997). Child development and neuroscience. *Child Development, 68*(5), 970–987.

Piaget, J. (1977). *The development of thought: Equilibration of cognitive structure.* New York: Viking.

Pianta, R.C., Belsky, J., Vandergrift, N., Houts, R., & Morrison, F.J. (2008). Classroom effects on children's achievement trajectories in elementary school. *American Educational Research Journal, 45*(2), 365–397.

Shonkoff, J.P., & Phillips, D.A. (Eds.). (2000). *From neurons to neighborhoods: The science of early childhood development.* Washington, DC: National Academies Press.

Siegler, R., DeLoache, J., & Eisenberg, N. (2003). *How children develop.* New York: Worth.

Snow, C.E., & Van Hemel, S.B. (2008). *Early childhood assessment: Why, what, and how.* Washington, DC: National Academies Press.

Stipek, D., & Byler, P. (2004). The Early Childhood Classroom Observation Measure. *Early Childhood Research Quarterly, 19*(3), 375–397.

U.S. Department of Health and Human Services. (2000). *Head Start child outcomes framework.* Washington, DC: Author.

Vygotsky, L.S. (1978). In M. Cole, V. John-Steiner, S. Scribner, & E. Souberman (Eds.), *Mind in society: The development of high psychological processes.* Cambridge, MA: Harvard University Press.

Vygotsky, L.S. (1986). In A. Kozulin (Ed.), *Thought and language* (Rev. ed.). Cambridge: The MIT Press.

Wood, D. (1980). Teaching the young child: Some relationships between social interaction, language, and thought. In D.R. Olson (Ed.), *The social foundation of language and thought* (pp. 259–275). New York: Norton.

Wood, D. (1998). Aspects of teaching and learning. In M. Woodhead, D. Faulkner, & K. Littleton (Eds.), *Cultural worlds of early childhood* (pp. 157–177). New York: Taylor & Francis.

Language Development

with Robert A. Stechuk

8

Learning Objectives

1. Understand the theories presented to account for young children's language development—ecological theory, social constructivist theory, verbal behavior theory

2. Recognize the features of young children's language development

3. Reflect on the development of multiple languages with young children

4. Identify how language development can be addressed across different learning centers and academic areas

5. Understand how children interact with teachers and peers as they develop effective language

6. Recognize how play affects language development

7. Describe how a teacher can assess whether he or she is providing quality opportunities for young children to learn effective language development

8. Understand how teachers can assess young children's language development so that they can adapt curricula and monitor the progress of their students

9. Understand how language development relates to other ideas discussed in this book—approaches to learning, social and emotional development, cognitive development and learning, and physical and motor development

How do 3- to 5-year-old children understand and use language? What are the parts of the language system? Why do children vary in the ways they use language? Should learning centers be set up in a special way so that children are more likely to talk with each other? How do culture, language, family income level, and cognitive ability affect young children's language development? Can preschool children learn English and a second language at the same time? What is the role of family, community, country, and culture? How do preschoolers develop such a sophisticated language system? There is a child in the class who does not talk; does that mean she has autism? How do play and children's conversations with adults and peers affect language development? How do we assess language and figure out language instruction?

These are the types of questions addressed in this chapter on preschool children's language use and development. The chapter begins by addressing different theorists, especially those whose ideas affect contemporary language development in early childhood education (ECE) practice. Next, we discuss communication and language systems and children's language development, including how its growth is supported through play, conversations, and studies in literacy, numeracy, science, social studies, and the creative arts. We further review ways teachers can assess the opportunities they are providing for language development and student language performance. Variation in language development is addressed throughout the chapter, as are individual and group factors that produce variation in children's language trajectories.

Theoretical Accounts: Using and Understanding Language

The theoretical accounts of cognitive development presented in this section were chosen in light of current ECE practices. The theoretical accounts presented in Chapters 5–7 also are relevant in this discussion of cognitive development in the following ways:

- Social learning theory (Bandura, 1977): Children learn through imitation of behavior (in this case, language) modeled by adults and peers.

- Constructivist theory (Piaget, 1977): Cognitive development precedes language development; therefore, language development only reflects cognitive development.

- Narrative construction of reality theory (Bruner, 1996): Culture affects story construction.

- Dynamic systems perspective (Fisher, 2009): There are diverse pathways of language development.

- Information processing theories: Processes of attention and memory relate to information input, elaboration, and output (Atkinson & Shiffrin, 1968).

- Critical theories: Language development and use can be viewed in relation to power (Dahlberg & Moss, 1999; Harry & Klinger, 2006; Nieto, 2010).

Two theories that were presented previously—ecological theory and social constructivist theory—are included in this chapter, with details that are particularly relevant to language learning and development. The section concludes with an additional theory that is currently used in ECE—verbal behavior theory.

Ecological Theory

Ecological theory was introduced in Chapter 6. Ecological theory (Bronfenbrenner & Morris, 1998) is helpful when considering the complexity of young children's language use, development, and variability. A wide variety of current and historical interconnected forces (e.g., cultural, social, economic, political) define this variability. The theory is central to language development because it affects the following aspects of children's development:

- Microsystems: the language of the child's family and friends and peers, along with the language of individuals from the child's childcare center, schools, and neighborhood

- Mesosystems: linkages between microsystems, such as consistency of language between family and individuals at the child's school or neighborhood advocates available for parents who speak a language different than individuals at the child's school

- Exosystems: issues outside of the child's immediate environmental context that are highly involved in child success in school and life, such as when a parent loses a job and is no longer able to afford the child's weekend language program

- Macrosystems: broader values of society, such as when the child's home language is devalued in the current society

- Chronosystems: sociohistorical conditions of children and families over a long time period, such as the perception of African American dialect given the history of race relations in the United States

Social Constructivist Theory

Social constructivist theory examines the processes involved in the transmission of language and thought from the social environment. It includes the potential for language to lead development in other areas, such as cognitive development and approaches to learning. Language use could propel development by leading the child to new insights and realizations.

According to Vygotsky (1978, 1986), language and thought originate independently of each other. During this phase, infants and toddlers use language that is not rooted in cognitive processes; they also think, but they think in ways that are not bound by language. At approximately 2 years of age, however, the development of language and thought merges. From this point forward, language and thinking are interconnected. Vygotsky (1986) used the term *reciprocal* to describe the relationship following the merger: Within the child's overall development, language and cognition are combined into a unitary system, while the development of one inevitably influences the development of the other.

In his analysis, Vygotsky (1978) believed that language plays a profound role in young children's development. Some of his observations included that language and thought combine to assist children in solving problems, as well as enabling them to plan how to carry out an activity. Language also gives children a greater potential to engage in action. Language exercises a controlling mechanism on children's behavior. As a child uses language to carry out an activity, the language serves to regulate the child's actions and to control impulses.

Language has a dynamic relationship with a child's perceptions, sensory-motor functioning, and attention. Language not only influences the development of each individually but also affects the relationships between these systems. For example, if you look at a classroom, your visual perception is integrated because you take in the whole of your visual field. However, if you describe a classroom, you need to arrange your description sequentially by linking individual words within a sentence or expanding this to link several sentences together. For Vygotsky (1978), visual perception is integral while language is essentially analytical. As children develop the capacity to speak, their perception of reality undergoes a transformation. With the ability to label objects, children are able to see the world as a place of sense and meaning. In turn, this transformation of perception through language also gives rise to new forms of sensory-motor functioning; children are able to participate in activities that are meaningful and purposeful rather than random. In terms of attention, a child's earliest attention is directed toward objects; however, the speaking child is the director of his or her own attention. That is, the child

> Can view changes in his immediate situation from the point of view of past activities, and he can act in the present from the point of view of the future"; thus, children's attention is no longer limited to one level of consciousness, but can take on "a whole series of potential fields. (Vygotsky, 1978, p. 36)

Children are also able to use language to gain information from adults. When faced with a problem or task that they cannot solve or perform, a child will often turn to an adult to describe the problem, ask for assistance, or seek additional information. Children's language undergoes a significant shift in its relationship to the child's actions. Whereas at an early time "language accompanies the child's actions," at a later time, "it comes to precede action" (Vygotsky, 1978, p. 28). This transition organizes a child's thoughts and behaviors, allowing the child to develop higher levels of functioning.

Verbal Behavior Theory

This section transitions to behavioral theory and how it accounts for the development and use of language. Verbal behavior theory (Skinner, 1957) and similar approaches are currently being implemented in ECE and care, especially in programs that include children with disabilities. The theory posits that language is based on children's current environmental **contingencies**, those of the past, and heredity/biology. Emphasis, however, is on environmental contingencies: Success occurs when learning is errorless because it is based on small enough steps for each individual child, directions are clear and repeated as needed, and reinforcement for accurate performance is immediate and positive.

contingencies
Dependence on a future event or condition.

Operant-based teaching of language development incorporates the following features, including both receptive and expressive language, in ECE and care (McCauley & Fey, 2006):

- Imitation: Another person asks the child to say a particular word or phrase; the child repeats it and receives positive reinforcement.

- Interverbal: Another person asks the child a question; the child answers that question and receives positive reinforcement.

- Initiation: The child directly makes an initiation to another person and receives positive reinforcement.

The language learner simultaneously uses features of the environment (tact) and of the listeners (audience) as nonverbal stimuli that affect verbal behavior. A **tact** is a label or vocabulary (Carbone et al., 2006). For example, if a child sees a fire truck pulling out of the station and says, "fire truck," then *fire truck* is the tact. Although verbal behavior theory and total communication (i.e., using manual signs with the corresponding spoken language) has been shown to increase verbal behavior at a higher rate than use of verbal behavior alone among children with

tact
A term in verbal behavioral theory for a feature of the environment.

developmental disabilities or autism spectrum disorders, it is devalued and misunderstood in ECE (Nordquist, Twardosz, & Higgins, 2007)—possibly because professionals working from different perspectives feel that use of one approach might undermine another approach, or because theorists often do not focus on the integration of various approaches.

✳ ✳ ✳ Section Summary ✳ ✳ ✳

Language development and learning has been studied from a number of different perspectives. The theories presented in this section were chosen in light of current ECE practices. Many theoretical accounts presented in Chapters 5–7 also are important in a discussion of language development. Social learning theory, constructivist theory, narrative construction of reality theory, dynamic systems perspective, information processing theories, and critical theories all contribute to the understanding of language learning and use. Further elaborated in this section were ecological theory and social constructivist theory. Ecological theory helps tremendously in the understanding of the multiple systems affecting language development, such as variations in language use and culture, as well as society's judgment of different variations related to language use and development. Social constructivist theory has a special role in understanding language development, particularly as it relates to approaches to learning and cognitive development. In addition, we introduced a theory of language use and understanding—verbal behavior theory—and its important empirical basis (and underuse) in ECE programs.

Crucial to language use and understanding is recognizing that there is not one theory that is absolute truth. All theoretical perspectives are in the process of refinement, specification, and growth. Finally, although we can study different areas of development, it is important to acknowledge that children do not function in an exclusive fashion; for example, young children's social and emotional development affects their language development, and vice versa.

Features of Language Development

Various features of language development are discussed in this section, including communication, **shared language systems**, individual differences in language development, language subsystems, and **metalinguistics**.

Communication

Culture and home language play a pivotal role in the child's developing communication abilities. Children develop their sense of language first in their home and cultural circles; these initial experiences help children learn and begin to understand how language is used in their social worlds. Scientists who study human communication divide it into two types of systems: individual and shared (see Figure 8.1).

Individual, exclusive communication systems have a foundation in the individual and extend to a limited number of others in a **social network**. This system uses facial, body, and natural expressions that are usually not comprehended beyond small familial circles or some friends. For example, a mother often knows

shared language systems
Shared systems of communication across numbers of people.

metalinguistics
Understanding about the form of language aside from its use and meaning (e.g., how young children pick out and enjoy rhyming).

social network
The set of contacts with which a person interacts on a regular basis.

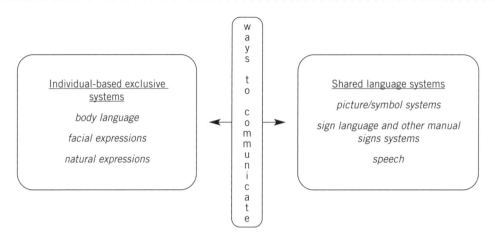

Figure 8.1. Communication systems.

that a particular gesture has a specific meaning for her daughter, although that gesture might not have the same meaning for the community at large:

> My 3-year-old daughter often makes a certain look with her eyes—making them wide, looking directly at me—when she wants her glass refilled with whatever she is drinking. She knows how to ask for a refill, but sometimes for a variety of reasons she is unwilling or unable to do so. Some children know how to sign to ask for more. This particular look certainly works with me. It does not work with her teacher, however, because they do not share this particular means of communication. In this case, my daughter needs to use her words to ask for a refill or use the sign in order to communicate more.

Speech and American Sign Language (ASL) are examples of shared language systems. A shared language system is one that is experienced across people. People communicate in many ways—through body language, facial expressions, natural expressions, picture systems, sign language, tone, intonation, and speech, just to name a few. However, not all of these systems are based on a shared language system. Even though body language, facial expressions, and natural expressions are forms of communication, they are not language systems. Rather, they are individually based systems that are heavily influenced by social and cultural norms.

Sign language is a shared form of communication.

In a preschool classroom, a young child will have to communicate fundamental needs with other adults and children through a shared language system rather than the more idiosyncratic system of expressions and body language. Early school education settings can stimulate language development if they incorporate the languages the children bring to school. The following section focuses on the features of a language system that lead to rich child language development during early schooling.

Shared Language Systems

Speech and hearing are the means by which the majority of preschool children use language. Speech is expressive language—that is, what the child is trying to convey, produce, or communicate with language. Hearing is receptive language—that is, what the child understands while listening to someone else communicate. Receptive language, also known as hearing and understanding, is in most cases achieved before expressive language (i.e., speaking). For example, a child can understand a parent's two-step command before being able to make a two-step command. Hence, receptivity develops greater complexity earlier than productivity for most children. Figure 8.2 shows very broad indicators of what type of language preschool children use. Know that a child might not meet these goals for many reasons, including being shy, learning a new language, or having a language related disability. In early childhood settings there are additional children who may not demonstrate their language abilities because of differences in cultural norms or language use at home.

All children—whether **monolingual**, bilingual, or multilingual—develop their languages as they engage in their social and physical worlds. Language use is directly influenced by culture. Culture is the ecosystem in which children develop; these ecosystems vary considerably. Considering language and culture in terms of an ecosystem is helpful in that there is often a geographical relationship between the types of vocabulary used and the social activities within the culture. For instance, young children learn the names of different types of snow in the Inuit language and culture in Alaska while preschoolers in Italy know the names of different types of pasta as they learn Italian (Tomasello & Mervis, 1994). Additionally, in

monolingual
An individual who uses and understands only one language.

Age group	Hearing and understanding	Talking
3–4 years	• Hears you when you call from another room • Hears television or radio at the same loudness level as other family members • Answers simple "who?" "what?" "where?" and "why?" questions	• Talks about activities at school or at friends' homes • People outside of the family usually understand child's speech • Uses a lot of sentences that have 4 or more words • Usually talks easily without repeating syllables or words
4–5 years	• Pays attention to a short story and answers simple questions about them • Hears and understands most of what is said at home and in school	• Uses sentences that give lots of details (e.g., "The biggest peach is mine") • Tells stories that stick to topic • Communicates easily with other children and adults • Says most sounds correctly except perhaps a few like *l, s, r, v, z, ch, sh, th* • Says rhyming words • Names some letters and numbers • Uses the same grammar as the rest of the family

Figure 8.2. Language skills for typically developing 3- to 5-year-olds. (Reprinted with permission from *How does your child hear and talk?* Available from the web site of the American Speech-Language-Hearing Association: http://www.asha.org/public/speech/development/01 .htm. All rights reserved.)

cultures in which young children are expected to demonstrate a high level of compliance to social rules, children learn to say *no* at an earlier age (Shatz, Grimm, Wilcox, & Niemeier-Wind, 1989).

The intricate relationship between cultural experiences and language development demonstrates the need for ECE professionals to validate multilingual realities for all children. Early childhood dual-language schooling that balances two languages and cultures needs to develop a new ecosystem across a different geo-ecological space (King & Fogle, 2006). Learning two or more languages during the preschool years does not lead to delay in language development (Paradis, Genesee, & Crago, 2011; Petitto & Holowka, 2002) and can lead to increased development of specific areas of cognition. For example, bilingual children have been shown to have a greater awareness of aspects of the language systems, such as print concepts or phonological awareness, than monolingual children (Bialystok, 2001). Bilingual and multilingual children may switch between two or more languages during a bilingual conversation, but this does not mean that they have language confusion.

Young children move between language and dialects easily, switching code. A child's ability to move between home and school language demonstrates the process of internalizing language, thereby increasing cognition. Multilingual children need to be supported and encouraged to switch between languages. Heath (1983) helped to inform teachers about academic language, or the language of school, and how a disconnect between home and school language forms might affect students' educational experiences. Her research showed how deeply imbedded children's language development is in their cultural worlds and how different development, language style, and interests occur in different communities.

Ballenger (1999) provided a similar description of language development and its roots in family and cultural experiences. Ballenger described her experiences as a teacher with children and families of Haitian backgrounds whose home language was Haitian Creole. Although she knew the language, she did not understand the Haitian Creole culture and realized that knowing the home language of children is not enough. She demonstrated the importance of developing relationships and shared understanding with families and children, especially when the family experiences might differ from the teacher's experiences.

Generally, speech is the means for language output and hearing for language input. However, this is not entirely true for deaf children. Deaf children often communicate using ASL and other manual signs systems such as cued speech, although some deaf children have cochlear implants and use oral language (speech and hearing). When deafness is identified during infancy, manual language can be taught in the same ways that oral language would be taught to a hearing infant (Goldin-Meadow & Morford, 1985; Goldin-Meadow, Mylander, & Butcher, 1995).

augmentative and alternative communication (AAC) systems
Communication systems that allow individuals without oral fluency to communicate (e.g., gestures, pictures, writing, communication boards).

AAC devices provide a shared form of communication.

Picture and symbol systems are additional means by which preschool children communicate. One example is the Picture Exchange Communication System (Pyramid Educational Consultants; see Figure 8.3), an **augmentative and alternative communication (AAC) system** that uses pictures or symbols as a way to communicate. These systems are often used if a child has a severe speech or language disability that might be caused by physical, sensory, or intellectual disability, including autism spectrum disorders. These systems can be com-

Figure 8.3.   Sample pictures from the Picture Exchange Communication System (Pics for PECS images are used with permission from Pyramid Educational Consultants, Inc., www.pecs.com; all rights reserved.)

bined with electronic voice output systems to increase the complexity and speed of communication (Beukelman & Mirenda, 2005; Calculator, 2007). These pictures can also be used to help support children learning English in school. The pictures can provide a shared form of communication that allows for speakers of other languages to be part of the classroom community no matter what language they speak.

Individual Differences in Language Development

Individual children demonstrate great variation in their language development. Temperament, such as being introverted or extroverted, influences risks that children take in expressing language. Children with autism spectrum disorders often have bigger differences in their expressive and receptive languages, with expressive language being more delayed. On the other hand, children with developmental disabilities such as Down syndrome are delayed in both receptive and expressive language across all of the aspects of language (Berko-Gleason & Ratner, 2009; see Figure 8.4), including pragmatics, phonology, morphology, syntax, semantics, and vocabulary. The degree of cognitive delay is correlated with the extent of language delay: Children with severe cognitive delays generally have significant language delays, whereas those with mild cognitive delays generally have minor functional language delays. Children with specific language impairments have significant language delays, most often without cognitive delays. Children with other disabilities have impairments in a particular area; for example, children with cerebral palsy involving the oral muscular structures have difficulty with expressive oral phonology.

Language Subsystems

This section addresses how expressive and receptive language are described by linguists. There are three main aspects of the language system: language use, the form of language, and the content of language (Snow, Burns, & Griffin, 1998; Snow, Griffin, & Burns, 2005).

Pragmatics (see Figure 8.4) is knowing how (and sometimes when) to use language in different cultural and social contexts to achieve the desired goals of the speaker. In some cultures, by the age of 3 children will respond to both indirect requests (e.g., "It's time for your nap," "It's time to close the door") and direct requests (e.g., "Go to bed," "Close the door"). A child accustomed to both forms has the pragmatic knowledge that both messages mean the same thing.

Preschool children also learn how to talk differently with parents, siblings, grandparents, friends, and teachers, as well as how to talk to people in different places, such as home, school, or restaurants. They learn that social interactions vary according to the role of the speakers and the setting in which they are currently located.

Preschool children use language for many purposes: expressing their emotions, thoughts, and feelings; developing identity; gaining and conveying knowledge and information; telling stories; self-regulating; communicating wants and needs; utilizing and developing cognitive and thinking processes; and learning about their cultures and the rules of society (see Figure 8.5). Language development cannot be totally separated from cognitive, socioemotional, sociocultural, and motor development. For example, speech is dependent on motor development because the small muscles of the mouth must move to form words. Cognitive development and the development of memory affect the understanding of new words. Socioemotional development influences interactions with others, which is

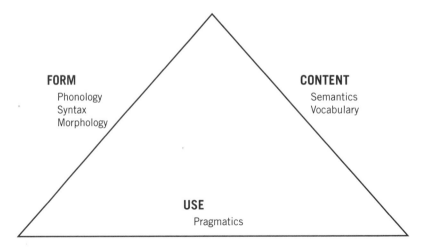

Figure 8.4.   Aspects of language.

Figure 8.5. Purposes for using language.

then influenced by sociocultural development. Sociocultural development is integral to pragmatic development—that is, how to use language in different contexts to achieve the goals of that use of language.

Two other aspects of the language system are form and content. Commonly identified aspects of the form of language are phonology, morphology, and syntax. *Phonology* refers to the language structures that relate to the sounds of language. Most sounds of any language are arbitrary and bear no relationship with the objects or conditions that they represent—that is, they are symbolic. The sounds used by a language are its phonemes. The source of sounds is air going through the vocal cords in the larynx (i.e., voice box). The lips, tongue, pharynx, nose, and lower jaw shape the sounds, giving each phoneme its distinct sound. Speech perception—the ability to perceive and process language differently from other sounds—is an ability that is present at birth.

Children's early attempts at words often sound different from adult pronunciations, which is normal. Usually by age 7, children have learned to produce the right sounds for the language they hear spoken around them (Berko-Gleason & Ratner, 2009). As children learn to talk, they learn to produce the right sounds, put them in sequences demanded by the language, and recognize variants of a phoneme and know they are the same phoneme (i.e., recognize accents).

Languages derive meanings by combining sounds within words and among words in a sentence. A haphazard arrangement of sounds, however, is not a language. For meaning, the series of sounds must be put and kept in the correct order. *Team* and *meat* use the same sounds in different orders and have different meanings. Languages have systematic ways of putting sounds together into recognizable words. A young child who speaks both Spanish and English, for example, may use the rules of Spanish when learning a new word even when speaking English (e.g., saying "yump" for *jump*).

Morphology refers to the ways words are formed (Berko-Gleason & Ratner, 2009). A morpheme is the smallest unit of meaning within a language. Consider the word *books*, for example. *Book* is a morpheme (unbound morpheme) and so is the letter *s* as used to denote a plural noun (bound morpheme), so the word *books* has two morphemes. Preschool children learn many aspects of morphemes at this age, including the use of past tense using *-ed*. During this learning process, preschool children often overgeneralize their new learning and apply it to words that do not directly follow the rule (e.g., "sleeped" for *slept*, "eated" for *ate*).

Syntax refers to the ways words are put together to form phrases, clauses, and sentences (Berko-Gleason & Ratner, 2009). Words must be arranged appropriately if they are to carry meaning. Usually there are several ways a language can arrange its words, with the different arrangements changing the meaning of the sentence (e.g., *The ball is red* conveys a different meaning than *Is the ball red?*). Syntax can differ from language to language. For instance, a child speaking Spanish would use the phrase *la pelota roja* (i.e., *the ball red*), whereas a child speaking English would use the phrase *the red ball*.

Phonology, morphology, and syntax are different aspects of the form of language. Each is an important feature for children to develop and understand at different levels of complexity as they move from birth and throughout their lives. There are major differences in these subsystems across languages. However, this does not mean that the students consciously know the different rules of language forms. Teachers should develop a fairly sophisticated understanding of the known mechanisms of phonology, morphology, and syntax and use of that knowledge so that the students develop expressive and receptive language abilities.

The final aspects of the language system presented in this section are semantics and vocabulary. *Semantics* is the study of meaning. Children learn to assign meaning both to words (lexical semantics) and to phrases and sentences (sentential semantics). Skills for knowing the meaning of words and the meaning of phrases are independent but interrelated. Children typically learn the meanings of words first and then progress to understanding sentences and longer discourse structures. Once again, it is helpful to know how different languages sort out meaning differently. In Hebrew, there are separate and distinct verbs for wearing a pair of socks, wearing a hat, and wearing a blouse. However, in English, there is one common verb—*to wear*.

Vocabulary is an important component for language development. The speed of vocabulary expansion is particularly fast during ages 3 through 5. Because of this speed, "researchers have not yet been able to make accurate calculations (especially about vocabulary comprehension), or work out any norms of spoken lexical frequency" (Crystal, 2005, p. 205). Children often know words in their social and language environments before adults are aware that the child knows the new words (Fenson et al., 1994). At this age, children typically learn nine new words per day and produce four new words per day. They typically understand 1,500 different words and can use 230 different words in any given hour, which is more than the usual total number of words that they know at age 2. By age 5, children know well over 4,000 words (Berko-Gleason & Ratner, 2009).

Children's vocabulary grows rapidly in size and also in complexity. Words are connected to concepts and are related to other words—often referred to as **semantic networks**. As vocabulary grows, finer distinctions are made to the best use of a particular word. There are a number of important studies of young children's vocabulary development, including the work of Hart and Risley (1995, 1999). They found that the number of different words (amount and variety of words) that parents use with their children between the ages of 1 and 2 years was an indicator of the size of child's vocabulary at age 3. Later on, children's school achievements in third grade—especially reading ability—were associated with their vocabulary size at age 3. It was very important that parents talked not just about their daily routines, but that they had additional discussion related to outside activities. In addition to the amount and variety of words used, it is also important for parents to be positive and supportive in tone and responsive to children's initiations (Hart & Risley, 1995, 1999).

semantic networks
A representation of the relationships between concepts, organized by the meaning of the concepts.

Metalinguistics

Metalinguistics refer to an expanded appreciation of the language and cognitive abilities of young children. The *meta-* construct attempts to make explicit a process that appears to be largely implicit: children's ability to attend to language forms rather than to meaning. Bialystok mentioned Cazden's work as "one of the first references" to the notion of metalinguistic awareness "as a unique construct" (2001, pp. 121–122):

> The ability to make language forms opaque and attend to them in and for themselves, is a special kind of language performance, one which makes special cognitive demands, and seems to be less easily and less universally acquired than the language performances of speaking and listening. (Cazden, 1974, p. 24)

Since Cazden's definition of the term, the metalinguistic construct has been investigated in the multiple lines of research that have included its role in and relationships to many other areas of children's development.

One aspect of metalinguistic development is **word awareness**. By understanding what a word is, children demonstrate that they have abstracted a linguistic concept from the language they use to communicate. Chaney (1992) believed that this ability does not suddenly appear, but instead increases gradually, from rather basic origins. Children must first understand that spoken language can be broken into sounds and syllables, and that words are "different sounds put together" (Chaney, 1992, p. 490). Chaney used 12 different measures to explore three major domains of metalinguistic abilities: phonological, word, and structural. A majority of 3-year-old children in the study were able to demonstrate an initial level of awareness of what a word is; a developmental trend that likely begins at 2 years. Chaney observed significant correlations among the three metalinguistic domains and between overall language skills and the domains as a whole.

word awareness
The ability to differentiate between words and understand their meaning.

A second aspect of metalinguistic development is *phonological awareness.* The term *phonological awareness* "refers to a general appreciation of the sounds of speech as distinct from meaning" (Snow et al., 1998, p. 51). A large and continuing body of studies identifies phonological awareness as a strong predictor for future reading achievement (Mathes, Torgesen, & Allor, 2001; Roth, Speece, & Cooper, 2002).

Children's everyday environments can be a source of much exposure to metalinguistic information. Ely, Gleason, MacGibbon, and Zaretsky (2001) observed 22 middle-income families of preschool children as they ate dinner. The researchers recorded and coded transcripts of these dinner conversations for the presence of terms reflecting metalinguistic abilities. The team found that family conversations contained numerous references to language forms and thus constituted a valuable means by which children could obtain, reflect upon, and experiment with observations of language forms.

❋ ❋ ❋ Section Summary ❋ ❋ ❋

Language is a shared communication system that includes oral (expressive and receptive) processes, as well as writing (expressive) and reading (receptive). Language is affected by cultural and individual differences. Language has complex subsystems including those identified as form (phonology, morphology, syntax), content (semantics and vocabulary), and use (pragmatics). Metalinguistic development addresses children's abilities to attend to different aspects of language in relation to its features rather than meaning per se.

Supporting Children's Effective and Diverse Language Development

This section presents information on ways that preschool children engage as language learners. All children, whether monolingual or multilingual, develop their language as they engage in their social and physical world. For all children, the same high-quality program described throughout this book is central. What differs is the need to address language use in ECE classrooms.

Language learning is promoted through interaction with adults and peers as presented in the theories and research described previously in this chapter. The physical setup of the language learning centers and materials included in them need to support language (see Chapter 4 for descriptions of the learning centers). Further, as an ECE professional, your beliefs about the level of talk allowable in learning centers has to be consistent with an environment that promotes language and your active role in addressing different aspects of language. Pragmatic aspects of language should be used as different centers afford different types of language use. Children learn concepts and vocabulary (semantic knowledge) across content areas. Through discussions, the forms of language, syntax, morphology, and phonology are heard, modeled, and expressed. The goal of this section is to describe how these aspects are put together with language development and with various curriculum content areas.

This section specifies activities that are integrated across creative arts, social studies, numeracy, science, and literacy using the model in Figure 8.6. However, note that these activities are only examples, provided as models; they are not necessarily the activities that you will be using, nor those that are the most important to include as opportunities for your young children's cognitive development. You will develop your own understanding of what activities to use and which centers to integrate as you get to know your individual children.

Creative Arts

Creative arts provide a rich context for language use. Consider having a puppet theater as part of the dramatic play area. Children can then use the information gleaned from their home, community, and classroom experiences to present a play.

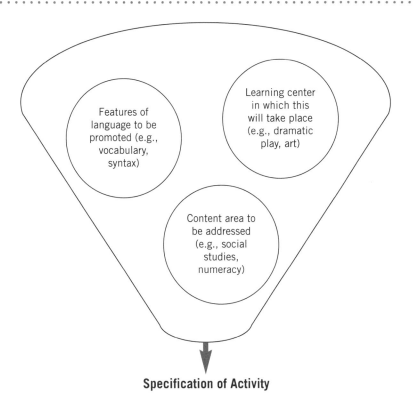

Specification of Activity

Figure 8.6. Contributors to specification of activity.

Certainly language will be used here; children can use whatever language with which they are comfortable communicating. The narrative will be developed and parts decided so that children at all language levels can be included in the activity. Teachers can take a part in the play and model specific syntactic features of language that might be a learning goal for a number of the children in the classroom. In regard to Figure 8.6, this activity highlights the creative arts as the academic content area, narrative and syntax as the features of language, and dramatic play as the learning center.

Social Studies

Social studies activities assist children in endless possibilities for developing and enhancing their broad understandings of their world, including their family, community, country, and other parts of the world where they have lived. They can begin to think about how their experiences are the same as and different from those of others. Suppose that children in this class are depicting the neighborhood in which the child care center is located and in which they all live. Each child should make a representation of their house. New vocabulary can be introduced as the parts of the houses and types of living situations are discussed. Teachers might even identify vocabulary that is not used as often in prekindergarten. For example, words such as *represent* and *concrete* can be used when pointing out that the gray construction paper represents the concrete walkway to a house. In regard to Figure 8.6, this activity highlights social studies as the academic content area, vocabulary as the feature of language, and the center for special projects as the learning center.

Numeracy

Opportunities to develop numeracy will lay the foundation for mathematics understanding. Young children working in the block center make many constructions that call for the concepts of *more* or *less,* especially when the use of those words is encouraged by the environment. For example, children can discuss *more* or *less* to negotiate how many blocks they are asking for when they request a peer "to get them some blocks off the shelf." If the children do not raise the concepts spontaneously, teachers can encourage them through an assortment of different interactions. For example, uses of *more* and *less* can take place when space for block play is being negotiated between two children (e.g., "Robin, are you asking Justin to get you *more* blocks?" or "Why do you need *more* blocks?"). These questions are just a part of the ongoing play. Also, a template can be used that would encourage children to be specific about the number of blocks that they are using to build an item. In regard to Figure 8.6, this activity highlights numeracy as the academic content area, concept formation as the feature of language, and the block area as the learning center.

Science

Science activities provide plenty of opportunities for developing language (Chaille & Britain, 2002). The curriculum *Science Start!* (French, 1985) was actually developed with language development as a main goal. For example, there are a number of language concepts that can be explored while playing at the water table: seeing items float or sink, seeing ice get smaller but not seeing the melting water because the ice is in water, and seeing certain little toys grow in size when they are put in water. In regard to Figure 8.6, this activity highlights science as the academic content area, science concepts as the feature of language, and the water table as the learning center.

Literacy

scribe
A person assigned to write what one or more other people say.

The science activity described in the previous section can be incorporated with an early writing activity. In fact, the water table could be strategically placed next to the writing center so that children can take turns playing a scientist and **scribe**, with one child exploring the items in the water table and the other writing down notes on the scientist's findings about floating, sinking, melting, and growing toys. Depending on the time of the school year, children can even write the other child's name (or first letter) on the science report so that they have a record of who made the science observations and who was the scribe. The language components include the concepts as well as the functions of printing (e.g., it goes from left to right in English) and phonological skills as a way to figure out the letters to use in writing down the peer's name. In regard to Figure 8.6, this activity highlights literacy as the academic content area, writing concepts as the feature of language, and the literacy center and water table as the learning centers.

Interaction and Play

Notice that the sample activities described in the previous sections require a great deal of planning on the part of teachers. Just as important is how teachers interact with students during these learning activities. The adult's role in these respective academic areas is to creatively arrange the environment and adjoining potential learning materials and activities, and then encourage children to interact with the environment and the many aspects of those diverse settings in ways that best promote the fruition of children's language development.

Further, conversations with adults and peers are a major source of opportunity for language development. These conversations also provide the opportunity for social shared meaning. They happen as adults integrate into play and other activities throughout the day, such as mealtimes. They give young children the chance for language practice. Adults and more advanced peers can model sounds, words, and functions of language. They can describe ongoing actions taking place in the child's world. They can create opportunities for communication, making sure that children have time to talk and to get feedback from teachers.

It is important that communication extends interactions. In extended interactions, all participants tend to interact in the conversation, and it is very important that the child get ample and possibly even more opportunity to talk. The adult should match the child's pace and style of talk, with the adult intentionally making sure that the child has time and the ability to contribute to the interaction. The topic should stay close to the child's topic. Adults should ask questions that expand on that topic and confine these questions to ones that are real, indicating that they are truly interested in the child's response. Adults keep attuned to children's receptive language skills, asking questions that the child has the prior experiences needed to answer and that the child understands. Growth-enhancing conversations with young children should always be positive in tone.

Learning new vocabulary is influenced by the amount of more sophisticated language used around and directed toward children. In a study of racially diverse children from low-income families, significant positive correlations were found between rare word use in the homes of 3- to 5-year-old children and their reading comprehension at Grade 4. Similarly significant positive correlations were found between teacher's use of rare words in free play, large group, and mealtime settings and children's reading comprehension at Grade 4 (Snow, Tabors, & Dickinson, 2001).

Routines such as interactive reading are effective in developing language (Hargrave & Senechal, 2000; Lonigan & Whitehurst, 1998). The most important reason for using interactive reading is to focus on oral language development (listening and speaking). A type of interactive reading, **dialogic reading** can be used effectively as an intervention for children with low vocabulary levels (Whitehurst et al., 1994). Positive outcomes include increases in expressive and receptive vocabulary, the length of conversational exchanges, and use of a larger number of different words. Although some positive effects have been found from participating in dialogic reading for a short period of time, longer interventions have the most sustained impact (Whitehurst et al., 1994).

dialogic reading
A type of book reading with young children in which the goal is conversation around the book to develop children's vocabulary and syntax.

There are a number of other effective interventions for children whose language development is slower than that of other children but who also do not have a perceptual grasp of the cognitive causes for the delay. For these children, a systematic and explicit use of expanded vocabulary is effective. The adult should restate a child's one- or two-word utterance in a more elaborate form. For children with more severe disabilities, the adult should scaffold the use of more complex syntax in a manner that does not interrupt the conversation. The focus here is on expressive language. Children with significant receptive language delays require similar explicit strategies. It is important for teachers to be careful to rule out that young children's behavior problems are not the result of language delays.

Interactive Reading: Making Book Reading a Conversation

As adults and more advanced peers model sentences that are a little longer and complex than the child's sentence, they bring in new vocabulary for the child to learn. One way that this happens is when adults and children have extended conversations while reading books. In interactive reading, the adult uses systematic techniques to encourage the child to participate in reading and provides feedback to the child. Thus, the child becomes an active participant in the reading of the story. This technique encourages multiple exchanges between the adult and child on aspects of the book, which often extends the conversation. The child may recall previous experiences, draw inferences, or make predictions.

The following is an example of interactive reading between teacher and student while reading *Whistle for Willie* by Ezra Jack Keats (1964):

Ms. Peggy: "So instead he began to turn himself around—around and around he whirled . . . faster and faster . . ." What was it like when he whirled? "He whirled . . . faster and faster . . ."

Ralph: He falls.

Ms. Peggy: He falls? Not totally, but almost! So when he "whirled" he went around and around in circles, right?

Ralph: Fast, fast, fast!

Ms. Peggy: Fast, fast, fast. When he whirled he went around and around in circles really fast.

Ralph: Fast, went around in circles fast.

Ms. Peggy: Let's do it! [Ms. Peggy and Ralph go around and around in circles] I'm whirling! I'm whirling! I'm whirling!

Ralph: I'm whirling! I'm whirling!

Underfunded preschool programs may have inadequate language environments, with less support for child talk and fewer opportunities to build a rich vocabulary. It is especially important that these programs are of high quality and that added support for child talk and vocabulary expansion are included. Many indicators of high-quality language environments are included in the assessment section later in this chapter.

Adults and peers best serve as language facilitators in preschool settings within the context of play. Play is critical to language development because it promotes grounding of social shared meaning for both physical and social worlds (Bruner, 1996). Play is the context for exchange of culture and language among children as well as between adults and children. Sociodramatic play is a type of play in which language plays the central role; in fact, Bodrova and Leong (2008) defined extensive language use as being a key feature of mature play. For example, children can develop a scenario that they want to play out. This might be one chosen from a book that had been recently read in class or from events in their lives. Children can use these opportunities to learn new words and use this new language by exercising verbalization, vocabulary, and language comprehension (Smilansky, 1968; Smilansky & Shefatya, 1990). The scenarios may be played out in the block center or dramatic play center. Children will often use vocabulary relevant to the scenario and change their speech to reflect their roles. Both Smilansky and Shefatya (1990) and Bodrova and Leong (2008) identified key features of children's socio-dramatic play: using language to plan the play, deciding and negotiating the roles they will play, and acting out those roles.

Leong, Bodrova, and Hensen (2007) also pointed out how such sociodramatic play can be encouraged with fewer children or even by a child playing alone, for example, in the sand table or at the art center. In these cases, toy people or animals can be included in the centers so that a child can assign roles to figures and pro-ceed to act out a scenario, taking on the roles of multiple figures. Leong et al. sug-gested that this type of play should be highly encouraged in all classroom learning centers.

Teachers should support specific play that enhances language development. They should intentionally promote language use in play and be aware of family structure that children act out in sociodramatic areas. For children with disabilities, teachers might say part of the dialogue for a child and encourage the child to imi-tate it or provide assistive devices to help the child communicate. To encourage the learning of new words, teachers should name objects, actions, and events. Teach-ers should also introduce specific props (or help children figure out how to make a generic object, such as a block, stand for a specific prop) that help children bind to their ideas in pretend play.

Peers also should be encouraged to get everyone involved to play their parts and use words. Teachers should help negotiate the cultural differences present within the playgroup. For example, if one child looks concerned that the mother is hurrying the grandmother because it is taboo in the child's culture, the teacher might intervene so that the concerned child's perspective is taken into account. For deaf children and children who are new to learning the main language spoken in class, teachers should include enough visual and tactile cues or assistive technol-ogy devices so that these children can take part in the conversation.

❊ ❊ ❊ Section Summary ❊ ❊ ❊

Language development is supported in the preschool years through rich learning centers in which there is ample opportunity for play and conversation between adults and children and between peers. Thoughtful use of materials in learning cen-ters, including books and writing materials, promotes language learning and use. In-clude specific toys that promote sociodramatic play, especially toy people that can be used by children to take on particular roles in play and prompt them to talk to each other. Finally, throughout the day extended conversations between teachers and children are critical to preschool children's language development and use.

Assessing Language

Speech-language pathologists will perform formal language evaluations, and teachers often address language outcomes related to the curriculum guides they are using in their programs. This section discusses assessment of the language op-portunities that early childhood teachers and other professionals provide for young children in their early care and education programs. It is important for teachers to assess whether they are providing instructional activities for young children, as well as adapt curricula to meet individual children's learning needs and monitor if children are making progress (Copple & Bredekamp, 2009).

The availability of opportunities for language experiences can be assessed with the Early Childhood Classroom Observation Measure (ECCOM; Stipek & Byler, 2004) and the Early Language & Literacy Classroom Observation (ELLCO) Pre-K Tool (Smith, Brady, & Anastasopoulos, 2008). The ECCOM focuses on types of teacher practices, including directed, teaching for understanding, and child-centered teaching practices, whereas the ELLCO focuses on overall teacher practices, determining whether they are deficient to exemplary. Examples of high-quality instruction that address teaching for understanding from the ECCOM in the area of language are presented in Figure 8.7. Examples of high-quality practices from the ELLCO are presented in Figure 8.8.

Teacher and children participate equally in instructional conversations around clearly defined topics

Teacher solicits children's questions, ideas, solutions, or interpretations around a clearly defined topic.
   Example: "Can you tell me how you solved this problem?"

Teacher listens attentively to children and allows them to complete their thoughts, but steers conversation back to topic if child's contribution is tangential.
   Example: A child shares his experience about milking a cow and begins drifting into other topics. Teacher summarizes his story and brings the group back to discussion about farm animals (e.g., "So you were surprised at how hard it is to get the milk to come out. Who else has visited a farm or milked a cow?").

Teacher asks probing questions or uses some other strategy to get children to engage in conversation or expand on their ideas.
   Example: In a science lesson on five senses, teacher has children feel different textures in a bag and describe the sensations (e.g., "Daniel, you said it feels squishy. What other squishy things can you think of?").

Teacher uses inadequate solutions and/or children's underdeveloped understandings to enhance discussions.
   Example: Teacher begins a discussion of the moon by making a list of what the children already "know" (e.g., it's made of cheese, a man lives inside) and uses this list to initiate group discussion.

Teacher encourages children to ask questions, and respond to or elaborate on classmates' comments.
   Example: Teacher encourages others to ask a child questions to determine what he has brought in the surprise box.

Figure 8.7.   Example items from the Early Childhood Classroom Observation Measure in the language domain. (From Stipek, D., & Byler, P. [2004]. The Early Childhood Classroom Observation Measure. *Early Childhood Research Quarterly, 19*[3], 375–397; reprinted by permission.)

8. Discourse Climate

5 Exemplary	4 Strong	3 Basic	2 Inadequate	1 Deficient
There is **compelling** evidence of a positive discourse climate that actively engages children in conversations that facilitate the mutual exchange of ideas, opinions, and feelings.	There is **sufficient** evidence of a positive discourse climate that actively engages children in conversations that facilitate the mutual exchange of ideas, opinions, and feelings.	There is **some** evidence of a positive discourse climate that actively engages children in conversations that facilitate the mutual exchange of ideas, opinions, and feelings.	There is **limited** evidence of a positive discourse climate that actively engages children in conversations that facilitate the mutual exchange of ideas, opinions, and feelings.	There is **minimal** evidence of a positive discourse climate that actively engages children in conversations that facilitate the mutual exchange of ideas, opinions, and feelings.
• Teachers deliberately foster a climate in which expressing individual opinions and ideas is valued. They listen attentively to children and encourage them to listen and respond to one another.	• Teachers make efforts to listen attentively to children and create opportunities to elicit differing opinions and ideas, including some attempts to connect children's ideas and opinions with those of others.	• Teachers listen to children and acknowledge their contributions, but deliberate efforts to elicit children's thoughts or connect their ideas and opinions with those of others are less evident.	• There are limited opportunities for the exchange of ideas between teachers and children and among children. Teachers may, at times, be unresponsive to children and appear tuned out.	• There are few or no opportunities for children to express their own ideas or opinions. Teachers may discourage children's personal contributions to conversations. Children are expected to listen to teachers, and most interactions focus on procedural or managerial topics. Teachers may appear to interact with children in a harsh or punitive manner.
• Teachers explicitly and appropriately encourage the participation of all children, including those from differing linguistic, gender, racial, and cultural groups. Teachers build on similarities and differences to foster further discussion.	• Teachers appropriately encourage the participation of all children, including those from differing linguistic, gender, racial, and cultural groups. However, their efforts to explicitly involve particular children may be less evident.	• Teachers display fairness in treatment of children from differing linguistic, gender, racial, and cultural groups. They spend some time in conversations with children, but the quantity and quality of discussion may vary noticeably.	• Teachers may interact differently with children from differing gender, racial, and cultural groups. They may appear unaware of varying levels of involvement of particular children in conversations and verbal exchanges.	• Teachers' patterns of interaction reflect preferential treatment of children from certain gender, racial, or cultural groups.

Figure 8.8. Example items from the Early Language and Literacy Classroom Observation Measure in the language domain. (From Smith, M.W., Brady, J.P., & Anastasopoulos, L. [2008]. *Early Language and Literacy Classroom Observation Tool (ELLCO) Pre-K*. Baltimore: Paul H. Brookes Publishing Co.; reprinted by permission.)

(continued)

Figure 8.8 *(continued)*

9. Opportunities for Extended Conversations

5 Exemplary	4 Strong	3 Basic	2 Inadequate	1 Deficient
There is **compelling** evidence that teachers understand the role that extended conversations play in children's oral language development and learning.	There is **sufficient** evidence that teachers understand the role that extended conversations play in children's oral language development and learning.	There is **some** evidence that teachers understand the role that extended conversations play in children's oral language development and learning.	There is **limited** evidence that teachers understand the role that extended conversations play in children's oral language development and learning.	There is **minimal** evidence that teachers understand the role that extended conversations play in children's oral language development and learning.
• Teachers select topics and use strategies that engage children in conversations about their ideas, experiences, and curriculum activities. These support broader intellectual purposes (e.g., analyzing, predicting, problem solving, reflecting on learning).	• Teachers select topics and use strategies that engage children in conversations about their experiences and curriculum activities. The focus of conversations is typically context specific (e.g., description of what each child might do next to build a tower) and does not require broader intellectual engagement (e.g., discussion of how various blocks might affect the stability of the tower).	• Teachers engage children in conversations, but topic selection and/or use of strategies to engage children may be less clearly connected to children's content learning or their oral language development.	• The subject of teachers' comments is mostly informational (e.g., "Your drawing is over here") or evaluative (e.g., "Good job") and rarely extends content or oral language learning.	• The subject of most discussions is procedural, directing children to the next activity or task.
• Teachers create varied opportunities for interaction that engage a range of children in a balance of individual, small-group, and large-group conversations. They also take advantage of opportunities for informal and personal exchanges.	• Teachers make consistent efforts to engage a range of children in conversations, though the balance may favor certain settings (e.g., predominantly large groups) or conversational types (e.g., listing favorite things). Teachers regularly engage in informal conversations with children.	• Teachers make some efforts to engage children in conversations, although the settings may be less varied (i.e., in large-group formal settings, such as circle or book reading) and less extended.	• Teachers' attempts to talk with children are generally formulaic and are not conducive to an exchange.	• Teachers' efforts to engage children in extended conversations are minimal across formal or informal settings in the classroom.
• Conversations and exchanges maximize talk that informs learning, either to extend content knowledge or build specific oral language skills. For example, teachers orchestrate a discussion about how the class will create their own post office, including brainstorming and listing the supplies they will need.	• While most conversations tend to lead toward learning, they are not as extended (i.e., they do not contain as many turns or are less complex).	• Conversations include a balance of instructional and management talk.	• Management talk is commonplace, although teachers may make an occasional, ineffectual attempt to focus discussion on a topic, such as a question posed during book reading or circle time.	• Management talk predominates, with occasional efforts to quiet children and limit children's attempts to engage in productive conversation.

Adapting Curriculum and Monitoring Progress

Criterion-referenced or curriculum-based assessments are used to meet individual children's learning needs and monitor their progress. Children can be observed, asked questions, or even recorded. The focus here could be on an assessment system within a curriculum model. Some assessment measures are used across curriculum models, such as *Speaking and Listening for Preschool Through Third Grade* (Resnick & Snow, 2009). Figure 8.9 presents a partial list of the preschool expectations from *Speaking and Listening*.

Talking a Lot

Activities involving high-quality, purposeful talk and attentive feedback are critical for the development of language skills. Such talk can occur simultaneously with learning activities, playtime and mealtime. Talking a lot every day provides practice with various genres of talk for specific purposes. But children should experiment and *play* with language daily. Specifically, we expect preschool children to:

- talk daily for various purposes;
- engage in play using talk to enact or extend a story line (for example, taking on roles, using different voices, solving problems);
- playfully manipulate language (including nonsense words, rhymes, silly songs, repetitious phrases);
- express ideas, feelings and needs;
- listen and respond to direct questions;
- ask questions;
- talk and listen in small groups (during playtime or mealtime or more formally at workshop areas or craft tables); and
- share and talk daily about their own experiences, products, or writing (for example, explaining their pictures or "reading" their writing attempts).

Conversing at Length on a Topic

Daily conversations with others are critical if children are going to develop their language skills. Preschoolers begin to advance from simple yes or no answers to lengthier exchanges on a single, familiar topic or experience. Specifically, we expect preschool children to:

- initiate and sustain a conversation with comments or questions through at least four exchanges;
- recognize the topic of the conversation and make topic-relevant responses (for example, "I know Ernie. Yeah, on 'Sesame Street,' but I like Bert better.");
- recognize invitations to converse questions intended to elicit a brief response; and
- listen to others and avoid "talking-over."

Narrative

The spoken narrative is a precursor to the forms of fiction and nonfiction narrative accounts that children eventually will read. In addition, relating past experiences is a prerequisite for transitioning from speech to print. Preschool children can produce longer narratives if adults extend the production with questions that increase structure, such as "Tell me more" or "What was the dog doing?" or "Was the bike broken?"

Though typically more successful with factual accounts of personal experiences, preschoolers may produce some combination of fact and fiction.

Specifically, by the end of preschool we expect children to:

- give a simple narrative (with adult prompting if necessary), recounting two or more events that are not necessarily in chronological order (for example, "Puppy chase me, and he lick my knee" or "We rode the merry-go-round. Mommy took us. We got our tickets."); and
- recount knowledge gained through observation, experience or text.

Figure 8.9. *Speaking and Listening for Preschool Through Third Grade* assessment examples. (From Resnick, L.B., & Snow, C.E. [2009]. *Speaking and Listening for Preschool Through Third Grade* [Rev. ed.]. Newark, DE: International Reading Association; Copyright © 2011 by the International Reading Association [www.reading.org]; reprinted by permission.)

(continued)

Figure 8.9 *(continued)*

Preschool children should learn to include these elements for telling more complete and varied narratives:

- orient the listener by giving some setting information about people, objects, and where and when events occured (for example, "I had a shot once. With a needle. He [doctor] gave me a big hole in my arm.");
- describe information and evaluate or reflect on it (for example, "I went down the blue slide. It was real fun.");
- include quotations (for example, "He went, 'Get out of here,' and I said, 'No, I won't.'"); or
- mark the end of the story directly or with a coda (for example, "That's what happened.").

Producing and Responding to Performances

When preschoolers respond to a performance (whether it's a live storyteller, video or play) they are taking the first tentative steps toward what eventually will become reflection and critique of works of art, music or literature. Offering polite attention, giving a simple reaction or asking thoughtful questions is a sufficient start at this age.

By three or four years of age, children are very ready to produce brief performances, especially in small groups accompanied by music, rhyme or body movement. This is an excellent entree into acquiring the skills needed for reading aloud, giving reports and public speaking in later years. Specifically, we expect preschool children to:

- attend to a performance (for example, watching and listening to a performance 10 or more minutes long);
- describe the experience and/or their reaction to the performance (for example, "I was scared" or "I liked the clown. He was funny.";
- ask questions about things that they don't understand (for example, "Why is Tiny Tim so sad?");
- join in appropriately;
- draw from a rehearsed repertoire to give a brief performance (for example, in highly practiced forms like the "ABCs," "Itsy-Bitsy Spider" and "I'm a Little Teapot");
- as a performer, look at the audience as appropriate;
- speak, sing or act in a loud-enough voice; and
- speak, sing or act out a few sentences.

Rules of Interaction

Preschoolers need to feel confident speaking, whether they use standard English, a nonstandard dialect of English or some other language. Appropriate and expected modes of speaking and listening may differ widely from school to home and may be complicated further by cultural differences. A general respect for language differences and social rules of school interaction is critical for children's willingness to talk—and talk is critical to academic success. Specifically, we expect preschool children to:

- know and be able to describe rules for school interactions (for example, using "inside" voices, taking turns, raising a hand to speak); and
- learn rules for polite interactions (for example, saying "please" and "thank-you").

Word Play, Phonological Awareness and Language Awareness

Children's enjoyment of language and capacity to play with language enrich their lives as preschoolers and offer opportunities to learn things about language that will be helpful to them later on with formal reading and writing. The focus of this standard is on *play*—playing with sounds, words and word meanings rather than on *producing* particular words. While children play and experiment with words, they develop foundation skills for reading and writing. Specifically, we expect preschool children to:

- listen for and play with the rhythm of language (for example, clapping to the words in a chant or rhyme);
- recognize and enjoy rhymes (for example, nursery rhymes);

- play with language through songs, alliteration and word substitution (for example, "Ring Around the Rosy," "Five Little Monkeys");
- play with words and their meaning (for example, a three-year-old changes the expected to the unexpected, "Daddy, doggie, meow!");
- experiment with unconventional uses of words (for example, "soda in my arm" for an arm falling asleep);
- recognize and enjoy metaphorical language;
- in a string of sounds or words, listen for and identify the first, middle, or last sound or word in the string;
- in a string of sounds or words, listen for and identify the missing sound or word;
- try oral blending of familiar word parts (for example, "If I say 'hop . . . scotch,' 'butter . . . fly,' or 'valen . . . tine,' what do I have when it comes together?");
- build letter recognition (names and shapes only);
- recognize violations of word order;
- engage in sentence play; and
- transition from speech to print (for example, provide the words or label for a picture, dictate words of a story, or begin to use letters and words).

Vocabulary and Word Choice

There is a direct correlation between vocabulary development and academic success, so students' acquisition of new words should be emphasized from the start. Learning new words and the ideas and concepts associated with those words should occur daily. The most effective way to increase children's vocabulary at this age is by reading to them—reading (and rereading favorite books) every day. Specifically, we expect preschool children to:

- add words to familiar knowledge domains;
- sort relationships among words in knowledge domains;
- add new domains from subjects and topics they are studying (for example, in math, shapes like circle and triangle or in science, reptiles like snake and lizard);
- learn new words daily in conversation;
- learn new words daily from what is being explored or read aloud;
- show a general interest in words and word meanings, asking adults what a word means or offering definitions;
- recognize that things may have more than one name (for example, "Fluffy is a cat, the cat is a pet, the pet is an animal");
- categorize objects or pictures and tell why they go together (for example, group the following objects into toy or food categories: ball, skates, grapes, kite, bread, milk);
- increase vocabulary of verbs, adjectives and adverbs to exercise options in word choice;
- use some abstract words and understand that these words differ from concrete things, places or people; and
- use verbs referring to cognition, communication and emotions.

❊ ❊ ❊ Section Summary ❊ ❊ ❊

This section discussed a few assessments that teachers can use to determine the quality of the language experiences in their classrooms. Examples from several of these measures were provided. In addition, we addressed measures that teachers can use to determine whether they are adapting curricula to meet individual children's learning needs and monitoring if children are making progress (Copple & Bredekamp, 2009).

KEY CONCEPTS

- Theory and research about language development has an impact on ECE teacher practice. Theories presented in previous chapters—ecological theory, social constructivist theory, social learning theory, constructivist theory, narrative construction of reality theory, and dynamic systems perspective—all contribute to the understanding of language learning and use.

- Ecological theory explains the multiple systems affecting language development, such as variations in language use and culture, as well as society's judgment of different variations related to language use and development.

- Social constructivist theory is central to examining the interrelations between language and other areas of development, such as approaches to learning and cognitive development.

- Verbal behavior theory provides an important empirical basis in ECE programs.

- Important features underlie language development. These are that language systems are systems of communication that are shared across people and are affected by cultural and individual differences.

- Language has complex subsystems including those identified as form (phonology, morphology, syntax), content (semantics and vocabulary), and use (pragmatics). Metalinguistic development addresses children's abilities to attend to different aspects of language in relation to its features rather than meaning per se.

- Learning and academic centers provide ample opportunities for language development when they provide opportunities for play and conversation between adults and children and between peers. Books and writing materials as well as specific toys that promote sociodramatic play, especially toy people that the children can use to take on particular roles in play and talk to each other, are a must.

- Throughout the day extended conversations between teachers and children are critical to preschool children's language development and use.

- Teachers should use assessments that measure the quality of the education in the area of language development that they are providing young children and refer to measures available that describe high-quality ECE opportunities.

- Ongoing classroom assessments provide teachers with information necessary to reflect on and adapt language curriculum to be responsive to each individual child's needs.

- Teachers should constantly reflect on their education and care of children in the area of language use and development and understand how this area of development has an impact on all other areas of development—approaches to learning, social and emotional development, cognitive development, and physical development.

Integration of Information

You have just read a chapter on language development. Language development affects all areas of development and learning of young children. What do you think? Does language learning stand out to you as extremely important for early childhood educators to be familiar with? Do you think you will enjoy teaching young children to develop and use language?

Self-Reflective Guide

This self-reflective guide will help you assess whether you learned the information in this chapter. It also provides an opportunity to identify areas in which you want or need more information. Are there some new ideas learned that will affect your immediate practice with children?

1. Reflect on the theories presented to account for young children's language development: ecological theory, social constructivist theory, verbal behavior theory. Are there aspects of these theories that align with your observations of young children's language learning? Does a particular theory resonate with you? Make a few notes.

2. Recognize the features of language development. Have you seen young children use these? List two aspects of language development that you think are extremely important for young children to learn and why.

3. Identify how language development can be addressed across different learning centers and academic areas. List one center and one academic area that are fruitful contexts for developing language. Elaborate on why these are important contexts.

4. Understand how children interact with teachers and peers as they develop effective language. Describe a type of interaction that you want to develop as an ECE teacher. Elaborate on why this type of interaction is important.

5. Reflect on how play affects language development. Elaborate on why play is important in children's learning and development in this area.

6. Connect what you have learned about dual-language learners and those from different cultural backgrounds. Identify a child you know who is from a different language or cultural background than most of your students. What are the key pedagogical principles to keep in mind?

7. Describe how teachers can assess whether they are providing quality opportunities for young children to learn language.

8. Determine how teachers can assess young children's language so that they can adapt curricula and monitor the progress of students. Identify a child with a disability (note the specific disability) and describe how such assessment information could help you adapt your instruction to meet this child's needs.

(continued)

Self-Reflective Guide (continued)

9. Reflect on language development and how this area of development relates to others discussed in this book—approaches to learning, social and emotional development, cognitive development, and physical and motor development.

10. Identify other information learned that can have an immediate impact on your current practice if you are a practicing teacher or caregiver at this time.

11. List areas you need to explore further. Who can help you learn about your concerns?

Helpful Web Sites

American Speech-Language-Hearing Association

www.asha.org/academic/curriculum/slp-artic/deskref.htm
This section of the American Speech-Language-Hearing Association's site provides information for teachers of early language. There are many subsections on this site with important information.

BookHive

www.plcmc.org/bookhive/zingertales/zingertales.asp
This site, which is produced by the Charlotte Mecklenburg Library, provides video recording of story tellers.

Born Learning

www.bornlearning.org/default.aspx?id=36
Born Learning is a public service campaign that has grown out of a partnership between media professionals and a variety of civic and professional associations. This site incorporate basic information about language.

Children's National Medical Center

www.childrensnational.org/DepartmentsandPrograms/default.aspx?Type=Dept&Id=382&Name=Hearing%20and%20Speech
This site includes information on language that is important for all teachers. Look especially at Cozmo the therapy dog for an interesting way to elicit language with children with more severe language problems.

PBS Kids Games

http://pbskids.org/games
This Public Broadcasting Service site provides a wide range of children's games and extensions to popular children's literature characters.

Reading Rockets

www.readingrockets.org/article/18935
This site includes tip sheets for parents of preschoolers that include many supports for language development. In addition to English, the tip sheets come in 10 languages—Spanish, Arabic, Traditional Chinese, Haitian Creole, Hmong, Korean, Navajo, Russian, Tagalog, and Vietnamese. Posting such materials in the classroom demonstrates that languages other than English are embraced.

References

American Speech-Language-Hearing Association. (n.d.). *Three to four years.* Retrieved December 19, 2010, from http://www.asha.org/public/speech/development/34.htm

Atkinson, R.C., & Shiffrin, R.M. (1968). Human memory: A proposed system and its control processes. In K.W. Spence & J.T. Spence (Eds.), *The psychology of learning and motivation: Advances in research and theory* (Vol. 2; pp. 89–195). New York: Academic Press.

Ballenger, C. (1999). *Teaching other people's children: Literacy and learning in a bilingual classroom.* New York: Teachers College Press.

Bandura, A. (1977). *Social learning theory.* Englewood Cliffs, NJ: Prentice Hall.

Berko-Gleason, J., & Ratner, N.B. (2009). *The development of language* (7th ed.). New York: Allyn & Bacon.

Beukelman, D.R., & Mirenda, P. (2005). *Augmentative and alternative communication: Supporting children and adults with complex communication needs* (3rd ed.). Baltimore: Paul H. Brookes Publishing Co.

Bialystok, E. (2001). Metalinguistic aspects of bilingual processing. *Annual Review of Applied Linguistics, 21,* 169–181.

Bodrova, E., & Leong, D. (2008). Developing self-regulation in kindergarten: Can we keep all the crickets in the basket? *Young Children, 63*(2), 56–58.

Bronfenbrenner, U., & Morris, P.A. (1998). The ecology of developmental processes. In W. Damon & R.M. Lerner (Eds.), *Handbook of child psychology: Vol. 1: Theoretical models of human development* (pp. 993–1028). New York: Wiley.

Bruner, J. (1996). *The culture of education.* Cambridge, MA: Harvard University Press.

Calculator, S.N. (2007). Augmentative and alternative communication. In R.S. New & M. Cochran, (Eds.), *Early childhood education: An international encyclopedia* (pp. 52–55). Westport, CT: Praeger.

Carbone, V.J, Lewis, L., Sweeney-Kerwin, E.J., Dixon, J., Louden, R., & Quinn, S. (2006). A comparison of two approaches for teaching VB functions: Total communication vs. vocal alone. *Journal of Speech Pathology and Applied Behavior Analysis, 1,* 181–192.

Cazden, C.B. (1974). Play with language and metalinguistic awareness: One dimension of language awareness. *International Journal of Early Childhood, 6*(1), 12–24.

Chaille, C.M., & Britain, L. (2002). *The young child as scientist: A constructivist approach to early childhood science education* (3rd ed.). Columbus, OH: Allyn & Bacon.

Chaney, C. (1992). Language development, metalinguistic skills, and print awareness in 3-year-old children. *Applied Psycholinguistics, 13*(4), 485–514.

Copple, C., & Bredekamp, S. (2009). *Developmentally appropriate practice in early childhood programs serving children from birth through age 8.* Washington, DC: National Association for the Education of Young Children.

Crystal, D. (2005). *How language works: How babies babble, words change meaning, and languages live or die.* New York: Penguin Group.

Dahlberg, G., & Moss, P. (1999). *Beyond quality in early childhood education.* Philadelphia: Falmer.

Ely, R., Gleason, J.B., MacGibbon, A., & Zaretsky, E. (2001). Attention to language: Lessons learned at the dinner table. *Social Development, 10*(3), 355–373.

Fenson, L., Dale, P.S., Reznick, S.J., Bates, E., Thal, D.J., & Pethick, S.J. (1994). Variability in early communicative development. *Monographs of the Society for Research in Child Development, 59*(5), 1–173.

Fischer, K.W. (2009). Mind, brain, and education: Building a scientific groundwork for learning and teaching. *Mind, Brain, and Education, 3,* 2–15.

French, L.A. (1985). Real-world knowledge as the basis for social and cognitive development. In J.B. Pryor & J.D. Day (Eds.), *Social and developmental perspectives on social cognition* (pp. 179–209). New York: Springer-Verlag.

Goldin-Meadow, S., & Morford, M. (1985). Gesture in early child language: Studies of deaf and hearing children. *Merrill-Palmer Quarterly, 31*(2), 145–176.

Goldin-Meadow, S., Mylander, C., & Butcher, C. (1995). The resilience of combinatorial structure at the word level: Morphology in self-styled gesture systems. *Cognition, 56*(3), 195–262.

Hargrave, A.C., & Senechal, M. (2000). A book reading intervention with preschool children who have limited vocabularies: The benefits of regular reading and dialogic reading. *Early Childhood Research Quarterly, 15*(1), 75–90.

Harry, B., & Klinger, J. (2006). *Why are so many minority students in special education: Understanding race and disability.* New York: Teachers College Press.

Hart, B., & Risley, T.R. (1995). *Meaningful differences in the everyday experience of young American children.* Baltimore: Paul H. Brookes Publishing Co.

Hart, B., & Risley, T.R. (1999). *The social world of children learning to talk.* Baltimore: Paul H. Brookes Publishing Co.

Heath, S.B. (1983). *Ways with words: Language, life, and work in communities and classrooms.* New York: Cambridge University Press.

Keats, E.J. (1964). *Whistle for Willie.* New York: Penguin Group.

King, K., & Fogle, L. (2006). Bilingual parenting as good parenting: Parents' perspectives of family language policy for additive bilingualism. *International Journal of Bilingual Education and Bilingualism, 9*(6), 695–712.

Leong, D.J., Bodrova, E., & Hensen, R. (2007). *Tools of the Mind curriculum project preschool manual* (4th ed.). Denver, CO: Center for Improving Early Learning, Metropolitan State College of Denver.

Lonigan, C.J., & Whitehurst, G.J. (1998). Relative efficacy of parent and teacher involvement in a shared-reading intervention for preschool children from low-income backgrounds. *Early Childhood Research Quarterly, 17,* 265–292.

Mathes, P.G., Torgesen, J.K., & Allor, J.H. (2001). The effects of peer-assisted literacy strategies for first-grade readers with and without additional computer-assisted instruction in phonological awareness. *American Educational Research Journal, 38*(2), 371–410.

McCauley, R.J., & Fey, M.E. (2006). *Treatment of language disorders in children.* Baltimore: Paul H. Brookes Publishing Co.

Nieto, S. (2010). *The light in their eyes: Creating multicultural learning communities* (10th anniversary ed.). New York: Teachers College Press.

Nordquist, V.M., Twardosz, S., & Higgins, W.B. (2007). Behaviorism. In R.S. New & M. Cochran (Eds.), *Early childhood education: An international encyclopedia* (pp. 62–66). Westport, CT: Praeger.

Paradis, J., Genesee, F., & Crago, M.B. (2011). *Dual language development and disorders: A handbook on bilingualism and second language learning* (2nd ed.). Baltimore: Paul H. Brookes Publishing Co.

Petitto, L.A., & Holowka, S. (2002). Evaluating attributions of delay and confusion in young bilingualists: Special insights from infants acquiring a signed and a spoken language. *Sign Language Studies, 3*(1), 3–33.

Piaget, J. (1977). *The development of thought: Equilibration of cognitive structure.* New York: Viking.

Resnick, L.B., & Snow, C.E. (2009). *Speaking and listening for preschool through third grade* (Rev. ed.). Newark, DE: International Reading Association.

Roth, F.P., Speece, D.L., & Cooper, D.H. (2002). A longitudinal analysis of the connection between oral language and early reading. *Journal of Educational Research, 95*(5), 259–272.

Shatz, M., Grimm, H., Wilcox, S.A., & Niemeier-Wind, K. (1989). *The uses of modal expressions in conversations between German and American mothers and their two-year-olds.* Paper presented at the biennial meeting of the Society for Research in Child Development, Kansas City, MO.

Skinner, B.F. (1957). *Verbal behavior.* Acton, Massachusetts: Copley Publishing Group.

Smilansky, S. (1968). *The effects of sociodramatic play on disadvantaged preschool children.* New York: Wiley.

Smilansky, S., & Shefatya, L. (1990). *Facilitating play: A medium for promoting cognitive, socio-emotional, and academic development in young children.* Gaithersburg, MD: Psychological and Educational Publications.

Smith, M.W., Brady, J.P., & Anastasopoulos, L. (2008). *Early Language and Literacy Classroom Observation Tool (ELLCO) Pre-K.* Baltimore: Paul H. Brookes Publishing Co.

Snow, C.E., Burns, M.S., & Griffin, P. (1998). *Preventing reading difficulties in young children.* Washington, DC: National Academies Press.

Snow, C.E., Griffin, P., & Burns, M.S. (2005). *Knowledge to support the teaching of reading: Preparing teachers for a changing world.* Indianapolis, IN: Jossey-Bass.

Snow, C.E., Tabors, P.O., & Dickinson, D.K. (2001). Language development in the preschool years. In D.K. Dickinson & P.O. Tabors (Eds.), *Beginning literacy with language* (pp. 1–25). Baltimore: Paul H. Brookes Publishing Co.

Stipek, D., & Byler, P. (2004). The Early Childhood Classroom Observation Measure. *Early Childhood Research Quarterly, 19*(3), 375–397.

Tomasello, M., & Mervis, C.B. (1994). The instrument is great, but measure comprehension is still a problem. *Monographs of the Society for Research in Child Development, 59*(5), 174–179.

Vygotsky, L.S. (1978). In M. Cole, V. John-Steiner, S. Scribner, & E. Souberman (Eds.), *Mind in society: The development of high psychological processes.* Cambridge, MA: Harvard University Press.

Vygotsky, L.S. (1986). In A. Kozulin (Ed.), *Thought and language* (Rev. ed.). Cambridge: The MIT Press.

Whitehurst, G.J., Arnold, D.H., Epstein, J.N., Angell, A.L., Smith, M., & Fischel, J.E. (1994). A picture book reading intervention in daycare and home for children from low-income families. *Developmental Psychology, 30,* 679–689.

Physical Development

with Myra Rogers

9

Learning Objectives

1. Understand your interests and strengths related to physical development, and different contexts in which the physical development of young children is enhanced
2. Recognize the features of young children's physical development
3. Identify how physical development can be addressed across different learning centers and academic areas
4. Understand how children interact with teachers and peers as the develop physically
5. Recognize how play affects physical development
6. Describe how teachers can assess whether they are providing quality opportunities for young children to enhance effective physical development
7. Determine how you would assess young children's physical development so that you can adapt curricula based on these findings and monitor the ongoing progress of your students

How do 3- to 5-year-old children grow physically? What is the relationship between physical, socioemotional, and cognitive development? Should I provide children with physically challenging activities? How do young children physically navigate their childhoods? I have a 3-year-old child in my class who does not have the use of his right hand; are there things I can do to help him develop? How can I challenge these young learners in their physical development without frustrating them? When children are frustrated, how can my understanding of physical development influence my interactions with them?

These are the types of questions addressed in this chapter on the physical development of preschool children. The chapter begins by addressing different theorists, especially those whose ideas affect physical development in early childhood education (ECE) practice. Next, we discuss features of physical development, including issues related to childhood obesity. We present how physical growth is supported through play. Providing an abundance of effective age-appropriate and developmentally appropriate healthy experiences during the early years of development is critical and can have a tremendous impact on how an individual physically develops over time. The active facilitation of physical development by teachers to reduce sedentary activity (Brown et al., 2009) is presented.

Theoretical Accounts: Physical Development

The theoretical accounts of physical development presented in this section were chosen in light of current ECE practices. Some theoretical accounts presented in Chapters 5–8 also are relevant in this discussion of physical development in the following ways:

- Social learning theory (Bandura, 1977): Children learn through imitation of behavior (in this case, fine and gross motor skills) modeled by adults and peers.

- Behavioral theory (Skinner, 1957): Children's motor behavior is influenced by current environmental contingencies, those of the past, and heredity/biology.

- Critical theories: Motor development is dependent on safe and open spaces being available in children's communities. When playgrounds, recreation centers, and neighborhood sports clubs are dilapidated and underfunded, schools and families are unable to provide appropriate activities for children's motor development (Dahlberg & Moss, 1999; Nieto, 2010).

One theory that was presented previously—ecological theory—is included in this chapter, with details that are particularly relevant to physical development. This section concludes with an additional area of research and theory that is currently used in ECE—brain development.

Ecological Theory

As discussed in Chapters 6–8, Bronfenbrenner (1989) noted a wide variety of intertwined forces (e.g., cultural, social, economic, political) that affect physical development patterns of children in different ways. Ecological issues such as housing availability, socioeconomic inequalities, and a school system's resources have varying degrees of impact on children's physical development. Many additional factors may affect children's abilities, as well as the availability of places to engage in gross motor activities.

Other researchers have built on Bronfenbrenner's theoretical perspectives, such as Gabbard, Cacola, and Rodrigues, who noted that "motor development considers environmental influences as critical factors in optimal growth and behavior" (2008, p. 5). For example, for many young children living in urban areas, outdoor sports activities are difficult to engage in because of a lack of well-maintained playing fields or playgrounds in their neighborhoods.

Brain Development

A key part of brain development in young children is sensory integration. Sensory integration is a child's ability to take in information from various senses (e.g., sight, sound, touch) to form brain connections and memory of an event or activity. Many of the modes of early learning are dependent on multiple sensory systems that integrate these to enhance learning and developmental patterns across all areas of development (e.g., socioemotional, cognition, physical, language; Jensen, 2005). The importance of focusing on the brain and physical development has been justified in research. Magnetic resonance imaging of the brain after exercise revealed that children who were physically fit had a larger basal ganglia (a section of the brain dedicated to motor development, coordinated actions), and thereby had better coordination skills and formed thoughts more clearly (Reynolds, 2010). Actively facilitating the ongoing nurturance of movement activities will assist children's overall physical development and stimulate their neurons and other brain functions that are critical for learning (Hendler & Nakelski, 2008). For instance, Blaydes (2000) highlighted how movement affects thinking abilities and enhances memory because an increased heart rate oxygenates the brain and supplies it with glucose, which is vital for learning. Recognizing the important relationship between increased physical activity and improved learning opportunities should assist teachers in including this part of overall child physical development in daily curricular activities.

❋ ❋ ❋ Section Summary ❋ ❋ ❋

In summary, as with cognitive and language development discussed in other chapters, children's physical development stands to affect all areas of their growth and learning. Ecological theory plays a central role in the understanding of young children's physical development. The multiple systems within which the child functions—such as microsystems, which include family and school, and macrosystems, which include how a child's culture is valued in the current society of residence—affect their physical development. Sophisticated research on development of the brain highlights the integration of sensory development with brain development as well as all other developmental areas.

Features of Physical Development

body awareness
An individual's awareness of his or her own body (e.g., pain) and of his or her body in space (e.g., proximity to another person).

Between the ages of 3 and 5, children are actively manipulating various art objects (e.g., paint brushes, markers, crayons) and making drawings. They are holding down paper with one hand and drawing with the other, showing great coordination of motor activity. They use all sorts of blocks to build. On the playground children are running, sliding, and kicking and throwing balls. Overall physical growth, rapid development, and expansion of the nervous system contribute to the important need for physical activity in early childhood. Active children grow up to be active adolescents and adults (Barros, Silver, & Stein, 2009).

Fundamental movement skills are developed during the preschool years.

Gross Motor Development

In the early years of life, young children grow rapidly. Their physical sizes, abilities, and interests in the world around them expand as they grow. In this area of gross motor development young children are acquiring and practicing many motor skills related to movement and **body awareness**. They are climbing, walking, running, skipping, and hopping in more and more coordinated movements. They are bending and stretching, pushing and pulling, twisting and turning, throwing and catching. Integral to these processes is coordination,

that is, eye–hand coordination (throwing toward a target) and eye–foot coordination (kicking toward a target), as well as balance, rhythm, and endurance. Children become responsible for body regulation as they learn to

• Move fast and slow

• Start and stop

• Sit on their chair and not fall off

• Move through their environment without bumping into furniture

Gross motor activities should be well supervised and available daily. They should occur both indoors and outdoors with enough space for all of the children to run, climb, jump, and so forth. Opportunities should be available for children with all levels of ability to participate. Teachers should show children how to use equipment, give words to guide their movements, explain what needs to be done, introduce new skills, and encourage practice. Children with limited gross motor skills should be monitored and encouraged to participate in play and become involved in peer interactions and play. Often the playground is the first and only opportunity for children with motor delays to use their bodies to attempt fun and challenging motor actives.

Encouraging Motor Development for Children with Physical Disabilities

Children with physical disabilities are often physically limited by adults because of fear and expediency. Physical activities often are performed for the child instead of the child performing the activity. It's quicker, for example, if someone else gets the toy that is out of reach instead of allowing the child the opportunity to plan, solve, and perform the steps needed (e.g., reach for the toy, crawl, maneuver around objects and furniture) to get what she wants and enhance her physical development.

Every part of the day's activities is an opportunity for mobility learning and exercise. Of course, as the classroom teacher it is your goal to move each child closer to independence. Functioning as independently as possible should always be the goal of any child in a preschool classroom, especially those children with limitations in fine and gross motor skills. Having children carry their backpacks, take out their folders from their backpacks (which involves unzipping, grasping folder, planning how to do that), and take off their jackets (which may be zipped or snapped) all support gross and fine motor development. Doing these activities while 15 other children are bustling around them is challenging and necessary, and requires attending to the environment and maintaining gate and balance. Often a child may have adaptive clothing, shoes, or braces to learn to use during the school day. Having children with disabilities perform these and other tasks on their own may take longer, it may be harder, and some things may be missed, but they can create a sense of satisfaction, pride, working through a task, and, equally important, muscle strength and cognitive development.

Don't shy away from providing opportunities to children with disabilities. They can do errands (real or made up), take a note to a neighboring classroom, pick up toys that they have used in the class, and so forth. Any opportunity to get children with disabilities moving gives them the chance to use their motor skills and gain much needed stamina and endurance.

Fine Motor Development

Fine motor development forms in these early years in the same rapid manner as gross motor development. Preschool children typically can now draw shapes and figures on paper, write letters and numbers, cut with scissors, tie strings and laces, manipulate puzzle and game board pieces, and button and use zippers and commonly used adult tools such as wrenches and screwdrivers. They use many types of grasps, beginning with ones that are cumbersome (e.g., holding a crayon in their fist) and moving toward a grasp using their first two fingers and thumb (**tripod grasp**). These same fine motor skills are applied to completing puzzles, building with blocks, and developing basic self-help skills such as zippering, buttoning, lacing, buckling, snapping, and pouring liquids. Eye–hand coordination, eye movement, and hand movement being in sync and building small muscle strength are central in these processes of development.

Fundamental fine motor skills include writing and drawing and including some letters and numbers.

tripod grasp
A grasp in which the writing instrument is held between one's first two fingers and thumb.

Many types of activities and materials are provided in the preschool classroom to help students develop eye–hand coordination skills (e.g., train tracks to assemble and trains to ride on those tracks, even through tunnels); manipulative skills (e.g., math materials that are sorted and combined in different ways); planning and organizing skills (e.g., art materials that are used in different ways to develop a product); and self-help skills such as dressing, personal hygiene, and eating. These small objects and materials should be organized, accessible, age appropriate, safe, and in sufficient amounts for all of the different levels and abilities of all of your children. Enough time and space should be provided for children to complete fine motor projects and activities. Allowing children to help one another with fine motor activities is important to encourage modeling of higher-level skills. The development of fine motor skills is a priority because it serves to develop prewriting skills as well as functional life skills, such as buttoning and zipping, that will be needed to be productive and successful year after year (Copple & Bredecamp, 2009).

Physical Development, Nutrition, and Physical Fitness

Children often do not spend enough time involved in fine and gross motor activities that influence their physical development (Gabbard et al., 2008). Children should be provided multiple opportunities to participate in developmental activities related to muscular strength, endurance, flexibility, and cardiorespiratory endurance. Physical development of young children is directly related to their overall health and nutrition.

Consuming a nutritious diet also assists physical development beginning in childhood. The majority of 2- to 5-year-old children in the United States are currently consuming poor diets. The continuous (mis)consumption of poor nutrients in a child's diet can set the tone for poor dietary intake throughout a lifetime, which can negatively affect children's developmental outcomes well into adulthood (Children's Defense Fund, 2010).

Childhood obesity is a central factor influencing the need to discuss healthy food and exercise habits with young children. Approximately 17% of 2- to 19-year-olds are obese in the United States (Ogden, Carroll, Curtin, Lamb, & Flegal, 2010). The Centers for Disease Control and Prevention (2009) identified approximately 14% of preschool children from low-income homes as obese in 2008. Obesity rates for these children were stable between 2003 and 2008; however, there were differences in the prevalence of obesity for specific ethic groups of children—those being Hispanic, American Indian, or Alaska Native. Renewed focus on promoting physical activity and changes in the federal food programs have been changed as a result of concerns about obesity.

For example, in 2010 Congress passed The Healthy, Hunger-Free Kids Act of 2010 (PL 111-296), which allows the United States Department of Agriculture (USDA) to reform school lunch and other programs designed to feed young children throughout the United States. Enhancements to the Women, Infants, and Children (WIC) program—a program that provides healthy nutrition to low-income mothers and children up to 5 years of age—to include breastfeeding support and promoting healthy food choices stands to have a significant impact on preschool-age children and their families. The WIC Food Packages program allows for more flexibility for families to purchase fruits and vegetables and cultural food preferences, something that was not allowed previously. Many children consume two meals per day at school, this includes children in all USDA–subsidized child care and Head Start programs. Changes to school lunch include strict adherence to nutrition guidelines, education, and improved quality of the food distributed. In addition, changes to the USDA's food pyramid for children, such as presenting the fruits and vegetables and grains in extra large sections with larger images and providing user-friendly formats in various languages, reflects the importance of proper nutrition for all children.

Lack of physical activity is a key factor in childhood obesity; therefore, efforts have been launched to promote sustained physical activity in young children. For example, First Lady Michelle Obama launched the Let's Move Campaign in 2010 as a direct result of the White House Task Force on Childhood Obesity's (2010) report *Solving the Problem of Childhood Obesity Within a Generation.* The Task Force outlined improvements to accessibility of quality foods and increased activity, such as making a garden at schools where children work on all aspects of growing vegetables (which also serves as a physical activity) and participate in eating those vegetable, some being ones they have never tried before.

Early childhood teachers should plan and provide good, tasty nutritional snacks for preschoolers. When asking for parent participation in providing food for snacks, teachers should request a variety of healthy snacks that all of the students have an opportunity to taste and eat.

*** Section Summary ***

Features of motor and physical development that are especially important for ECE include gross or large motor development, fine or small motor development, and nutrition and physical fitness. Development in all of these areas is central to a child's overall growth across domains, including approaches to learning, social and emotional, cognitive, and language development, and is crucial to brain development.

Supporting Children's Effective and Diverse Motor and Physical Development

Teachers, caregivers, and parents play key roles in the highly interactive processes of the physical development of young children (Hyson, 2003). An awareness of the range of possible activities and their impact on physical development is a central

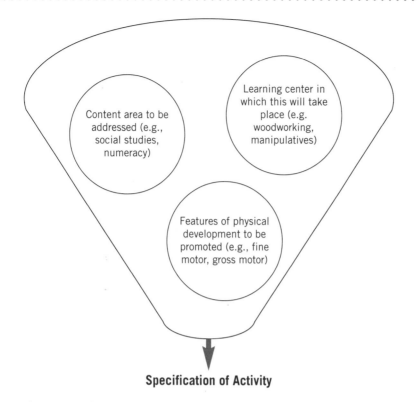

Specification of Activity

Figure 9.1. Contributors to specification of activity.

part of young children's developmental progression over time. This knowledge affects our belief systems and understandings and our practical applications in our home, the classroom, or on the playground and greater community. With experiential and curricular opportunities, it is important to begin with basic needs, being attentive and tuned into where children are developmentally. Through classroom learning centers (e.g., creative arts, social studies, science, numeracy, literacy), it is possible to provide young children the key tools needed to expand their physical development.

Academic content can be put together with physical development and enacted in different learning centers. This section specifies activities that are integrated across creative arts, social studies, numeracy, science, and literacy using the model in Figure 9.1. However, note that these activities are only examples, provided as models; they are not necessarily the activities that you will be using, nor those that are the most important to include as opportunities for your young children's physical development. You will develop your own understanding of what activities to use and which centers to integrate as you get to know your individual children.

Creative Arts

Providing an abundance of activities in the creative arts can enhance effective physical development. Recall the activity in Chapter 5 in which children design a collage while listening to music. During this activity, children could also be motivated to be highly involved in large motor physical development by actively moving their bodies throughout the space to the beat, tone, and sound of the music. The physical development characteristics that might be emphasized include **locomotion**, developing pincer control, coordination, balance, and developing gross motor skills. Body awareness can be emphasized as children actively and carefully move their body parts about, organizing their bodies in a limited space. In regard to Figure 9.1, this activity highlights creative arts as the academic content area; motor regulation, large motor skills, coordination, and balance as the features of physical development; and the music area as the learning center.

locomotion
Gross motor activity that moves a child through space.

Social Studies

Social studies activities provide children with opportunities to learn about the world. Recall the activity from Chapter 8 in which the children physically construct houses like those in their respective neighborhoods using a wide assortment of large and small blocks. The physical development skills emphasized in the activity are movement skills and developing fine motor skills, perceptual awareness, and coordination. In regard to Figure 9.1, this activity highlights social studies as the academic content area; movement skills, manipulative coordination, fine motor skills, and developing perceptual awareness and coordination as the features of physical development; and the block area as the learning center.

Numeracy

Numeracy and physical development are closely intertwined when considering how children manipulate objects as they take systematic approaches to the skills and concepts that lay the foundation for mathematics understanding, including counting, comparing sizes, sorting, and classifying. Wooden trains are often available in preschool classrooms and provide a great intersection between numeracy and fine motor development. Planning and counting the number of tracks that need to be put together to make the train line is rich in measurement and number skills. Choosing the trains to then run on the track may include sorting trains according to size as well as function. Running the trains require the fine motor skills needed to manipulate the route as well as surmount obstacles such as passing through a tunnel. In regard to Figure 9.1, this activity highlights numeracy as the academic content area; developing perceptual awareness, coordination of eye–hand development, and refining grasp as features of physical development; and the woodworking area as the learning center.

Science

Physical development and science go hand in hand. So many of the traditional early childhood science activities and experiences involve group work and active manipulation of the environment (e.g., working with machines, experimenting with found materials, working with a classmate). Traditional early childhood science experiences provide opportunities for children to foster physical development, for example, as children put food coloring in different jars of water and look at the results, then mix jars of colored water together and find a new result. In regard to Figure 9.1, this activity highlights science as the academic content area; enhancing fine motor skills and eye–hand coordination as the features of physical development; and the science area as the learning center.

Literacy

Physical development can be incorporated with literacy activities in numerous ways. Recall the activity from Chapter 5 in which children write letters to each other. In this activity, many physical development skills can be addressed, including **posture** and body mechanics, developing fine motor skills, formulating patterns, and refining grasp. First, children decide to whom in the class they want to write a letter. They will then spend time at the writing center using markers and papers and developing a message they want to convey to the recipient of the letter. A completed letter is then addressed and delivered. In regard to Figure 9.1, this activity highlights literacy as the academic content area; coordinating eye and hand movement (using a hole punch), refining grasp (tripod grasp), and developing hand control (scissors) as the features of physical development; and the writing center as the learning center.

posture
The physical arrangement or orientation of a person's body.

Interaction and Play

As we noted earlier, the adult's role in these respective developmental and academic areas is to creatively arrange the environment and potential learning materials and curricular activities. Adults should then encourage children to creatively interact with the environment and the many aspects of those diverse settings in ways that best promote the fruition of children's motor skills and physical development (Morrison, 2009).

parquetry blocks
Geometrically shaped blocks that children use to make patterns and designs.

bristle blocks
Blocks for children's constructive play that are usually of varied primary colors, with small nubs that allow the blocks to interlock for building or making patterns.

The multiplicity and diversity of settings where children spend different amounts of time physically involved and developing in their early years will have significant influence on their whole development (Malina, 1994). For example, young children with siblings tend to spend more time interacting with their sibling than with anyone else (McHale & Crouter, 1996). An older, more active brother or sister can, therefore, influence the physical developmental patterns of a younger sibling in various ways. As each of these subcomponents of a larger system stress, the physical development of children is heavily affected in both positive and negative ways by individual and group experiential factors, as well as the interactive patterns (or lack thereof) within these contexts (Halberstadt, Denham, & Dunsmore, 2001).

LEGOs
Construction blocks that are interlocking and that are often different sizes, colors, and shapes with some realistic features that can be attached to the blocks.

A vital aspect of enhancing physical development is providing a wide range of diverse play opportunities inside and outside of the preschool classroom. One of the most popular forms of play in early childhood classrooms is block play. Most high-quality classrooms include a block center and blocks as one of the basic classroom and playground materials. There are currently many types of block systems on the market, including unit blocks, picture and alphabet blocks, **parquetry blocks**, large hollow blocks, superblocks, large cardboard blocks, **bristle blocks**, **LEGOs**, and other interlocking systems. All of these block systems have their individual merits and uses in early childhood programs; in this chapter we consider the use of unit blocks.

Many physical development skills are emphasized in complex block-building (e.g., movement skills, fine motor skills, perceptual awareness, coordination).

Research on block play has covered a variety of topics. Much has been written about the benefits of block play for young children, often stressing the importance of block play in any preschool program (Love & Burns, 2006; Stroud, 1995). Blocks are open-ended and predictable, so they are not threatening to children who may feel uncomfortable with paint, clay, or other messy materials. Blocks can also be a dramatic material. To build, use, change, destroy, and build again

and again is mastery, and children love to master objects. Using blocks, children learn to help each other in group activities. They learn to lead and to follow, to share ideas and skills, to communicate with each other, and to contribute to a group effort. Children process and learn a wealth of independent and integrated information by playing with blocks (Cartwright, 1987). One great advantage of block play is the development of motor skills such as reaching, **grasping**, balancing, stacking, and carrying. Some research has studied the quantity and type of blocks needed for effective block play. Bender (1978) studied the effect of children having 70 large hollow blocks as opposed to 20 to build with. A greater number of blocks was needed for the children to achieve a higher level of play.

grasping
A part of a child's fine motor development in which he or she grips or holds onto something.

Play supports physical development in ECE programs (Copple & Bredecamp, 2009). Play has an incredible therapeutic value in that it is self-expressive and releases tension. Play allows children to choose freely, yet it usually involves an element of risk or challenge. It involves repetition that helps children consolidate skills as they repeat steps over and over.

❖ ❖ ❖ Section Summary ❖ ❖ ❖

Many different features of young children's physical development are viewed as essential components of healthy child developmental processes, such as gross and fine motor skills development, motor development, progression from large to small motor skills development, and ways of enhancing physical development skills for children. The multitude of different interactions that children have with their family members, peers, teachers, and other community members affect the healthy or unhealthy trajectory of these physical developmental features and influence children's physical developmental patterns in childhood and potentially over a lifetime.

Assessing Physical Development

Parents, teachers, and other caregivers have a responsibility to assist children in enhancing their physical development by being good role models, which provides children with an effective foundation to grow up in a healthy-minded way (Breslin, Morton, & Rudisill, 2008). When professionals think about assessment of physical development, the classroom environment and materials come to mind as critical components for enhancing motor development. In this current framework of providing early educational opportunities for young children, teachers should focus on assessing whether they are providing instructional activities for young children, adapting curricula to meet individual children's learning needs, and monitoring if children are making progress in their physical development (Copple & Bredekamp, 2009).

Of central importance in assessment is consulting and implementing effective instruments developed to assess interactions within the early childhood environment, such as the Early Childhood Environment Rating Scale (ECERS; Harms, Clifford, & Cryer, 2005). The ECERS is a conceptual framework that is used to evaluate quality and consistency in ECE programs. For physical development, the criteria for Fine Motor and Music and Movement on the ECERS are indicators of whether opportunities for growth are being provided (see Figure 9.2).

Inadequate 1	2	Minimal 3	4	Good 5	6	Excellent 7
ACTIVITIES **19. Fine motor** 1.1 Very few developmentally appropriate fine motor materials accessible for daily use. 1.2 Fine motor materials generally in poor repair or incomplete (Ex. puzzles have missing pieces, few pegs for pegboard).		3.1 Some developmentally appropriate fine motor materials of each type accessible. 3.2 Most of the materials are in good repair and complete.		5.1 Many developmentally appropriate fine motor materials of each type accessible for a substantial portion of the day. 5.2 Materials are well organized (Ex. pegs and pegboards stored together, building toy sets stored separately). 5.3 Materials on different levels of difficulty accessible (Ex. both regular and knobbed puzzles for children with varying fine motor skills).		7.1 Materials rotated to maintain interest (Ex. materials that are no longer of interest put away, different materials brought out). 7.2 Containers and accessible storage shelves have labels to encourage self-help (Ex. pictures or shapes used as labels on containers and shelves; word labels added for older children).
21. Music/movement 1.1 No music/movement experiences for children. 1.2 Loud background music is on much of the day and interferes with ongoing activities (Ex. constant background music makes conversation in normal tones difficult; music raises noise level).		3.1 Some music materials accessible for children's use (Ex. simple instruments; music toys; tape player with tapes). 3.2 Staff initiate at least one music activity daily (Ex, sing songs with children; soft music put on at naptime, play music for dancing). 3.3 Some movement/dance activity done at least weekly (Ex. marching or moving to music; acting out movements to songs or rhymes; children given scarves and encouraged to dance to music).		5.1 Many music materials accessible for children's use (Ex. music center with instruments, tape player, dance props; adaptations made for children with disabilities). 5.2 Various types of music are used with the children (Ex. classical and popular music; music characteristic of different cultures; some songs sung in different languages).		7.1 Music available as both a free choice and group activity daily 7.2 Music activities that extend children's understanding of music are offered occasionally (Ex. guest invited to play instrument; children make musical instruments; staff set up activity to help children hear different tones). 7.3 Creativity is encouraged with music activities (Ex. children asked to make up new words to songs; individual dance encouraged).

Figure 9.2. Example items from the Early Childhood Environment Rating Scale in the physical development domain. (Reprinted by permission of the Publisher. From Thelma Harms, Richard M. Clifford, and Debby Cryer, *Early Childhood Environment Rating Scale, Revised Edition*, New York: Teachers College Press. Copyright © 2005 by Thelma Harms, Richard M. Clifford, & Debby Cryer. All rights reserved.)

Objective 5   Demonstrates balancing skills

Not Yet	1	2	3	4	5	6	7	8	9
		Balances while exploring immediate environment • Sits propped up • Rocks back and forth on hands and knees • Sits a while and plays with toys • Sits and reaches for toys without falling		**Experiments with different ways of balancing** • Squats to pick up toys • Stands on tiptoes to reach something • Gets in and out of a chair • Kneels while playing • Straddles a taped line on the floor • Sidesteps across beam or sandbox edge		**Sustains balance during simple movement experiences** • Walks forward along sandbox edge, watching feet • Jumps off low step, landing on two feet • Jumps over small objects • Holds body upright while moving wheelchair forward		**Sustains balance during complex movement experiences** • Hops across the playground • Hops on one foot then the other • Walks across beam or sandbox edge forward and backwards • Attempts to jump rope	

Color key bands: red (2), orange (4), yellow (5), green (6), blue (7), purple (8)

Objective 7   Demonstrates fine-motor strength and coordination

a. Uses fingers and hands

Not Yet	1	2	3	4	5	6	7	8	9
		Reaches for, touches, and holds objects purposefully • Bats or swipes at a toy • Transfers objects from one hand to another • Release objects voluntarily • Rakes or scoops objects to pick them up • Picks up food with fingers and puts in mouth • Bangs two blocks together • Crumbles paper		**Uses fingers and whole-arm movements to manipulate and explore objects** • Places shape in shape sorter • Points at objects and pokes bubbles • Releases objects into containers • Uses spoon and sometimes fork to feed self • Dumps sand into containers • Unbuttons large buttons • Rotates knobs • Tears paper		**Uses refined wrist and finger movements** • Squeezes and releases tongs, turkey baster, squirt toy • Snips with scissors, then later cuts along straight line • Strings large beads • Pours water into containers • Pounds, pokes, squeezes, rolls clay • Buttons, zips, buckles, laces • Uses hand motions for "Itsy Bitsy Spider" • Turns knobs to open doors • Uses eating utensils • Sews lacing cards		**Uses small, precise finger and hand movements** • Uses correct scissors grip • Attempts to tie shoes • Pushes specific keys on a keyboard • Arranges small pegs in pegboard • Strings small beads • Cuts out simple pictures and shapes, using other hand to move paper • Cuts food • Builds a structure using small Legos®	

Color key bands: red (2), orange (4), yellow (5), green (6), blue (7), purple (8)

Figure 9.3.   Example items from the Teaching Strategies GOLD® tool items in the physical development domain. (From Heroman, C., Burts, D.C., Berke, K., & Bickart, T. [2010]. *Teaching Strategies GOLD® Objectives for Development & Learning: Birth Through Kindergarten*. Washington, DC: Teaching Strategies; adapted by permission. *Key to colors in Teaching Strategies GOLD*: red, birth to 1 year; orange, 1 to 2 years; yellow, 2 to 3 years; green, preschool 3 class; blue, pre-K 4 class; purple, kindergarten.)

Adapting Curriculum and Monitoring Progress

Teaching Strategies GOLD Objectives for Development & Learning (Heroman, Burts, Berke, & Bickart, 2010) is an assessment tool that can be used across curriculum models, as it provides a comprehensive means of monitoring children's development as well as academic progress. Teachers document and observe children's development to help adapt curricula and provide differentiated instruction and support. Figure 9.3 provides a few examples of physical development, balancing skills, and fine motor strength and coordination from the Teaching Strategies GOLD tool. In the examples, the green band refers to expectations for children in a preschool 3 class, and the blue band refers to expectations for children in a pre-K 4 class. Please refer to the full assessment document for more information.

❖ ❖ ❖ Section Summary ❖ ❖ ❖

This section discussed assessment tools that teachers use to assess the quality of the physical experiences they are providing in their classrooms. Examples from several of these measures were described, but others are available. A main purpose for teachers using these instruments is to assess whether they are providing young learners with the opportunity to develop effective physical development. In addition, teachers need to know the measures used to determine whether they are effectively adapting curricula to meet individual children's learning needs and monitoring if children are making physical developmental progress (Copple & Bredekamp, 2009). Several examples of these types of measures and activities that promote physical development were provided.

KEY CONCEPTS

- Theory and research about physical development has an impact on ECE teachers practice.

- Ecological theory plays a central role in the understanding of young children's physical development at the microsystem level, given impact by families, neighborhoods, and schools. Macrosystems similarly have an impact on physical development given the child's culture and society of residence.

- Sophisticated research on brain development highlights the integration of sensory development with brain development, as well as all other developmental areas.

- Teachers need to understand features of physical and motor development to provide appropriate ECE. Specifically, features of gross and fine motor development as well as nutrition and physical fitness are integrated into a quality ECE program.

- Learning and academic centers provide ample opportunities for fine and gross motor activities.

- Interactions and opportunities for play that children have with family members, peers, teachers, and other community members have a significant

(continued)

KEY CONCEPTS *(continued)*

impact on healthy and unhealthy trajectories of physical and motor development.

- Teachers should assess their classrooms and their teaching to determine whether they are providing quality opportunities to enhance their young students' physical and motor development.

- Ongoing classroom assessments provide teachers with information necessary to reflect on and adapt their fine and gross motor curriculum to be responsive to each individual child's needs.

- Teachers should constantly reflect on their education and care of children in the area of physical and motor development and understand how this area of development has an impact on all other areas of development—approaches to learning, social and emotional development, cognitive development, and language development.

Integration of Information

You have just read a chapter on physical development, which introduced fine and gross motor development and associated areas of physical development, such as the need for physical activity and a healthy diet within the context of ECE. As is the case in all areas of development, the information included in this chapter overlaps with all other areas of development, including approaches to learning, social and emotional development, cognitive development, and language development. What do you think? Does physical development stand out to you as extremely important for early childhood educators to be familiar with? Do you think you will enjoy teaching young children to develop effective physical development?

Self-Reflective Guide

This self-reflective guide will help you assess whether you learned the information in this chapter. It also provides an opportunity to identify areas in which you want or need more information. Are there some new ideas learned that will affect your immediate practice with children?

1. Recognize theories that have an impact on young children's physical development. Name one. What aspects of this theory align with your observations of young children's physical development? Make a few notes.

2. Recognize the features of physical development. List two aspects of physical development that you think are extremely important for young children to learn and why.

3. Identify how physical development can be addressed across different learning centers and academic areas. List one center and one academic area that are fruit-

ful contexts for developing physically. Elaborate on why these are important contexts.

4. Understand how children interact with teachers and peers as they develop physically and learn. Describe a type of related interaction that you want to develop as an ECE teacher. Elaborate on why this type of interaction is important.

5. Reflect on how play affects physical development. Elaborate on why play is important in children's learning and gross and fine motor development in this area.

6. Describe how teachers can assess whether they are providing quality opportunities for young children to develop and learn in the physical development area.

7. Connect what and how you would assess young children's physical development so that you are able to adapt your curriculum based on findings and also monitor the progress of your students. Identify a child with a disability (note the specific disability) and describe how such assessment information could help you adapt your instruction to meet this child's needs.

8. Reflect on physical development and how this area of development influences and is influenced by other developmental areas discussed in this book, such as approaches to learning, cognitive development, using and understanding language, and social and emotional development.

9. Identify other information learned that can have an immediate impact on your current practice if you are a practicing teacher or caregiver at this time.

10. List areas you need to explore further. Who can help you learn about your concerns?

Helpful Web Sites

Action for Healthy Kids

www.actionforhealthykids.org
Action for Healthy Kids is a nonprofit organization focused on helping children, families, and teachers motivate and improve child health throughout the United States. This site includes information on programs by state, as well as lessons and activities by topic and grade level.

Council For Exceptional Children

www.cec.sped.org
This site offers information for children with disabilities, including those with physical disabilities. CEC promotes adaptive physical education so that all children can participate.

Cuidado De Salud

www.cuidadodesalud.gov/enes/
This site from the U.S. Department of Health & Human Services provides information in Spanish about health for families.

Kids.gov

www.kids.gov/k_5/k_5_health_issues.shtml
This site is the official kids' portal for the U.S. government. Information mostly addresses kindergarteners and older children, but important information for preschoolers is included as well.

Let's Move

www.letsmove.gov
This is the official site of the Let's Move Campaign, launched by First Lady Michelle Obama. The site provides information and activities related to raising healthy children by promoting a healthy diet and physical activity.

National Association for Sport and Physical Education

www.aahperd.org/naspe
This site provides national standards and position statements concerning physical education and development. Lessons and information are available in English and Spanish.

Office of Minority Health

http://minorityhealth.hhs.gov
The Office of Minority Health, an office within the U.S. Department of Health & Human Services, provides information about health, specifically addressing minority groups in the United States.

PBS Teachers PreK Health & Fitness Resources

www.pbs.org/teachers/classroom/prek/health-fitness/resources
This Public Broadcasting Service site provides information and lesson plans focused on health and fitness.

PE Central

http://pecentral.org
This site provides physical activities for young children and early childhood programs.

Team Nutrition

http://teamnutrition.usda.gov/library.html
The U.S. Department of Agriculture's food and nutrition service provides excellent resources and materials to help teach young children and families about healthy nutrition.

References

Bandura, A. (1977). *Social learning theory.* Englewood Cliffs, NJ: Prentice Hall.

Barros, R.M., Silver, E.J., & Stein, R.E.K. (2009). School recess and group classroom behavior. *Pediatrics, 123*(2), 431–436.

Bender, J. (1978). Large hollow blocks: Relationship of quantity to blockbuilding behaviors. *Young Children, 33*(6), 17–23.

Blaydes, J. (2000). *How to make learning a moving experience.* Richmond: Virginia Department of Education.

Breslin, C.M., Morton, J.R., & Rudisill, M.E. (2008). Implementing a physical activity curriculum into the school day: Helping early childhood teachers meet the challenge. *Early Childhood Education Journal, 35,* 429–437.

Bronfenbrenner, U. (1989). Ecological systems theory. *Annals of Child Development, 6*, 185–246.

Brown, W.H., Pfeiffer, K., McIver, K.L., Dowda, M., Addy, C.L., & Pate, R.R. (2009). Social and environmental factors associated with preschoolers' non-sedentary physical activity. *Child Development, 80*(1), 45–58.

Cartwright, S. (1987). Group endeavor in nursery school can be valuable learning. *Young Children, 42*(5), 8–11.

Centers for Disease Control and Prevention. (2009). *Obesity prevalence among low-income, preschool-aged children 1998-2008*. Retrieved March 3, 2011, from http://www.cdc.gov/obesity/childhood/lowincome.html

Children's Defense Fund. (2010). *The State of America's Children 2010*. Retrieved September 29, 2010, from http://www.childrensdefense.org/child-research-data-publications/data/state-of-americas-children-2010-report.html

Copple, C., & Bredekamp, S. (2009). *Developmentally appropriate practice in early childhood programs serving children from birth through age 8* (3rd ed.). Washington, DC: National Association for the Education of Young Children.

Dahlberg, G., & Moss, P. (1999). *Beyond quality in early childhood education*. Philadelphia: Falmer.

Gabbard, C., Cacola, P., & Rodrigues, L.P. (2008). A new inventory for assessing "affordances in the home environment for motor development." *Early Childhood Education Journal, 36*(1), 5–9.

Halberstadt, A.G., Denham, S.A., & Dunsmore, J.C. (2001). Affective social competence. *Social Development, 10*(1), 79–119.

Harms, T., Clifford, R., & Cryer, D. (2005). *Early Childhood Environment Rating Scale* (Rev. Ed.). New York: Teachers College Press.

The Healthy, Hunger-Free Kids Act of 2010, PL 111-296, 42 U.S.C. §§ 1751 *et seq.*

Hendler, S., & Nakelski, M. (2008). Extended day kindergarten: Supporting literacy and motor development through a teacher collaborative model. *Early Childhood Education Journal, 36*, 57–62.

Heroman, C., Burts, D.C., Berke, K., & Bickart, T. (2010). *Teaching Strategies GOLD®: Objectives for Development & and Learning: Birth Through Kindergarten*. Washington, DC: Teaching Strategies.

Hyson, M. (2003). Putting early academics in their place. *Educational Leadership, 60*(7), 20–23.

Jensen, E. (2005). *Teaching with the brain in mind* (2nd ed.). Alexandria, VA: Association for Supervision and Curriculum Development.

Love, A., & Burns, M.S. (2006). 'It's a hurricane! It's a hurricane!': Can music facilitate social constructive and socio-dramatic play in a preschool classroom? *Journal of Genetic Psychology, 167*, 383–391.

Malina, R.M. (1994). Physical activity and training: Effects on stature and the adolescent growth spurt. *Medicine & Science in Sports & Exercise, 26*(6), 759–766.

McHale, S., & Crouter, A. (1996). The family contexts of children's sibling relationships. In G.H. Brody (Ed.), *Sibling relationships: Their causes and consequences* (pp. 173–195). Norwood, NJ: Ablex.

Morrison, G.S. (2009). *Teaching in America* (5th ed). Columbus, OH: Pearson.

Nieto, S. (2010). *The light in their eyes: Creating multicultural learning communities* (10th anniversary ed.). New York: Teachers College Press.

Ogden, C.L., Carroll, M.D., Curtin, L.R., Lamb, M.M., & Flegal, K.M. (2010). Prevalence of high body mass index in US children and adolescents, 2007–2008. *Journal of the American Medical Association, 303*(3), 242–249.

Reynolds, G. (2010, September 19). The fittest brains: How exercising affects kids' intelligence. *New York Times Magazine*, p. 28.

Skinner, B.F. (1957). *Verbal behavior.* Acton, Massachusetts: Copley Publishing Group.

Stroud, J. (1995). Block play: Building a foundation for literacy. *Early Childhood Education Journal, 23*, 9–13.

White House Task Force on Childhood Obesity. (2010). *Solving the problem of childhood obesity within a generation.* Retrieved February 26, 2011, from http://www.letsmove.gov/pdf/TaskForce_on_Childhood_Obesity_May2010_FullReport.pdf

Learning in Early Childhood Is Continuous

10

This final chapter considers some aspects of early childhood education (ECE) not mentioned in previous chapters. Our goal for this book is to provide a comprehensive introduction to the field of ECE—one that is informative, useful, and provides a basis for reflection for new professionals entering the field. As early childhood educators who have worked in different programs across the United States, we recognize that we provide a predominantly American perspective. We are grateful that we have had the opportunity to work with multicultural and multilingual students and families, as well as children with disabilities and their families.

International Perspectives

World perspectives in ECE are briefly touched upon in this book. For more detail, we suggest that you review *Early Childhood Education: An International Encyclopedia* (New & Cochran, 2007), which includes perspectives on ECE from many different countries, including Australia, Brazil, China, the Czech Republic, France, Italy, Japan, South Africa, Sweden, and the United Kingdom. Additional information from other parts of the world are readily available in the literature.

ECE practice varies widely around the world. For example, consider the recommended teacher-to-child ratios for preschool classes in Mexico and Norway (Organisation for Economic Co-operation and Development, 2006). In Mexico, there is no official regulation governing child-to-staff ratios, but for planning purposes the Ministry of Education recommends a ratio of 25:1. The overall ratio of children to teachers is 22:1. In contrast, in Norway the ratio is 7–9 children per 1 trained preschool teacher when children attend more than 6 hours per day. For 3- to 6-year-old children, the ratio is 14–18 children per 1 teacher.

Exploring practices from other parts of the world will help you to look deeply at your own subjective practices as a teacher, as well as the ECE field as a whole. This personal reflection and the deeper understanding of current and historical practices will strengthen

Many similar early childhood activities are found in classrooms around the world.

your individual and collective identity as you continue to develop as an early childhood educator.

Advocacy

We did not specifically set out in this book to address advocacy, but it is important to remember that your actions (or lack thereof) may influence the larger field of ECE. For example, consider the impact of the No Child Left Behind Act of 2001 (PL 107-110) and its lingering effects on children and early childhood practices. In some cases, it has redefined the preschool years by overstressing the standardization of education and putting newfound pressure on preschool. In some cases, this pressure has pushed down the first-grade curriculum into the kindergarten classroom, so now preschoolers must complete what were previously kindergarten curriculum activities (Stipek, 2006). The federal government's 2010 Race to the Top education initiative builds on this history (U.S. Department of Education, 2010). It will affect preschool children in multiple ways and continue to redefine the field of practice. The voices of ECE professionals, parents, caregivers, and community members need to be heard as practices in ECE get redefined over the course of your career.

An additional area that provides an excellent example of your need to advocate in ECE is related to professional development for early childhood educators and salary levels in the ECE field. Recall from Chapter 1 that there is a wide range in both of these areas. Early childhood educators from all backgrounds need the opportunity to access quality professional development and associated degrees. Pathways that are economically achievable as well as accessible by location and time of delivery of program need to be available. Wages, especially those in child care, need to be equitable.

Reflection Is Never Ending

Just as advocacy and knowledge are a never-ending process in education, so too is reflection. It is an ongoing cycle of learning and refining one's practice. As an ECE professional, you are responsible for understanding current changes in the field. Experts can provide insight, but you should also look both inside and outside your own classroom, school, and county to keep growing. Here are some additional guidelines:

Be critical of new information and practices that come to you as a teacher.

Question curricula that do not seem to be working for your young learners and their families, then change what is not working.

Have high expectations for learning and development of children living in poverty.

Embrace the richness that children and families from culturally and linguistically diverse backgrounds bring to your program.

Be careful about stereotypes of families with different structures.

Understand that young children with disabilities have varying developmental and learning needs.

A Rewarding Challenge

Whether you teach ECE or early childhood special education in a public or private school or in a child care center, you will encounter children from diverse backgrounds who themselves have individual characteristics that lead to the need for a thoughtful, professional teacher. Knowledge, skills, and dispositions to meet the needs of the children will be a rewarding challenge. You will be involved with all kinds of families, enriching your work. You will be asked to meet professional standards and will continue to improve your practice. Your own interests and strengths will propel you to excellence.

References

New, R.S., & Cochran, M. (2007). *Early childhood education: An international encyclopedia*. Westport, CT: Praeger.

No Child Left Behind Act of 2001, PL 107-110, 115 Stat. 1425, 20 U.S.C. §§ 12501 *et seq.*

Organisation for Economic Co-operation and Development. (2006). *Starting strong II: Early childhood education and care*. Paris, France: Author. Retrieved December 22, 2010, from http://www.oecd.org/dataoecd/14/32/37425999.pdf

Stipek, D. (2006). No Child Left Behind comes to preschool. *The Elementary School Journal, 106*(5), 455–465.

U.S. Department of Education. (2010). *Race to the Top fund*. Retrieved February 22, 2011, from http://www2.ed.gov/programs/racetothetop/index.html

Glossary

AAC *see* augmentative and alternative communication (AAC) systems

accommodations Changes made in the early childhood environment (both indoor and outdoor) so that children with disabilities can participate (e.g., wheelchair ramp).

ADA *see* Americans with Disabilities Act (ADA) of 1990 (PL 101-336).

adaptations Any means used to help a child with a disability (e.g., wheelchairs, communication devices, special eating utensils).

Americans with Disabilities Act (ADA) of 1990 (PL 101-336) Federal legislation that requires accommodations so that individuals with disabilities have access to goods and services available to the general public.

assistive technology A type of adaptation that is specific to an individual with a disability so that he or she can function in activities that would be impossible or very difficult to participate in without such a device.

attribute A construct associated with characteristics of items (e.g., color, shape, size).

augmentative and alternative communication (AAC) systems Communication systems that allow individuals without oral fluency to communicate (e.g., gestures, pictures, writing, communication boards).

bilingual The ability to speak two languages.

body awareness An individual's awareness of his or her own body (e.g., pain) and of his or her body in space (e.g., proximity to another person).

bristle blocks Blocks for children's constructive play that are usually of varied primary colors, with small nubs that allow the blocks to interlock for building or making patterns.

center-based care (education) Care or education that occurs within a child development center with multiple classrooms for preschool, in contrast to home or school settings.

constructivist theory A perspective on children's development and learning that highlights how children construct their own knowledge through interaction with the environment, both physical and social.

contingencies Dependence on a future event or condition.

coordination Effective interaction of movements (e.g., eye–hand coordination to build with blocks, eye–foot coordination to kick a soccer ball).

corporate-sponsored child care Child care or education that is provided by a parent's employer.

criterion-referenced assessment Children are measured on whether or not they have a particular skill using a tool that includes skills across developmental or academic areas.

cubbies   Private spaces in the classroom that are individually assigned to children, where they can hang their coats and keep other personal items.

cultural awareness   The awareness of cultural richness in a particular setting such that it is a source of new learning as well as a marker for respecting cultural differences.

cultural competence   Having the awareness, insight, knowledge and skills to interact with others from a different cultural group than one's own.

cultural transmission of information   Cultural information that is passed to children from adults, peers, and community.

cultural values   A cultural preference that guides thoughts and actions.

curriculum theme   A topic that defines a curriculum for a particular period of time.

curriculum-based assessment   An assessment in which a child is measured on whether or not they have mastered an activity or skill that is part of a particular curriculum.

developmental trajectory   A developmental course followed by an individual as determined by child development milestones for typical development; multiple developmental trajectories acknowledge that there are variations in development (e.g., a child with a specific language impairment will develop in a different way and rate).

dialogic reading   A type of book reading with young children in which the goal is conversation around the book to develop children's vocabulary and syntax.

dual-language learners   Children who are learning at least two languages.

ecosystems   Independent aspects of an individual's life that interact with each other and affect each other.

educational opportunities   Learning and development opportunities that children have been given.

equivalence   Two items with the same quantity.

ethnic identity   An individual's identity with his or her ethnic group, which affects emotions, thoughts, and behavior.

expressive processes   Language processes in which a person acts on the physical and social world through such things as action, speech, and writing.

extended families   Families that include parents and children, as well as grandparents, cousins, aunts and uncles, nieces and nephews, and more distant relatives living together and taking part in care of children.

family child care   Child care provided in a private home for children who are not related to the homeowner.

family stories   Stories of an individual's family that have a meaningful impact on how he or she functions in the world.

family structure   Members of a family and their functions and hierarchical positions.

found materials   Materials for children that were not necessarily intended for use in a play activity (e.g., a cardboard box).

grasping   A part of a child's fine motor development in which he or she grips or holds onto something.

high-quality ECE   Programs deemed high quality given a particular valid and reliable measure or understanding of quality in early childhood education.

IDEA 2004   *see* Individuals with Disabilities Education Improvement Act (IDEA) of 2004 (PL 108-446)

IEP   *see* individualized education program (IEP)

IFSP *see* individualized family service plan (IFSP)

impulse control The ability to regulate oneself and resist or delay an activity.

inclusion The placement of children with disabilities in classrooms and programs for children without disabilities.

individualized education program (IEP) A written plan for a child with a disability including assessments, services, and placements for provision of an education.

individualized family service plan (IFSP) A written plan for an infant or toddler with a disability that focuses on early intervention that is family centered; can also be substituted for an IEP for 3- to 5-year-old children.

Individuals with Disabilities Education Improvement Act (IDEA) of 2004 (PL 108-446) The public law that provides for an appropriate education for children with disabilities. IDEA 2004 reflects changes and clarifications to parent involvement, which is particularly important for ECE.

instructional assistant A teacher in the class who assists a lead teacher in providing instruction.

intentional teaching Teaching that takes into account children's individual needs and interests, which includes differentiated instruction and culturally responsive practice.

internalized problems A child who has internalized problems tends to be withdrawn or fearful, and might have associated health problems.

knowledge, skills, and dispositions Characteristics that are considered by professional groups and researchers to determine the quality of teachers.

least restrictive environment A basic policy in IDEA to provide an environment in which children with disabilities can function and learn with typically developing children.

LEGOs Construction blocks that are interlocking and that are often different sizes, colors, and shapes with some realistic features that can be attached to the blocks.

locomotion Gross motor activity that moves a child through space.

manipulative toy An educational toy that can be handled with a child's hands.

memory strategy A strategy that can help an individual remember something, such as repeating or visualizing.

mental representation How objects and concepts are represented in an individual's mind.

mental tool A way that an individual uses his or her mind to learn (e.g., visualizing something in order to remember it).

metalinguistics Understanding about the form of language aside from its use and meaning (e.g., how young children pick out and enjoy rhyming).

monolingual An individual who uses and understands only one language.

morphology Meaning units in words.

multilingualism The ability to speak more than one language.

National Association for the Education of Young Children (NAEYC) The main professional organization for early childhood educators.

National Council of Teachers of Mathematics (NCTM) A professional organization for mathematics teachers.

nesting cubes Blocks that fit inside one another which are used to support the understanding of size and sequence.

nuclear families Families that include parents and their children, including single parents and same-sex parents.

opportunities to learn   Instruction and experiences provided in high-quality environments that support learning and development.

parallel play   Occurs when children play alongside one another without interacting in any way.

parquetry blocks   Geometrically shaped blocks that children use to make patterns and designs.

person-first language   Language used to indicate that a child is a person first, rather than a disability (e.g., a child with autism, *not* an autistic child).

phonology   The study of speech sounds and how they are sequenced and structured in words.

Plan-Do-Review   A method developed by HighScope to help children self-regulate and learn by planning what they want to achieve during learning center time and reviewing whether they achieved their goals afterwards.

planning time   A time during the preschool day when children have the opportunity to think about the play and activity they want to participate in that day.

posture   The physical arrangement or orientation of a person's body.

pragmatics   Language use and function of language across contexts.

prior knowledge   Information that was previously obtained.

private speech   Oral communication directed toward oneself.

prosocial behavior   Actions that demonstrate empathy for and awareness of the well-being of others.

readiness   The state of being prepared or willing; in early childhood education, often refers to whether children are prepared to be successful in kindergarten.

receptive language   Listening and understanding oral language or visually receiving and understanding sign language or print.

representation   The expression of some person, group, or object by a separate entity or symbol.

resiliency skills   Strategies used to bounce back or recover from difficult situations.

resilient   The ability to learn and develop even in difficult, negative, or frustrating circumstances.

scaffolding   Providing instruction that helps a child learn an activity but also requires that the child have as much responsibility for learning as possible (e.g., by including hints).

school mentor   A school-based knowledgeable and trusted guide to help with difficulties related to teaching young children.

scribe   A person assigned to write what one or more other people say.

script   The cultural processes involved in functioning in the world learned through experience and interactions with knowledgeable peers and adults (e.g., going to the grocery store, going to the library).

self-regulatory capacities   The abilities of individuals to govern or be in command of themselves.

semantic networks   A representation of the relationships between concepts, organized by the meaning of the concepts.

semantics   Study of the meaning of language.

SES   *see* socioeconomic status (SES)

shared language systems   Shared systems of communication across numbers of people.

siblings   Individuals who share one or both parents (biological or otherwise).

social network   The set of contacts with which a person interacts on a regular basis.

socioeconomic status (SES)   An individual's income and educational levels, as well as level of professional status in employment.

sociodramatic play   A type of play in which a child or children assume roles and act out a familiar scene in play.

stages of cognition   Distinct levels of mental abilities along the process of child development.

symmetry   The congruence of form or shape across a line dividing the object into two parts.

syntax   The order and combination of words that creates sentences.

tact   A term in verbal behavioral theory for a feature of the environment.

Teach for America   A U.S. organization that trains, supports, and places new teachers in high-need schools.

teenage parents   Individuals between the ages of 13 and 19 years who have children.

temperament   An individual's manner of behaving or thinking.

Title I   The largest federal program for elementary/secondary education geared to the needs of low-income children and families, which includes funds for prekindergarten education.

translator   A person who is responsible for mediating communication between parties who do not share a common language.

tripod grasp   A grasp in which the writing instrument is held between one's first two fingers and thumb.

universal prekindergarten   Voluntary public preschool for all children that is not based on a targeted group, such as income or disability.

verbal cues   Hints from the teacher to assist the student in accomplishing a task, provided through speech rather than physical signals.

word awareness   The ability to differentiate between words and understand their meaning.

zone of proximal development (ZPD)   A concept developed by Lev Vygotsky referring to the mental space between what a student can do independently and what that student can do with the assistance of a teacher or tutor.

Index

Throughout this index, *f* indicates a figure, *t* indicates a table, and *b* indicates a box on that page.

AAC, *see* Augmentative and alternative communication technology
Accommodations, 32, 33, 36
Accreditation of ECE program, 9, 13–14
ACEI, *see* Association for Childhood Education International
Achievement, school, 30, 165
Activities
  airplane template, 99*f*
  approaches to learning, 97–101, 97*f*
  cognitive development, 139–143, 140*f*
  in content areas, 97, 97*f*
  language development, 166–171, 167*f*
  physical development, 189–192, 189*f*
  social and emotional development, 120–124, 121*f*
Adaptations, 32
ADHD, *see* Attention-deficit/hyperactivity disorder
African Americans, 119
Ages & Stages Questionnaires® (Squires & Bricker, 2009), 38
Alaska Natives, 188
American Sign Language (ASL), 35, 158, 160
Americans with Disabilities Act (ADA) of 1990 (PL 101-336), 33, 33*f*
Approaches to learning, *see* Learning, approaches to
Art center, 68
Ascendent multilingual, 28*f*
Assessment
  of approaches to learning, 101–105, 103*f*
  cognitive development, 143–147
  of ECE program, 14–15
  language development, 171–177
  physical development, 192–195
  social and emotional development, 124–128
  standards in, 18, 18*f*
  through play, 75*b*
Assessment Profile for Early Childhood Programs (Abbott-Shim & Sibley, 1992), 14
Assistive technology, 35, 36, 37, 39
Association for Childhood Education International (ACEI), 51
Athetoid cerebral palsy, 36
Attachment, benefits of, 117
Attention, 93
Attention-deficit/hyperactivity disorder (ADHD), 39–40
Attributes, 137, 138

Augmentative and alternative communication (AAC) technology, 36*b*, 160
Autism spectrum disorders, 39, 157, 160–161

Balance, 186
Bank Street Nursery School, 54
Behavior management, 57
Behavioral theory, 184
Beyond the Pleasure Principle (Freud, 1920/1961), 51
Bias, 31, 118, 118*b*
Bilingual Education Act, 58
Bilingualism, 2, 3, 27, 28*f*, 160
Black Ants and Buddhists (Cowhey, 2006), 122
Blindness, 35
Blocks, 69, 74, 143, 191–192
Blow, Susan, 50
Body awareness, 185, 190
Books, 67, 120
  see also Literacy
Botulinum toxin (Botox), 37
Brain development, 136, 184, 185
Bristle blocks, 191
Bronfenbrenner, Urie, 57, 112
Bureau of Educational Experiments, 54

Caring for Our Children (CFOC) report, 13
Carnegie Foundation, 58
CDA, *see* Child Development Associate
CEC, *see* Council for Exceptional Children
Center-based care, *see* Early childhood education (ECE) programs
Centers, *see* Learning centers
Cerebral palsy, 36–37
Child abuse and neglect, 30–31
Child care centers
  accreditation of, 9, 13–14
  history of, 55
  increasing attendance in, 56
Child Care Development and Block Grant (1990), 59–60
Child Care Mandatory and Matching Funds of the Child Care and Development Fund, 7–8
Child development
  19th century theorists on, 46, 48–50, 49*f*
  20th century theorists on, 51–54, 52*f*, 56–57, 57*f*

Child development—*continued*
  brain development on, 136, 184–185
  constructivist theory on, 134–135
  critical theory on, 116
  dynamic skills perspective on, 136
  ecological theory on, 112–115, 114*f*,
    154–155, 184
  information processing theory on, 87–88,
    88*f*
  narrative construction of reality theory
    on, 135–136
  pyschosocial theory on, 115–116
  social constructivist theory on, 88–90,
    155–156
  social learning theory on, 87
  theory of mind on, 74*b*, 90
  verbal behavior theory on, 156–157
Child Development Associate (CDA), 10, 13
Child Find, 39*b*
Children with disabilities
  ADHD, 39–40
  assessing through play, 75*b*
  autism spectrum disorders, 39
  emotional and behavioral disorders, 40
  encouraging motor development in, 186*b*
  encouraging play for, 74
  federal legislation and, 32–34
  Gesell on, 53
  identification of, 39*b*
  intellectual disabilities, 37–38
  language development and, 161–162
  learning disabilities, 40
  multiple disabilities, 41
  overview of, 31–32
  physical and health disabilities, 36–37
  picture/symbol systems, 160–161
  sensory impairments, 34–36
  speech and language impairments, 40
  UN rights of, 59*b*
  verbal behavior theory and, 157
Chronosystems (ecological theory), 57, 113,
    155
Church/synagogue programs, *see* Early
    childhood education (ECE) programs
Clark, Kenneth, 118*b*
Clark, Mamie, 118*b*
Clark experiment, 118*b*
Classroom Assessment Scoring System™
    (CLASS™; Pianta, La Paro, & Hamre,
    2008), 14, 101–102, 103*f*, 125*f*, 126
Classroom Practices Inventory (Hyson,
    Hirsh-Pasek, & Rescorla, 1990), 14
Cochlear implants, 35*b*, 160
Cognitive development
  activities, 139–143, 140*f*
  assessment of, 143–147
  brain development and, 136
  features of, 137–139
  importance of interactions for, 142–143
  language development and, 139, 155,
    161, 162

  learning center for, 140–143, 140*f*
  multilingualism and, 160
  Piaget on, 56
  supporting diversity in, 139–143
  theories of, 134–137
Columbia Greenhouse Nursery School, 54
Comenius, John Amos, 46, 47*f*
*The Common Sense Book of Baby and Child
    Care* (Spock, 1946), 55
Communication
  cerebral palsy and, 36
  culture and, 157, 159–160
  with families, 78
  hearing loss and, 35
  interactions and, 75–76, 101
  language development and, 157–158
  systems of, 158*f*
Communities
  deaf, 35*b*
  exploring in the classroom, 122–123, 123*f*
  exploring through social studies, 122,
    141, 167, 190
  links to in ecological theory, 113–114
  served by ECE professionals, 26
  standards on building relationships with,
    17, 17*f*
Community-based programs, *see* Early
    childhood education (ECE) programs
Concepts, learning, 137
Conflict resolution, 123*b*
Constructive play, 73
Constructivist theory, 56, 134–135, 154
Content areas
  activities and, 97, 97*f*
  approaches to learning in, 98–101
  cognitive development in, 140–143, 140*f*
  language development in, 166–171, 167*f*
  physical development in, 189–192
  social and emotional development in, 121*f*
Contingencies, environmental, 156
Convention on the Rights of the Child
    (1989), 59*b*, 60
Conversations
  approaches to learning and, 102, 102*b*
  from book reading, 170*b*
  language development and, 169, 175*f*
  see also Interactions
Coordination, 35, 185–186, 187
Corporate-sponsored child care, 59
Council for Exceptional Children (CEC),
    15–21, 16*f*–20*f*
Cowhey, Mary, 122
Creative arts
  approaches to learning in, 98
  cognitive development in, 140–141
  language development in, 167–168
  physical development in, 189–190
  social and emotional development in, 122
Creativity, 95
Criterion-referenced assessments, 102, 126,
    143, 175

Critical theory, 116, 154, 184
Cubbies, 66
Cued speech, 160
Cultural competence, 26
Cultural diversity
    awareness of, 12, 26–27
    in the classroom, 3, 4
    communication development and, 157,
        159–160
    considering during first week of school, 79
    deafness and, 35b
    demographics, 26–27
    pragmatics and, 162
    social constructivist theory and, 88
    sociodramatic play and, 171
    TESOL standards on, 17f
    values and, 26
    views on school and teacher roles, 113
Cultural transmission of information, 56,
    88, 135–136
Curiosity, 93
Curriculum themes, 68, 70
Curriculum-based assessments, 102, 126,
    143, 175

Deafness, 35–36, 160
Developmental trajectories, 136
Dewey, John, 52, 54
Dialogic reading, 169
Discrimination, 33, 33f, 118b
Division for Early Childhood, 34b
Down syndrome, 38, 161
Dramatic play, see Sociodramatic play
Dual-language learners, 8, 8b, 58, 160
    see also English-language learners
Dynamic skills perspective, 136, 137, 154

Early Childhood Classroom Observation
    Measure (ECCOM; Stipek & Byler,
    2004), 14, 101–102, 143, 145f, 172, 172f
Early Childhood Education: An International
    Encyclopedia (New & Cochran, 2007),
    201
Early childhood education (ECE) educators
    advocacy by, 202
    characteristics of, 11–15
    demographics of, 4–5
    history of training of, 50–51
    labor statistics, 9–11
    professional standards for, 15–21
    reasons for, 2–4
    salary, 9–11, 10f, 12, 202
    settings for, 5–9
Early childhood education (ECE) programs
    pre-19th century, 46–48
    19th century, 48–51
    early 20th century, 51–55
    later 20th century, 56–61
    advocacy in, 202

beginnings of, 57–58
core concepts of, 73–78
daily schedule, 71–72
demographics of teachers in, 4–5
exploring diversity of, 201–202
first weeks of, 78–80
funding for, 6–7, 58–60
high quality, 13, 15, 18, 58–60
historical timeline, 49f, 52f, 57f
salaries paid by, 9–11, 10t, 12, 202
setting up the environment, 66–71
socioeconomic status (SES) and, 9b, 30
underfunded, 170
Early Childhood Environment Rating Scale
    (ECERS; Harms, Clifford, & Cryer,
    2005)
    assessing cognitive development with,
        143, 144f
    assessing physical development with,
        192, 193f
    assessing social and emotional develop-
        ment with, 126, 126f
    overview of, 14
Early Childhood Inclusion (2009), 34b
Early childhood special education (ECSE)
    programs, 5–6, 6f, 7b
Early Head Start, 58
Early Language and Literacy Classroom
    Observation Measure (ELLCO; Smith,
    Brady, & Anastasopoulos, 2008), 14–15,
    172, 173f–174f
ECCOM, see Early Childhood Classroom
    Observation Measure (Stipek & Byler,
    2004)
ECE, see Early childhood education pro-
    grams
Ecological theory, 57, 112–115, 114f,
    154–155, 184
Economic Opportunity Act of 1964
    (PL 88-452), 58
Ecosystems (ecological theory), 112
Education
    ECE teachers, 10
    importance of, 12
    parental, 29
    social development and, 52
    state requirements for, 12–14, 13t
Education for All Handicapped Children
    Act of 1975 (PL 94-142), 8b, 58
The Ego and the Id (Freud, 1923/1949), 51
Egocentrism, 135
Elaborative processes, 92f, 93–94, 96
Elementary and Secondary Education Act
    (ESEA) Amendments (PL 90-247), 58
Eliot, Abigail, 55
Elliott, Jane, 118b
Emerging Academic Snapshot (Ritchie,
    Howes, Kraft-Sayre, & Weiser, 2001), 15
Emile (Rousseau), 48
Emotional and behavioral disorders, 40
Endurance, 186

English-language learners, 18*f*
   see also Dual-language learners
Environment
   for assessment, 75*b*
   creating a community in, 122–123, 123*f*
   of the early childhood program, 66–71
   high-quality, 101
   materials in, 142–143
   metalinguistics and, 165
   for naps, 70–71
   positive, 12
   in the social constructivist theory, 88
   in the social learning theory, 87
   stimulation from, 73
   supporting development, 135
   theorists on, 46, 53, 56
Environmental contingencies, 156
Epilepsy, 37
Erikson, Erik, 56, 115–116
Ethnic identity, 115, 118
Exosystems (ecological theory), 57, 113, 155
Explanatory talk, 104*f*
Expressive language, 159, 159*f*, 161,
   162–166, 175*f*
Expressive processes, 92*f*, 95–96
Extended family, 28

Families
   building relationships with, 17, 17*f*,
     77–78
   characteristics of, 26–30
   knowledge of child, 117
   paying for ECE programs, 6
   served by ECE professionals, 26
   structure of, 28–30
   see also Parents
Family child care providers, 9
Federal legislation, 32–34, 55
   see also Individuals with Disabilities Edu-
     cation Improvement Act (IDEA) of
     2004 (PL 108-446)
Fetal alcohol syndrome, 38
Fine motor development, 35, 36, 162, 187
Following directions, 104*f*
Free and appropriate public education
   (FAPE), 58
Freud, Sigmund, 51–52
Froebel, Frederick, 49
Frustration tolerance, 95
Functional behavioral assessment, 38*b*
Funding, 6–9, 58–60

Gay and lesbian parents, 29
Gender, 4–5
Geometry, 138
Gesell, Arnold, 53, 55
Grasping, 192
Gross motor development, 35, 36, 70,
   185–186

Handicapped Children's Early Education
   Program, 58
Head Start Child Outcomes Framework
   (U.S. Department of Health and
   Human Services, 2000), 137
Head Start program
   beginnings of, 58
   benefits of, 2
   demographics of teachers in, 4–6, 6*f*
   federal funding for, 8, 58
   goals of, 58*b*
   overview of, 8*b*
   performance standards of, 91
   teacher education requirements, 10
   theories influencing, 57
Healthy, Hunger-Free Kids Act of 2010
   (PL 111-296), 188
Hearing loss, 35–36
HighScope (Hohmann, Weikart, & Epstein,
   2008), 126, 137
HighScope Educational Research Foundation, 58
Hill, Patty Smith, 55
Hispanics, 26–27, 188
Hull House kindergarten training, 51
Hydrocephalus, 37

IDEA, *see* Individuals with Disabilities
   Education Improvement Act of 2004
   (PL 108-446)
Identity, 118
IEP, *see* Individualized education program
IFSP, *see* Individualized family service
   plans
Imitation (verbal behavior theory), 156
Immigrant families, 27
Improving Teacher Quality State
   Grants, 7
Impulse control, 93, 155
Incipient multilingual, 28*f*
Inclusion, 3, 32, 34*b*
Individual-based exclusive communica-
   tion systems, 158*f*
Individualized education program (IEP),
   32, 32*f*
Individualized family service plans (IFSP),
   32–33
Individuals with Disabilities Education Act
   (IDEA) of 1990 (PL 101-476), 32
Individuals with Disabilities Education
   Improvement Act (IDEA) of 2004
   (PL 108-446), 7, 7*b*, 32, 39*b*, 58
   see also Federal legislation
Information processing theory, 87–88, 87*f*,
   154
Initiation (verbal behavior theory), 156
Initiative, 92–93
Instructional assistant, 4, 13*t*
Instructional planning, 19, 19*f*, 72*b*
Intellectual disabilities, 37–38

Intentional teaching, 50, 76, 76*b*, 77*f*, 142
Interactions
     activities and, 122–124, 142–143, 168–171,
          191–192
     approaches to learning in, 74–77, 77*f*, 100
     for assessing language development, 176*f*
     communication and, 75–76, 101
     as core of ECE programs, 74–77, 77*f*
     planning for, 100
     play and, 100–101
     quality of, 114
     see also Conversations
Interactive reading, 169, 170*b*
Internalized behavior, 40
International Kindergarten Union, 51
International Reading Association, 15
Interverbal (verbal behavior theory), 156
Irreversibility (constructivist theory), 135
Irwin, Elizabeth, 54

Johnson, Harriet, 54
Johnson, Lyndon B., 6

Kaiser Company, 55
Keats, Ezra Jack, 170*b*
Kindergarten, 48, 49, 50
Kindness, 12

Labeling, classroom, 66
Laboratory School at University of Chi-
          cago, 54
Language development
     activities and, 166–171, 167*f*
     assessment of, 171–177
     awareness of language and, 176*f*–177*f*
     children with disabilities and, 161–162
     for cognitive development, 139, 155, 161,
          162
     communication and, 157–158
     features of, 157–166, 162*f*
     importance of, 89
     multilingualism and, 27, 28*f*
     purposes of, 162, 163*f*
     sociodramatic play and, 73
     theories of, 154–157
     typical, 159*f*
     see also Shared language systems
Lanham Public War Housing Act
          (PL 76-849), 55
Learning, approaches to
     activities and, 97–101, 97*f*
     assessment of, 101–105, 103*f*
     conversations to develop, 102, 102*b*
     elaborative processes in, 92*f*, 93–95
     expressive processes in, 92*f*, 95–96
     features of, 91–92
     receptive processes in, 92–93, 92*f*
     supporting diversity in, 17*f*, 96–101

     theories in, 87–91
     through interactions, 74–77, 77*f*, 100
Learning centers
     approaches to learning and, 97*f*
     cognitive development, 140–143, 140*f*
     introducing, 79
     language development, 167*f*
     physical development, 189–192, 189*f*
     setting up, 66–70
     social and emotional development,
          120–124, 121*f*
     talk allowed in, 166
Learning disabilities, 40
Least restrictive environment (LRE), 7, 7*b*,
          32
LEGOs, 191
Let's Move Campaign, 188
Licensing/registration, 9
Literacy
     approaches to learning in, 99–100
     deafness and, 36
     learning center for, 67
     supporting cognitive development
          through, 142
     supporting language development
          through, 168
     supporting physical development
          through, 191
     supporting social and emotional devel-
          opment through, 120–121
     see also Books
Locke, John, 46
Locomotion, 190
Low-income families/communities, 7, 60
     see also Socioeconomic status (SES)
LRE, *see* Least restrictive environment

Macrosystems (ecological theory), 57, 113,
          155
Manipulative skills, 66–67, 187
Math/numeracy
     approaches to learning in, 98–99
     learning center for, 66–67
     supporting cognitive development
          through, 138, 141
     supporting language development
          through, 168
     supporting physical development
          through, 190
     supporting social and emotional devel-
          opment through, 121
Meek, Lois (Stolz), 55
Memory, 94, 101*b*, 162
Memory strategies, 89, 94, 94*b*
Mental representations, 124
Mental tools (social constructivist theory),
          88, 89
Mentor, 72*b*
Mesosystems (ecological theory), 57, 113,
          155

Metalinguistics, 157, 165–166
Microsystems (ecological theory), 57, 113, 155
Minimum Essentials for Nursery Education (National Committee on Nursery School, 1929), 55
Mitchell, Lucy Sprague, 54
Modeling, 87, 167
Monolingual, 159
Montessori, Maria, 52–53
Morphemes, 164
Morphology, 40, 164
Motivation, 87
Multidimensional development and learning, 16, 16f
Multilingualism, 27–28, 28f, 58, 160
Music, 140, 190
Myelomeningocele, 37

Naps, 70–71
Narrative construction of reality theory, 135–136, 154
Narratives, 136, 175f–176f
National Association for Nursery Education (NANE), 55
National Association for the Education of Young Children (NAEYC)
    accreditation by, 9, 13–14
    foundations of, 50
    on inclusion, 34b
    standards, 15–21, 16f–20f
    theorist influences on, 56
    trying to increase quality of ECE, 13
National Council of Teachers of Mathematics, 15
National Dissemination Center for Children with Disabilities, 34
National Education Goals Panel, 58
National Federation of Day Nurseries, 50
National Home Start Program, 58
Native Americans, 119, 188
Nesting cubes, 53
New York Seminary for Kindergarteners, 51
No Child Left Behind Act of 2001 (PL 107-110), 58, 202
Nuclear family, 28
Numeracy, *see* Math/numeracy
Nursery School at Columbia University, 54
Nutrition, 187–188

Obama, Michelle, 188
Obesity, 187–188
Office of Child Care, 7
Organization/planning skills, 94–95, 187
Oshkosh Normal School, 51
Outdoor play, 70
Owen, Robert, 48

Parallel play, 69
Parent Cooperative Schools International, 59
Parents
    as child's first teacher, 46, 165
    as expert on their child, 117
    in the family structure, 28–29
    immigrant, 27
    involvement of, 77–78
    see also Families
Parquetry blocks, 191
Patterns/measurement, 138–139
Peabody, Elizabeth, 50
Peers, 74–77, 171
Persistence, 95
Personal Responsibility and Work Opportunity Reconciliation Act of 1996 (PL 104-193), 59–60
Person-first language, 3
Pestalozzi, Johann, 48
Phonological awareness, 165, 176f–177f
Phonology, 40, 163
Photos/pictures, 66
Physical development
    activities and, 189–192, 189f
    assessment of, 192–195
    brain development and, 184, 185
    features of, 185–188
    theories of, 184–185
Physical fitness, 187–188
Piaget, Jean, 56, 134
Picture Exchange Communication System, 160, 161f
Picture/symbol systems, 139, 160, 161f
PL 76-849, *see* Lanham Public War Housing Act
PL 88-452, *see* Economic Opportunity Act of 1964
PL 90-247, *see* Elementary and Secondary Education Act Amendments
PL 94-142, *see* Education for All Handicapped Children Act of 1975
PL 101-336, *see* Americans with Disabilities Act of 1990
PL 101-476, *see* Individuals with Disabilities Education Act of 1990
PL 104-193, *see* Personal Responsibility and Work Opportunity Reconciliation Act of 1996
PL 107-110, *see* No Child Left Behind Act of 2001
PL 108-446, *see* Individuals with Disabilities Education Improvement Act of 2004
PL 111-296, *see* Healthy, Hunger-Free Kids Act of 2010
Plan-Do-Review sequence (HighScope), 96b
Planning time, 19, 72b, 96, 97
Plato, 46
Play
    accessibility of areas of, 33f
    approaches to learning in, 100

assessment through, 75*b*
as core of ECE programs, 73–74
Froebel's views on, 49
importance of to children, 124
interactions and, 100–101
manipulative toys for, 66–67
memory and, 101*b*
outdoor, 70
supporting cognitive development
    through, 142–143
supporting language development
    through, 168–171
supporting physical development
    through, 191–192
supporting social and emotional devel-
    opment through, 122–124
see also Toys
Positive behavioral support, 38*b*
Posture, 191
Pragmatics, 40, 162
Pratt, Caroline, 54
Preoperational thought, 135
Preschool, *see* Child care centers
Preschool Classroom Mathematics Inventory
    (Frede, Weber, Hornbeck, Stevenson-
    Boyd, & Colon, 2005), 15
Pretending, 73
Private speech, 89, 95, 135
Problem solving, 95, 97, 123*b*
Professional development
    advocacy for, 202
    federal programs for, 7
    standards on, 16*f*, 20, 20*f*
Professional standards, 15–21, 20*f*
Property taxes, 7
Prosocial behavior, 74
Protective factors, 31, 119–120
Psychosocial theory, 115–116

Questions, 96, 156, 169

Race to the Top (2010), 202
Racial identities, 5
Reading, 169, 170*b*
Receptive language, 40, 159, 159*f*, 161,
    162–166
Receptive processes, 92–95, 92*f*, 96
Reinforcement, 87
Relationships
    building with families, 77–78
    as central element to the classroom, 123
    learning through, 77, 77*f*
    parent-teacher, 12
    as a protective factor, 31
Representations, 96, 97, 124
The Republic (Plato), 46
Resiliency, 30, 31, 119–120
Response to intervention (RTI), 39*b*

Rhythms, 140, 186
Role play, 69
Rousseau, Jean, 48

Safety, 66
Salaries, 9–11, 10*f*, 12, 202
Sales tax, 7
Sand and water center, 68
Scaffolding, 56, 76, 77*f*, 89, 169
Schedules/routines, 71–72, 79
School, *see* Child care centers
School of Infancy (Comenius), 46
School readiness, 8, 91, 96, 142
Schurz, Margarethe, 50
Science
    approaches to learning in, 99
    learning center for, 67
    supporting cognitive development
        through, 141
    supporting language development
        through, 168
    supporting physical development
        through, 190
    supporting social and emotional devel-
        opment through, 121–122
Science Start! (French, 1985), 168
Scripts, 46, 94
Section 504 of the Americans with Disabili-
    ties Act (ADA), 33
Security, sense of, *see* Attachment, benefits
    of
Self-reflective practices, 12, 15, 202
Self-regulation, 79, 93, 119, 155
Self-talk, 104*f*
Semantic networks, 165
Semantics, 40, 164
Sensitivity, teacher, 12
Sensory impairments, 34–36
Sensory integration, 184
SES, *see* Socioeconomic status
Sets, 137, 141
Shared language systems, 139, 157,
    158–161, 158*f*
    see also Language development
Siblings, 29, 191
Single-parent family, 29
Skinner, B.F., 56–57
Social and emotional development
    activities and, 116–120, 121*f*
    assessment of, 124–128
    language development and, 162–163
    theories of, 112–116
    theorists on, 52
Social constructivist theory, 88–90, 155–156
Social learning theory, 87, 154, 184
Social networks, 157
Social play, 75*b*
Social studies
    approaches to learning in, 98

Social studies—*continued*
supporting cognitive development through, 141
supporting language development through, 167
supporting physical development through, 190
supporting social and emotional development through, 122
Sociodramatic play
interactions in, 124
language development and, 166–167, 170–171
learning center for, 69–70, 73
social studies content area and, 141
Socioeconomic status (SES), 7, 8*b*, 26, 29–30
see also Low-income families/communities
Solving the Problem of Childhood Obesity Within a Generation (Task Force on Childhood Obesity, 2010), 188
Sound production, 163
Spastic cerebral palsy, 36
Spatial sense, 138
Speaking and Listening for Preschool Through Third Grade, Revised Edition (Resnick & Snow, 2009), 102, 104*f*, 175, 175*f*–177*f*
Special Education (U.S. Department of Education program), 8
Special project center, 70
Speech and language impairments, 40
Spina bifida, 37
Spock, Benjamin, 55
Stages of cognition, 134
Stimulation, 136
Stride Rite Corporation, 59
Symbolic thinking, 95*b*
Synapses, 136
Syntax, 40, 164

Tabula rasa, 46
Tact (verbal behavior theory), 156
Task Force on Childhood Obesity, 188
Taxes, 7
Taylor, Katharine Whiteside, 59
Teach for America, 3
Teachers of English to Speakers of Other Languages (TESOL), 15–21, 16*f*–20*f*
Teacher-to-child ratio, 201
Teaching Strategies GOLD Objectives for Development and Learning (Heroman, Burts, Berke, & Bickart, 2010), 127*f*, 128, 145, 146*f*, 194*f*, 195
Teasing, 29
Teenage parents, 29

Temperament, 31, 39–40, 117, 161
TESOL, *see* Teachers of English to Speakers of Other Languages
Themes, curriculum, 68, 70
Theory of mind, 74*b*, 90
Title 1 funds, 6–7, 8–9, 58
Tools of the Mind (Leong, Bodrova, & Hensen, 2007), 145
Toys, 49, 53, 66–67, 191
see also Play
Training, teacher, 12–14, 13*t*
Training requirements, teacher, 10, 12–14, 13*t*
Transductive reasoning, 135
Translators, 4
Traumatic brain injury, 37
Tripod grasp, 187

Unauthorized immigrants, 27
United Nations, 59*b*
Universal education, 46
Universal prekindergarten, 9*b*
U.S. Department of Agriculture, 188
U.S. Department of Education, 7
U.S. Department of Health and Human Services, 7

Verbal behavior theory, 56–57, 156–157
Verbal cues, 89
Visual impairment, 35
Vocabulary, 138, 164, 167, 169, 177*f*
Vygotsky, Lev, 56, 76, 89

Wages, 9–11, 10*f*, 12, 202
Water and sand center, 68
Whistle for Willie (Keats, 1964), 170*b*
White House Conference on Children and Youth, 54, 60
Women, Infants, and Children (WIC) program, 188
Woodworking center, 70
Word awareness, 165
Word play, 176*f*–177*f*
Work Projects Administration (WPA), 55
Writing center, 67

Yale Child Study Clinic, 53

Zone of proximal development (ZPD), 76, 89